Henry David Thoreau

The American Men of Letters Series

Henry David Thoreau

Joseph Wood Krutch

William Morrow & Company, Inc.
New York   1974

Dedication: to Charlie and Mary

Library of Congress Catalog Card Number 73-16724

ISBN 0-688-06774-3 (pbk.)

The greater part of what my neighbors call good I believe in my soul to be bad, and if I repent of anything, it is very likely to be my good behavior. What demon possessed me that I behaved so well?

Walden

Contents

Sources, Acknowledgements, etc.

The Writings of Henry David Thoreau in twenty volumes (Houghton Mifflin, 1906) devotes fourteen volumes to the *Journal* and is the most important single source for the study of Thoreau. Next in importance, and from the same publisher, is *Familiar Letters of Henry David Thoreau;* edited with an introduction and notes by F. B. Sanborn. Ellery Channing's recollections, *Thoreau, the Poet Naturalist*, appeared in 1873; and F. B. Sanborn's *Henry David Thoreau* in 1882, the latter to be followed by the same author's *The Life of Henry David Thoreau* in 1917. H. S. Salt's *Life of Henry David Thoreau* (1890) should also be listed among the early treatments, and Emerson's *Journals*, Hawthorne's *Notebooks*, and *The Journals of Bronson Alcott* should be cited as primary sources. The most important recent biography is Henry Seidel Canby's *Thoreau* (Houghton Mifflin), which contains important new facts and hitherto unpublished material. Mark Van Doren's *Henry David Thoreau* (1916) was the first interpretation based upon a careful study of the *Journal;* and among the more recent interpretations two of especial in-

terest are *Henry Thoreau, the Cosmic Yankee* by Brooks
Atkinson and *Walden Revisited* by George F. Whicher.

A Bibliography of Henry David Thoreau by Francis
H. Allen is standard, but is supplemented by *A Henry
David Thoreau Bibliography 1908-37* by William White
and *A Contribution to a Bibliography from 1909 to 1936
of Henry David Thoreau* by Joseph Sanford Wade. A
very extensive current bibliography is kept up to date in
the *Bulletin of the Thoreau Society*.

Walden has been reprinted in various editions, an interesting recent one being that illustrated with 142 photo-
graphs and preceded by an introduction by Edwin Way
Teal. *Collected Poems by H. Thoreau*, edited by Carl
Bode, includes some hitherto unpublished work. Arthur
Christie's *The Orient in American Transcendentalism*
treats extensively the subject, barely mentioned in this
book, of Thoreau's use of Oriental writings. Mr. Christie
also left, after his recent death, a large amount of material
on the general subject of Thoreau's reading. Scudder Mid-
dleton's *Concord* is an entertaining and instructive history.

The "last letter" mentioned in the text of this book
(page 240) is in the Huntington Library and was published
by Carl Bode in *The New England Quarterly* for June
1946. Although there seems to be no strictly contemporary
documentation for the story of Thoreau's reply to the
question whether he had made his peace with God, it is
told in the Salt biography and seems so clearly marked
by Thoreau's personality as to be beyond serious question.
The result of recent excavations on the site of the Walden
hut have been described in *Discovery at Walden* by Richard Wells Robbins.

Grateful acknowledgment is hereby made to the Houghton Mifflin Company for generous permission to quote extensively from Thoreau's works, from the *Familiar Letters*, and from H. B. Sanborn's *The Life of Henry David Thoreau*. Similar acknowledgment and thanks go to the publishers for permission to quote from the following works: Ellery Channing's *Thoreau, the Poet Naturalist* (C. E. Goodspeed); *The Heart of Emerson's Journals*, edited by Odell Shepard (Houghton Mifflin Company); *The Journals of Bronson Alcott*, edited by Odell Shepard (Little, Brown & Company); and Hawthorne's *American Notebooks* (Houghton Mifflin Company). Mr. Canby kindly gave me permission to quote some hitherto unpublished material in his *Thoreau*.

I wish also to thank the following: My fellow editors of the American Men of Letters Series and also, especially, Professor Ralph Rusk of Columbia University for valuable suggestions made after a reading of my manuscript; Miss Mary Stout for a careful typing of my messy original; and Mrs. Elizabeth C. Moore, whose editorial assistance I have had previous occasion to be grateful for.

Henry David Thoreau

When the Smoke is Blown Away

*T*HE LESSON which Henry David Thoreau had taught himself and which he hoped he might teach to others was summed up in the one word: "Simplify!"

Obviously this same word would also sum up better than any other possibly could what the world of his day was not doing and what the world has continued, increasingly, not to do ever since. So far as his mere reputation is concerned, it has grown steadily and it was never higher than it is now. *Walden* is one of the very few American works to have won international acceptance as a classic, and it is also—which does not necessarily follow—one of the most widely read of nineteenth-century books. But hearers are not always heeders and very few of Thoreau's professing admirers are willing to accept in its full rigor his central doctrine.

Even his present-day fame and present-day popularity would astonish his contemporaries if they could know of it, and very probably would astonish him also. To most citizens of Concord he had long been a familiar figure and, though they made him their official surveyor, he seemed to them only a somewhat irresponsible eccentric who had never stuck at anything long enough to be a success. To the small circle of New England intellectuals he was simply a man who had never fulfilled his early promise and was less likely to be remembered long than a Margaret Fuller or a Bronson Alcott—not to speak of an Emerson or a Hawthorne. Even he himself had probably become as nearly reconciled as a writer ever can be to the assumption that, so far as any considerable audience was concerned, he was a failure.

His first book had been printed at his own risk in an edition of one thousand copies and when, four years later, fewer than three hundred had been sold he had taken over the remainder with the wry comment: "I have now a library of nearly nine hundred volumes, over seven hundred of which I wrote myself." His masterpiece had had to wait several years to find a publisher willing to undertake it, and though it got rather better than a mixed reception in the press it was not reprinted until after his death. It is true that he continued in his enormous manuscript *Journal* to talk to himself and that during his later years he placed a few magazine articles; but even as a lecturer in a lecture-hungry region he was invited so seldom to speak— sometimes two or three times a year, sometimes not at all— that he was obliged to congratulate himself on being thus permitted to stay at home and, finally, to conclude: "As for lecture-goers, it is none of their business what I think."

Most literary reputations merely linger; and though there are a few which grow, it is not so very often that a writer who failed in his own time and who was, moreover, dismissed as a mere eccentric after his death recaptures the ear and the imagination of a public as Thoreau has done. Nor is the sheer brilliance of his writing even chiefly responsible for the phenomenon. What he had to say is what has really counted and what still arrests and fascinates even those who are less than half convinced by the arguments he sets forth. He disapproved of the way America was going and he refused point-blank to go along with it. Since his day, both America and the world have gone much farther along the road they chose, and they seem even less likely than they did in Thoreau's day to heed his injunctions or even to see how they could possibly be heeded. But the dissatisfaction which he expressed with things as they are has come to seem more and more justified and his prophecies have in many respects been fulfilled.

His contemporaries lived in an age of growing complexity and hope; we in an age of growing complexity and despair. "Progress" was not in his day a word of which even progressives were critical, and the great world is at the present moment so ready to admit that it needs saving as to be willing to listen rather more readily than Thoreau's contemporaries did even to a savior whose deepest conviction it is not willing to accept. Many of his exhortations and his gibes strike home as they never did before and give pause to many who are very far from being Thoreauists.

Men have an indistinct notion that if they keep up this activity of joint stocks and spades long enough all will at length ride somewhere, in next to no time, and for nothing; but though a crowd rushes to the depot, and the conductor shouts "All aboard!" when the smoke is blown away and the vapor condensed, it will be perceived that a few are riding, but the rest are run over . . . and it will be called, and will be, "A melancholy accident."

Even those who still believe that the difficulty can be solved if still more railroads are built; even those who continue to cherish the idea that if they keep up long enough this activity of joint stocks and spades, everyone will ride somewhere; even, in a word, those who insist that the cure for the evils of complexity is still more complexity —even these are more often than not arrested by the accuracy of Thoreau's short-time prophecy, and willing to admit that *so far* their solution has only served to accentuate the problem. A great many people have undoubtedly been run over; and if it is no longer true that "the mass of men lead lives of quiet desperation," that is only because the desperation of so many has become unquiet instead. Under the circumstances, a man who managed to solve, even for himself alone, the unsolvable problem, arouses at least a wondering interest. Radical remedies seemed called for and no man was ever more radical than Thoreau.

It has become the custom to wonder somewhat fatuously at the fulfillment of the "prophecies" made by Jules Verne and H. G. Wells. They were anticipated by others who worked a similar vein, and early in his career Thoreau reviewed a book by one of the wilder prophets of the technological millennium, a German immigrant named J. A. Etzler. Thoreau was not inclined to question much the possibility that all sorts of mechanical wonders might be created, but he did leap over to consider, not the Wellsian "things to come," but the still more distant things to come after them; or, in other words, to question the ultimate human worth of mechanical invention and the uses to which it would be put. Thus, if the Vernes and the Wellses saw far, Thoreau saw farther and he anticipated, not the age of invention, but the present age, which is just beginning to recognize the full urgency of the questions he raised. Many a man of today who can read coldly the much-admired descriptions of the aeroplanes, submarines, televisors, etc., which in the nineteenth and early twentieth centuries were still to come, will find far more pertinent than any nineteenth-century man did what Thoreau had to say about the danger of being run over.

Great writer though he was—and even today many wonderful pages full of humor and original sensibility are buried almost unread in the pages of his *Journal*—it is, then, evident that Thoreau's most vigorous fame is not merely literary in the narrowest sense of the word. Many of his most ardent admirers are those who have accepted him as some kind of teacher, who cherish his writings almost as though they were sacred books, and who feel with him a communion of spirit often personal and almost secret. But even those who regard themselves as in some sense disciples should be divided into two very different groups. On the one hand he has become the patron saint of nature lovers and solitaries everywhere, but on the other, he was also an acknowledged inspiration of Mahatma Gandhi and of various leaders of the British Labor party.

That the social reformer and the nature-loving hermit, whose attitudes seem so irreconcilable in every other respect, should nevertheless unite in their admiration for Thoreau is not, however, so strange as it might at first sight appear. His was an extremely personal philosophy which managed to reconcile, or at least managed to include, elements not usually compatible, and it needs only a variation in the stress upon this component or that to justify either the extreme individualist or the social reformer who claims his support. Certainly Thoreau began as an individual who found himself pursuing goods which the society of which he was a part did not recognize. Because of that fact he was unwilling to assume the responsibilities which society tried to impose upon him and what he faced first of all was the purely personal problem of survival in an alien environment. Self-justification led inevitably to a critique of society itself and this led no less inevitably to exhortation. Yet only in his last years (if ever) did he so much as waver in his conviction that reform is possible only in so far as each man reforms himself, and that all attempts to save mankind through concerted effort are vicious and self-destructive. It was always to a defiant individualism that he returned for strength, and he would always, as a last resort, take refuge in ultimate nonresistance and nonparticipation, in the resolution "not to live in this restless, nervous, bustling, trivial, Nineteenth Century, but stand or sit thoughtfully while it goes by."

The fundamental good which he pursued—a life devoted to contemplation in close contact with the phenomena of nature and relieved only by the simple activities attendant upon providing for himself the simplest necessities of life—is not a good which has in recent years received much official recognition. Most reformers propose that mankind should be redeemed from its slavery to material things, not by doing without them, but by means of an industry and a society so organized that everyone may ride somewhere in next to no time and for next to nothing. The contemplation of nature hardly figures as a good in most current social philosophies; and to most proponents of social change, those admirers of Thoreau who find that the heart of his teaching is his invitation into the woods and fields are merely "escapists." But for Thoreau himself this was not an escape from, but an escape into, reality, and without his faith in it he would have seen little reason to rebel against a society exclusively occupied with material things. In this respect he is, of course, at least closer to the followers of Gandhi than to the followers of Marx.

Only in recognizing the awful veracity with which he describes the present plight of mankind do the anarchical individualists agree with the reformers or the various reformers agree with one another, and it is chiefly the self-evident truth of his description of that plight which has won him his hearing and enabled *Walden* to become one of the great seminal books of the nineteenth century. It was full of seeds, many of which had hardly begun to germinate by the time his own life reached its end and which were, moreover, so various that from his scattering they have grown up into vigorous plants of very diverse species.

Thoreau can appeal to men with different fundamental aims because he starts from a premise which the most bigoted reformer and the most self-centered escapist can both accept. "The mass of men lead lives of quiet desperation." Once that obvious fact has been stated, its self-evident truth appeals equally to the reformer and to those so weary and so despairing of the world that they are ready to consider merely how they may save themselves. "Men labor under a mistake. . . . They are employed, as it says in an old book, laying up treasures which moth and rust will corrupt and thieves break through and steal. . . . I sometimes wonder that we can be so frivolous, I may almost say, as to attend to the gross but somewhat foreign form of servitude called Negro Slavery, there are so many keen and subtle masters that enslave both North and South. It is hard to have a

Southern overseer; it is worse to have a Northern one; but worst of all when you are the slave-driver of yourself."

What Thoreau proposes is passive resistance to society, the refusal of the individual to engage in activities and competitions which he does not want to engage in; and Thoreau's appeal to purely individual action has, for the reader, at least the psychological advantage that it suggests some immediate action and promises some immediate gain—not amelioration for all at some future and probably distant time but salvation now for any who want it badly enough to, as he phrased it, "move away from public opinion." The revolution he proclaims is a revolution without a leader and therefore a revolution which can begin now, not a revolution which is "coming," inevitably perhaps, but far off. There is no need to wait for a majority or for a minority large enough to promise success; here is a revolution which each man can make for himself.

He can, as a solitary individual, lay down the burden. If enough men do the same, society will be transformed; but if all but you and I insist upon carrying it, then at least you and I will have saved our souls. Moreover, Thoreau's individualism, his tendency even when most concerned with society and its possible reform, to hark back to the insistence that man must remake himself, has also the advantage of forbidding his disciples to indulge in that nerveless self-pity which expresses itself in the tendency to blame everything on "our times" or "the present system"; and he puts upon each man the responsibility for himself, at least. Though he often despaired of the world, he never, for long, despaired of himself, and though he often blamed the world for what it did to worldlings, he gladly assumed responsibility for his own soul. And that is, perhaps, one of the reasons why so many, even though they may be themselves less self-reliant, have found his writings curiously exhilarating.

Thoreau's principal achievement was not the creation of a system but the creation of himself, and his principal literary work was, therefore, the presentation of that self in the form of a self-portrait to which even those descriptions and expositions which seem most objective are in fact contributions. His starting point was not an idea but an impulse; and in a sense which must not be regarded as derogatory, his intellectual convictions were rationalizations of his needs and his desires. His philosophy of life grew with him as he lived, and though he tended, during most of his short pilgrimage, to examine more and more carefully its possible application to others, they were never his chief concern. The apology with which *Walden* opens is only mockingly apologetic. "I should not talk so much about myself if there were anybody else whom I knew as well." "Moreover," he goes on, "I, on my side, require of every writer, first or last, a simple and sincere account of his own life, and not merely what he has heard of other men's lives; some such account as he would send to his kindred from a distant land; for if he has lived sincerely, it must have been in a distant land to me." And even though the next paragraph is devoted to his Concord neighbors and to the "penance" to which it seems to him their lives are devoted, the book as a whole is not cast in the form of a treatise or an exhortation but purports to be merely the personal account of an adventure not recommended to others. It is to himself as a unique being with unique needs that he constantly returns.

Reform was never with him more than a secondary purpose. He did not, he said, come into the world primarily to make it better but to live in it, be it good or bad. Even in his essay on "Civil Disobedience" which Mahatma Gandhi acknowledged as an inspiration, he was stubbornly insisting that it is no man's inescapable duty to devote himself to the eradication of even the most enormous wrong, and that the most which can be required of him is to wash his hands of it; to refuse to give it his practical support. Though puritanism had, willy-nilly, its effect upon certain of his specific tastes and distastes, he was thus in full revolt, not only against the specifically puritan concept of life as a melancholy responsibility, but also against the whole pallidly puritan (or Victorian) conception of Duty as the supreme guide of life. For him, the *summum bonum* was joy, and the moments which most satisfied his conscience were the moments of ecstatic communion with nature. Indeed, what he despised most about the society in which he found himself was not its injustice but its joylessness. "Have the Gods," he was asking himself in his *Journal* long after his own great period had passed, "sent us into this world . . . to do chores, hold horses, and the like, and not given us any spending money?" and he went on to gibe at those who, seeking to make their lives more easy, keep a horse to feel their oats for them instead of feeling it themselves.

It was his own opinion, clearly expressed in the *Journal* of the Walden period, that the chief conflict in himself was not a conflict between individualism and social responsibility but between the impulse toward mystical contemplation and the instinct which impelled him toward the primitive and the savage, toward that whole revolt against civilized life which inspires some of the best of the pages to which Thoreau's nonpolitical admirers turn most eagerly. Despite the hours devoted to his *Journal*, and the lesser number spent in the composition of his published works, most of

Thoreau's life was not spent either in writing or even in physically inactive meditation but in doing the hundreds of outdoor things which he loved to do and in actively pursuing the duties of that office—inspector of snowstorms and rainstorms—to which he said he had appointed himself. "I sit in my boat on Walden, playing the flute this evening, and see the perch, which I seem to have charmed, hovering around me, and the moon traveling over the bottom, which is strewn with the wrecks of the forest, and feel that nothing but the wildest imagination can conceive of the manner of life we are living. Nature is a wizard. The Concord nights are stranger than the Arabian nights." A few years later he was writing to one of his mystical friends: "I have sworn no oath. I have no designs on society, or nature, or God. . . . I love to live. . . . I have heard no bad news. . . . When you travel to the Celestial City, carry no letter of introduction. When you knock, ask to see God—none of his servants. In what concerns you much, do not think that you have companions; know that you are alone in the world."

No great book can ever be accounted for by any presentation of its author's life. *Walden*, like all masterpieces, is better than anything which the author seemed capable of doing, and in all probability actually is better than anything he could have done at any time other than that at which it was written. The fact remains, nevertheless, that it grew more directly than many great books seem to grow, out of the experiences and the predicaments of the man who wrote it, and there is therefore more than the usual excuse for considering it in connection with those experiences and those predicaments.

A Joy Which Knew Not Its Origin

HENRY DAVID THOREAU—as he preferred to call himself—was born on July 12, 1817, and was christened David Henry three months later. His father was John Thoreau, the son of a Protestant emigrant from the Channel Islands; his mother the daughter of a Congregational minister named Asa Dunbar. On both sides, Henry's grandparents had been rather substantial people, but his father lost money in a business venture and the house in which Henry was born was a gray, unpainted structure just outside the village of Concord, Massachusetts. Another family occupied part of the building, and his father was farming the property for his wife's mother, the twice-married Widow Minott.

Before Henry's birth John Thoreau had been an unsuccessful storekeeper, and shortly thereafter he became precisely that again in the near-by village of Chelmsford. After a few years more he moved on to Boston to become a schoolmaster, and then, when Henry was six years old, returned to Concord where he took up as a home industry the making of graphite for lead pencils, that being already an industry established in the village. Thus a poverty which was genteel in Concord, but would have been less than that in many other communities, was Henry's early environment.

Concord township lies mostly in a valley traversed by quiet streams. In middle life Thoreau remarked that it was said to support two thousand inhabitants, and he himself lived on a street, though open country lay just beyond. Hence his family belonged socially with the townsfolk, not with the farmers close by; but Henry, unlike Emerson, was not a member of the Social Circle which met on Tuesday evenings and contained representatives from various trades, professions, and callings. Though distinctly respectable and respected, the Thoreaus were not among the obviously elect.

Years later Henry was to take the trouble to compile, with the aid of his mother, a list of the many houses in which he had at one time or another lived. From 1823 to 1826 the family occupied what he calls "the brick house"; then for a year "the Davis house"; and, finally, "the Shattuck house" until he left for Harvard in 1833. Besides himself and his parents, the immediate family consisted of his older sister, Helen, his older brother, John, and his younger sister, Sophia. Moreover the fertility and the clannishness of the Dunbar tribe made it inevitable that the future amateur of solitude should grow up far from solitary—so far at least as outward circumstances are concerned. At different times during his boyhood and adolescence, relatives, mostly female, were continually "coming to live with" his parents for shorter or for longer periods, and when nearly twenty he wrote in his *Journal:* "Here at my elbow sit five notable, or at least noteworthy, representatives of this nineteenth century—of the gender feminine."

John Thoreau, the father, was a quiet, gentle man who loved to read the newspapers or sit chatting in a village shop. "He belonged," wrote Henry, "in a peculiar sense to the village street. .... I think that he remembered more about the worthies (and unworthies) of Concord village forty years ago . . . than anyone else." John's wife, Cynthia, was, on the other hand, a bustling, strong-minded woman, active in practical affairs, given to taking in boarders, and described by one who knew her as "next to Madam Hoar, the mother of the Judge and the Senator, the most talkative person in Concord." Even Henry, who, like other admirers of silence, often held forth, deferred to her when she assumed control of the conversation.

Hovering about, either in the flesh or in legend, were perhaps rather more than the normal number of "characters" and eccentrics, including a Tory granduncle, whose efforts to supply the British Army with food had landed him in Concord jail two generations before Henry himself was lodged there; and including also, very much alive, Uncle Charles Dunbar, of whom Thoreau draws a delightful portrait. Uncle Charles was of great strength and famous for both his loud voice and his expertness with cards, though these did not constitute his most striking accomplishments. "Ever since I knew him he could," said Henry, "swallow his nose," and one of his tricks was to swallow the knives, forks, and some of the plates at a tavern table, then offer to give them up if the landlord would charge nothing for his meal. It was also this same Charles with whom the adult Thoreau had so exciting a discussion concerning the worthies of American history that, after both had gone to bed, "I heard his chamber door opened, after eleven o'clock, and he called out, in an earnest, stentorian voice, loud enough to wake the whole house, 'Henry, was John Quincy Adams a genius?' 'No, I think not,' was my reply. 'Well, I didn't think he was,' answered he." Sister Helen was an intellectual and an ardent abolitionist; sister Sophia, an unusually untalented artist who did very bad portraits.

John Junior was an amateur naturalist and no doubt it was he who introduced his younger brother to the fields and woods, though the parents also took "nature walks." Yet when Thoreau writes of his memories of boyhood, it is not "nature study" nor any of the intellectual interests of the family which come back to him, but rather recollections of the happy hours of thoughtless delight passed in the usual activities of a country boy. In autumn and spring he went barefoot to school and, as he himself recalled, "When I was young and compelled to pass my Sunday in the house without the aid of interesting books, I used to spend many an hour till the wished-for sundown, watching the martins soar." After theories had begun to be important for him, he hated killing, and in Maine he went with the moose hunters only as "chaplain" and "conscientious objector." But, as he once humorously confessed apropos his vegetarianism, "I am only half converted by my own arguments for I still fish," and on another occasion he remembered that: "In the country a boy's love is apt to be divided between a gun and a watch; but the more active and manly choose the gun. I have seen the time when I could carry a gun in my hand all day long on a journey, and not feel it to be heavy, though I did not use it once."

After his intellectual development had begun, he was, like all the group with which he was loosely allied, a reader of Wordsworth, and whether or not his recollections were colored by this fact, he remembered his boyhood as one passed in an instinctive and physical harmony with nature which was the source of delights the thoughtful man could never recapture. Though he seldom used terms so pietistic, heaven lay about him also in his infancy, and after he had passed through young manhood into the beginnings of middle age, he was convinced that the light was becoming more and more merely the light of common day. The young man no longer saw what the boy had seen, the middle-aged man no longer responded as the young man had. "I have," he thought, "experienced such simple joy in the trivial matters of fishing and sporting formerly, as might inspire the muse of Homer and Shakespeare." Again: "My life was ecstasy. In youth, before I lost any of my senses, I can remember that I was all alive, and inhabited my body with inexpressible satisfaction; both its weariness and its refreshment were sweet to me." Later he had to go about looking for what had once come unbidden, observing in the hope that he might be reminded of what had formerly thrust itself upon him, trying to recapture the time when he "walked with a joy which knew not its own origin." Already at twenty-three, he was convinced that "We seem but to linger in manhood to tell the dreams of our childhood, and they vanish out of memory ere we learn the language."

When, at the age of twenty, he began his *Journal* he expressed in the first published entry the significant aspiration: "I seek a garret. The spiders must not be disturbed, nor the floor swept, nor the lumber arranged." But that may have been a merely normal reaction against a family and tribal existence which was sometimes almost oppressively intimate quite as much as it was an early indication of the temperamental tendency to exalt the ideal of self-sufficiency. Certainly one must not suppose that he was ever either as uninterested in people or as detached from the members of his family as his formal writings would sometimes suggest. The despiser of gossip was his father's son in nothing more than in that concern with "The Concord worthies" which generates some of the most delightful pages of the *Journal;* and though the reader of his first published book might suppose from the infrequent, colorless references to the brother who accompanied him along the Concord and Merrimack rivers that Thoreau was scarcely aware of his brother's existence, the fact is that Henry remained, rather more than most men, dependent upon his family both spiritually and in practical affairs, so that it might, indeed, be argued that he never cut his mother's apron strings. Despite various comings and goings, which for the most part represented unsuccessful attempts to find a congenial way of making a livelihood, despite the brief and singularly unspectacular experiment of living alone at Walden, he spent a good part of his life under the parental roof and it was in the house of his mother, who survived him, that he finally died.

If he had any consciously intellectual interest during the boyhood which he liked to remember as a thoughtless, though ecstatic, participation in nature, no significant record of it remains. Nevertheless, Concord was not a place where a genteel family was likely to encourage a child to grow up into a savage, however much he might imagine that he was inclined that way. Most of the leading men of the village were Harvard graduates. The Concord Lyceum, before which Henry himself was later to lecture, had been established when he was twelve, and the older members of his family were well aware of "reformers" and "movements." Accordingly he was entered in Concord Academy, a private school supposed to be superior to the public one, and from there, at the rather late age of sixteen, he was sent on to Harvard, where his entirely respectable but not spectacular career indicated that he came adequately prepared. Though he was on a scholarship at college his formal education probably cost some sacrifice from his brother and sisters as well as from his parents, and it is obvious that he was regarded as the genius of the family even though his mother later became understandably disturbed by his failure to find any place for himself in the world.

Emerson's portrait of his friend and onetime handy man sums up his sense of Thoreau's unapproachability in the famous admission that he would as soon have attempted to take an elm by the arm. Undoubtedly most other genteel people outside the family group felt much the same and it may be that the very closeness and familiarity of his home life made it easier for him to indulge, outside it, his theoretical detachment. But the family life was close. At twenty he was sending playful, jaunty letters to his brother and his sister; at twenty-six, during a brief absence from home, he writes his mother: "Methinks I should be content to sit at the back-door in Concord, under the poplar-tree, henceforth forever," and then goes on to draw a nostalgic, genre picture in which Father, Helen, Sophia, and Aunt Louisa Dunbar all find their places. According to his friend Ellery Channing, he asked his mother, just before he left for college, what profession he should choose and when she replied: "You can buckle on your knapsack, and roam abroad to seek your fortune," he wept until Sister Helen put her arm around him and said: "No, Henry, you shall not go; you shall stay at home and live with us."

In the *Journal* Thoreau sometimes looks back upon his boyhood and youth and interprets them for us. When he does so, it is not merely from the vantage point of such philosophy as he had been able to achieve but also through the eyes of a personality which had deliberately dramatized itself. He omits, or at least plays down, all the everyday domestic aspects of his existence, and stresses the unthinking sympathy with wild nature as though the child were father not only to the man but also to the literary personality which the man adopted. No doubt this retrospective portrait of himself is true as far as it goes. The young Henry was an unusual youth, destined to grow up into a still more unusual man, and in all probability instinctive delight in wild nature was one of his earliest characteristics. But there is also no real reason for supposing that the youth who went off to Harvard, like any other genteel representative of Concord, was by that time as clearly set off from other men as Thoreau later liked to imagine he was.

A certain amount of unconventionality was in the New England of his day already a convention. When Emerson observed later that at Harvard all the branches of learning were taught, Thoreau was to reply: "Yes, indeed, all the branches and none of the roots." At thirty he was to remark in a similar vein, apropos of college diplomas: "Let every sheep keep but its own skin, I say." Yet though he may possibly, from the beginning, have expected little from a college education, the evidence seems to be that his moderately obscure career at Harvard was more the result of uncertainty, insecurity, and a certain rusticity than of any bold superiority. He belonged to no coterie, he took no part in the revels which some students indulged in. But he had roommates, he seems to have performed the routine tasks assigned to him with acceptable docility, and when he had time to himself, he spent it not in communion with nature but at the college library to which in later life he recurred. According to one of his classmates, Thoreau also owned a good many volumes of poetry "from Gower and Chaucer down through the era of Elizabeth," and "he was devoted to the old English literature." Before long, if not already, he was also to make the acquaintance of Goethe, Coleridge, Carlyle, Wordsworth, and the others whom the Concord group found sympathetic.

A certain kind of bookishness was as characteristic of his mature life as any of the pursuits which he preferred to consider peculiarly his own. Perhaps, indeed, he did not realize during his college years that his delight in the country could be intellectualized or in any way related to his intellectual aspirations. Later he might complain that he cannot remember "any page which will tell me how to spend this afternoon," and in his formal writings he quotes comparatively little except from rather out-of-the-way sources. But that was because he had made it his peculiar task to deal with an area of experience which he felt the writer had too much neglected, not because he even pretended to have got little from reading. "Decayed literature," he thought, "makes the richest of all soils."

At college he wrote a voluntary essay on *L'Allegro* and *Il Penseroso;* and, according to his friend Channing, *Lycidas*—not exactly a poem about wild nature—was one of his great favorites. Writing about the Maine woods he quotes *Paradise Lost* and even at Walden he occupied some time making a list of books which a reading of Hallam's history of literature had encouraged him to want to look into. Neither should it be forgot that by the time he left college he was able to read Latin and Greek for pleasure, knew French well, and had some acquaintance with Spanish, Italian, and German.

Not until his sophomore year was he required to write English compositions, but he preserved thirty college essays out of the more than fifty he was required to prepare. They furnish the first evidence, aside from a few letters, of what his mind at that time was like, and the evidence turns out to be mostly negative. Such topics as "The Comparative Moral Policy of Severe and Mild Punishments" or "The Literary Life" were assigned, and what was expected was apparently a rhetorical or forensic development of the theme. If Thoreau had any originality of opinion or personality, he kept it out of most of his assigned writing and gave what evidently proved acceptable—callow learning and callow moralizing. There is little trace of the pungency or even the eccentricity which was later to be his; above all no sign at all that he was thinking of himself as a man of the fields and woods rather than a man of the study. Indeed, it is only among those essays written comparatively late in his college career that one perceives anything not wholly conventional or, at most, conventionally unconventional, and the first tendency to branch out on a line slightly different from that of the earlier papers has been traced, no doubt correctly, to a reading of the first major pronouncement of his fellow townsman, Ralph Waldo Emerson, whose *Nature* had been published in 1836 and probably read by Thoreau shortly thereafter—although the first evidence that he knew the book comes when he gave a copy to a classmate the following year.

One interpretation of Thoreau's thought—and it is one which the present study will attempt—assumes that the kinship between him and Emerson was a good deal less close than at first sight it appears to be, that Thoreau himself was at the beginning deceived, and that he was compelled to achieve with great difficulty the independence which was almost lost forever when the vigorous pronouncements of his elder contemporary deceived him into the belief that their temperaments and aspirations were nearly identical. But upon this or any other assumption, it is evident that Emerson's was the first contemporary voice which seemed to him to be speaking a language fully meaningful to him.

Thoreau had done well enough at college to be granted the not too impressive distinction of being one of a considerable number who spoke at commencement. His performance consisted in maintaining, against an opponent, that "The Commercial Spirit" was evil, and a portion of his discourse was rescued and quoted by one of his early biographers. Thoreau observed that though the commercial spirit was a sort of by-product of the now universal assertion of freedom and to that extent good, it was nevertheless a corrupt manifestation because it was motivated by "a blind and unmanly love of wealth." "Let men," he urged, "cultivate the moral affections, lead manly and independent lives; let them make riches the means and not the end of existence, and we shall hear no more of the commercial spirit. . . . This curious world which we inhabit is more wonderful than it is convenient; more beautiful than it is useful; it is more to be admired and enjoyed than used." In these sentences is expressed nothing in which their author ever ceased to believe and one's first impulse is to declare that he had already found himself. But Emerson would have agreed heartily and there is so far from being anything unique in the sentiments expressed that it seems safest to conclude that Thoreau had by then found no more than that part of himself which Emerson had found for him.

Earlier in the same year he had written in a college essay: "The savage may be and often is a sage. Our Indian is more of a man than the inhabitant of a city. He lives as a man, he thinks as a man, he dies as a man." Vague though the meaning of those lines is, they may at least reflect, as nothing in the commencement speech does, that sympathy with actual wildness which is as characteristic of Thoreau as it is remote from Emerson. But a preceding passage in which Nature is named as the great educator uses, as the commencement address also does, the capitalized word in a way which makes it impossible to say that Thoreau himself had yet drawn any distinction between what it was to mean to him and what it meant to Emerson. In neither the essay nor the speech is there any evidence that he recognized the importance of the distinction between Emerson's serene assurance that Nature was what his quiet contemplation assured him it must be and a different conviction, which was certainly Thoreau's only a very little later—the conviction, that is to say, that Nature's lesson was not to be learned except by the man who observed, lived with, and participated in her phenomena.

Thoreau's four years at Harvard were not unbroken. He was frequently back in Concord, he passed through an illness there in the spring of 1836, and in the summer of 1836, as we know from a letter to a college friend, he built a boat in Concord for a trip on the Sudbury River. The winter before, in accordance with the custom of scholarship boys, he had been permitted to gain experience as a teacher by keeping school for some weeks in Canton, Massachusetts, where the Reverend Orestes A. Brownson took him in to board. Brownson, later to champion an economic radicalism closer to Marxism than most New England radicalism ever got and to end up at last in the Catholic Church, was at this time in his early thirties, and at the moment a Unitarian minister under the influence of Robert Owen. At their first meeting he and Thoreau are said to have "sat up talking till midnight." Writing Brownson a few years later concerning his qualifications for a teaching job, Thoreau declared that "the short six weeks" which the two had spent together "were an era in my life—the morning of a new *Lebenstag.*"

It has been suggested that Thoreau's long resistance to abolitionism—despite the fact that other members of the family espoused it ardently—may have been due to Brownson, who favored self-improvement and passive resistance as a method of producing reform. The extent of his influence at this moment is difficult to estimate, but the two men never had any subsequent personal relations of importance and it seems safer to attribute to Emerson's book the new interests and the new assurance which began to manifest themselves about the time that book appeared. Certainly in August 1837, when Henry returned home after graduation, he had already become one who intended to find himself, even if he had not yet done so, and he was provided with interests and opinions of a sort which we have no evidence he had had a few short years before. A somewhat pompous letter written to Sister Helen about three months after graduation protests against a state of affairs where "the sacred opinions one advances in argument are apologized for by his friends, before his face, lest his hearers receive the wrong impression of the man." At the moment, Mrs. Ward and her daughter Prudence, old friends of the Thoreaus, were boarding with the family, and though they admired Henry, it was probably to them that Helen had taken it upon herself to explain that he did not really mean all he said.

One sentence in Henry's commencement discourse suggests, even by the special rhythm of its phraseology, that it embodies a conviction of more direct and immediate significance for him than any of the glib, high-minded generalizations with which it is surrounded. "The order of things should," he proclaimed, "be somewhere reversed; the seventh should be man's day of toil, wherein to earn his living by the sweat of his brow; and the other six his Sabbath of the affections and the soul, in which to range this widespread garden, and drink in the soft influences and sublime revelations of Nature." But if this was indeed already, as it certainly very soon became, not merely a conversationally useful paradox but a simple fact upon the acceptance of which his whole life was resolutely to be built, he concealed for the moment his determination never to tie himself to any regular occupation; and under the eye of his mother, who would have expected no less, he looked about for a job.

Within two or three months after leaving college he undertook to teach the village school, and if one may believe the chatty, anecdotal account left by his jocose friend Ellery Channing, he soon abandoned that occupation after a characteristic demonstration of eccentric originality. Corporal punishment was contrary to his principles, but about a fortnight after he had taken over, a deacon walked in and instructed him that he must apply the ferrule lest the school should spoil. That afternoon he selected six pupils, apparently at random but including the maidservant at his own home, administered a therapeutic chastisement to each, and then wrote the school committee that if they did not like the way he managed their institution, they could run it themselves. One victim of his impartiality is said to have carried a grudge well into adult life.

After this fiasco Thoreau made a trip to Maine, hoping to find a school; considered going to Virginia; and, early in 1838, laid plans for going west to Kentucky with his brother John on a similar mission. Nothing came of the projects, but in June of the same year, after the family had moved into the Parkman house, Mrs. Thoreau boarded four boys from Boston whom John and Henry undertook to teach. Soon they took over the old Academy which Thoreau had himself once attended and had as many pupils as they could accommodate.

The success of this enterprise was apparently not impeded, but promoted, by the fact that the young Thoreaus had very modern ideas of schoolkeeping, some of which were probably borrowed from Bronson Alcott who had visited Concord for the first time the preceding year and of whom both Henry and John must by this time have been aware whether they had yet met him or not. No corporal punishment was administered, the day began with a moral lecture on some subject not immediately connected with the formal lesson, and once a week there was a walk, a sail, or a swim conducted by Henry who made these expeditions an occasion for "nature study." On one sail down the river he predicted from the situation of a certain spot on shore that evidence of an Indian encampment would be found there, and next week he impressed his young charges by taking them to visit the spot and uncovering with a spade the remains of a fireplace.

Prudence Ward, already mentioned as a boarder in the Thoreau household, introduced into it and then into the school an eleven-year-old boy who was a son of her sister and of the Reverend Edmund Quincy Sewall, a Unitarian minister. Thoreau was immediately drawn to the boy; he wrote into the *Journal* a passage describing his recent contact with "a pure uncompromising spirit"; and the passage is so little different in tone from what he was later to write about the women he liked best that it may be taken as a warning. It is dangerous to read into any of his very youthful and very mystical comments upon the persons to whom he felt drawn even the faintly erotic meaning which one is tempted to seek when the subject happens to be a member of the female sex.

Two days after the prose passage, he copied into the *Journal* a poem of six stanzas entitled "Sympathy" which begins:

> Lately, alas, I knew a gentle boy,
> Whose features all were cast in Virtue's mould.

Later occurs the line "I might have loved him, had I loved him less"; and this, it is not impertinent to remark, is almost as warm as anything he was ever to write about any woman.

Then in July 1839, young Sewall's sister Ellen came for a three weeks' visit. She was pretty as well as vivacious and both Henry and his brother John were attracted to her immediately. Henry took her for a boat ride as well as here and there in the village. Presently he was writing in his

Journal: "There is no remedy for love but to love more"—
though even that sentence, so it seems to at least one reader
well aware of Thoreau's general addiction in this callow
period to orphic utterances, cannot with perfect assurance
be identified as a reference to Ellen Sewall.

Of the two brothers John was much the more what is
called a normal youth. He had been capable six years before of writing a spoofing letter to a friend warning him
against "the lips of a strange woman" and declaring himself exempt from all such temptations "as there is naught
here save a few antiquated spinsters, or December virgins."
At no period in his life could Henry have been capable of
even this sort of harmless vulgarity, but the relatively casual
John soon thought that Ellen Sewall was probably for him.
The next summer she came for another visit, and on a jaunt
to the beach at Scituate he proposed marriage. She accepted; but almost immediately broke off the engagement
at the insistence of her parents who thought the whole
Thoreau family far too advanced in its ideas. A porten-
tously obscure passage in Henry's *Journal* dated July 19,
1840, and referring to the two preceding days as an aeon
during which a Syrian empire might have had time to rise
and fall, has been conjectured to mean that the writer knew
of his brother's intentions to propose and that he heroically
kept silent concerning his own love. Another entry, less
than three weeks later, speaks of a wave of happiness which
"flows over me like moonshine over a field," and this has
been similarly conjectured to refer to Henry's relief at
hearing that Ellen was not, after all, to be his brother's wife.

The evidence for this much of the story has long been
available, but in 1939 Henry S. Canby, author of a new
biography of Thoreau, made public for the first time in-

formation obtained from certain pages omitted from the published *Journal* and now in the hands of a private collector. It seems that on October 17, 1840, Thoreau was referring to "a friend" in whose presence "I am ashamed of my fingers and my toes." There are other references in the same obscure vein, but a letter dated Nov. 18th from Ellen to her Aunt Prudence Ward is perfectly explicit concerning the fact that, shortly before, she had at her father's request written "H.T." a short, explicit, and cold reply to a communication from him. Exactly what this letter contained is not known, but the available evidence does seem to suggest that Thoreau, the most perfect and apparently congenital of bachelors, did nevertheless once escape marriage, if not by the grace of God, then at least by grace of an ineptitude at wooing which God had given to tide him over the brief period during which even predestined celibates are likely to lose sight of their own vocations.

Others may, of course, consider the incident of more importance than has here been suggested. Mr. Canby, indeed, seems to feel that it gives us the key to Henry's secret and that had the incident (or something else like it) never occurred, we should not have the literary personality which we know as Thoreau. Speaking later of his women friends and especially of his intimacy with Mrs. Emerson—which certainly never, even in Thoreau's imagination, went beyond what New England propriety would have regarded as innocent—he writes: "There is nothing [nothing, that is, except the assumption that erotic impulses were frustrated] in Thoreau's philosophy . . . to explain the fierceness of his embrace of solitude and the passion of his reactions toward human love. There is nothing to account for the passionate intensity of his love for nature."

Surely, on the other hand, Thoreau himself would have been astonished at the suggestion that a passion for nature was inexplicable except on the theory that it substituted for some other passion which had been frustrated; and though this, of course, may not be acceptable evidence, the fact remains that Thoreau was already committed to what most men would regard as an abnormal way of life before he had ever laid eyes on Ellen Sewall. Mr. Canby himself admits that it is impossible to feel distressed that Thoreau was unsuccessful in his strange wooing. "I doubt," he writes, "whether he wanted to marry her," and that itself would seem almost enough to suggest that by that time he was already set into a pattern which allowed no place for any sexual expression of love. Less than a month before his proposal was rejected, he had written in the *Journal* a passage devoted to his "friend": "There is more than maiden modesty between us"; and if the reference really is to Ellen, the most probable inference seems to be not that her rejection caused, but rather that the rejection itself was determined by, Thoreau's absolute inability to recognize love in which sexual desire plays an essential part.

Few passages in his writings, public or private, are so misty, so paradoxical, and so self-contradictory as those devoted to Friendship in *A Week on the Concord and Merrimack Rivers;* and ostensibly, at least, that book relates a journey made just after the meeting of the brothers with Ellen and before John made his proposal of marriage. The best friends, it appears, according to Henry's account, say little, see one another seldom, and get the most profit out of their friendship while meditating upon it in solitude. On another occasion, setting down his thoughts on friendship and love for the benefit of an inquiring acquaintance, he wrote: "Love is the profoundest of secrets. Divulged, even to the beloved, it is no longer Love." If the author of those sentiments felt the same in 1840 and acted accordingly, it is no wonder that Ellen Sewall was as surprised as she seems to have been at receiving a proposal of marriage through the post.

That Thoreau was not physiologically sexless may be taken for granted. Perhaps, therefore, it should also be taken for granted that his sexuality was somehow sublimated or blocked. But the block, if block there was, was on some very deep level and the sublimation highly effective—much too highly so to admit the supposition that it was not achieved until, in his twenties, a pretty girl turned him down. At the very most it may be said, not that disappointment in love drove him into a scheme of life and an attitude toward nature, but that his one brief experience with a sexual attraction strong enough to make him contemplate the possibility of sexual relationship failed to disrupt or permanently change either his habits or his convictions. Perhaps for the first time it revealed him clearly to himself, but instinctive bachelorhood was what it revealed.

A wife was one of the many things which the way of life he had chosen compelled him to give up, and there is little evidence that the renunciation caused him more regret than the renunciation of various other things which, like sexual love, were not for him "necessaries of the soul." Mr. Clifton Fadiman once remarked that Thoreau could, after all, get more out of ten minutes with a chickadee than most men could get out of a night with Cleopatra, and it is perhaps not insignificant that a little more than two months after Ellen Sewall had rejected him he was writing one of those elaborate descriptions of a joyous encounter with a wild animal which became a recurrent feature of his *Journal* and which deserve to be better known than they are as an aspect of both his literary and his personal character.

Suddenly, looking down the river, I saw a fox some sixty rods off, making across to the hills on my left. As the snow lay five inches deep, he made but slow progress, but it was no impediment to me. So, yielding to the instinct of the chase, I tossed my head aloft and bounded away, snuffing the air like a fox-hound, and spurning the world and the Humane Society at each bound. It seemed the woods rang with the hunter's horn, and Diana and all the satyrs joined in the chase and cheered me on. Olympian and Elean youths were waving palms on the hills. In the meanwhile I gained rapidly on the fox; but he showed a remarkable presence of mind, for, instead of keeping up the face of the hill, which was steep and unwooded in that part, he kept along the slope in the direction of the forest, though he lost ground by it. Notwithstanding his fright, he took no step which was not beautiful. The course on his part was a series of most graceful curves. It was a sort of leopard canter, I should say, as if he were nowise impeded by the snow, but were husbanding his strength all the while. When he doubled I wheeled and cut him off, bounding with fresh vigor, and Antæus-like, recovering my strength each time I touched the snow. Having got near enough for a fair view, just as he was slipping into the wood, I gracefully yielded him the palm. He ran as though there were not a bone in his back, occasionally dropping his muzzle to the snow for a rod or two, and then tossing his head aloft when satisfied of his course. When he came to a declivity he put his fore feet together and slid down it like a cat. He trod so softly that you could not have heard it from any nearness, and yet with such expression that it would not have been quite inaudible at any distance. So, hoping this experience would prove a useful lesson to him. I returned to the village by the highway of the river.

Thoreau's humor, especially his ability to see the comic value of his own eccentricities, developed rather slowly. So too did his realization that humor made more effective the picture he drew of a world in which everyone except himself was out of step with common sense as well as out of step with the Divine Intention. Indeed he was in the beginning capable of warning himself to keep humor out of his *Journal*, and, for long stretches, he was capable of succeeding. But within a few days after he had established successful relations with the fox and therefore within less than three months after he had as conspicuously failed to achieve the same with Miss Sewall, he was comparing his determination not to yield an inch from the position in the universe which he had taken up with a similar determination in regard to late-comers at a town meeting—even though these late-comers might be of the female sex. And the passage, throughout which humor is beginning to gleam, will serve also to suggest why Thoreau, who had always been surrounded by spinsters and got along well enough both with them and with married ladies, nevertheless did not have or want to have what is ordinarily called "a way with women."

I will rest as the mountains do, so that your ladies might as well walk into the midst of the Tyrol, and look for Nature to spread them a green lawn for their disport in the midst of those solemn fastnesses, as that I should fly out of my orbit at their approach and go about eccentric, like a comet, to endanger other systems. No, be true to your instincts, and sit; wait till you can be genuinely polite, if it be till doomsday, and not lose your chance everlastingly by a cowardly yielding to young etiquette. By your look say unto them, The lines have fallen to me in pleasant places, and I will fill that station God has assigned me. . . .

When presumptuous womanhood demands to surrender my position, I bide my time—though it be with misgiving—and yield to no mortal shove, but expect a divine impulse. Produce your warrant, and I will retire; for not now can I give you a clear seat, but must leave part of my manhood behind and wander a diminished man, who at length will not have length and breadth enough to fill any seat at all. It was very kind in the gods who gave us a now [sic] condition, or condition of rest, in which we might unhurriedly deliberate before taking a step. When I give up my now and here without having secured my then and there, I am the prodigal son of a kind father and deserve no better than the husks which the swine eat, nor that the fatted calf be killed for me.

Thoreau Signs Off

THOREAU'S SCHOOLMASTERING was brought to an end early in 1841 when brother John, an easier, less original young man but the executive spirit of the enterprise, fell ill and the school was closed. John's malady was probably the tuberculosis to which the family was prone, but next year, before it had had time to develop, he suffered a slight accident and died in agony from a tetanus infection. Henry was deeply shaken by his brother's loss, he made no move to reopen the school, and he had probably never really considered himself so firmly settled in the profession of teaching as his mother had liked to suppose. On previous occasions he had helped his father with the manufacture of pencils, and even during his college years he had gone at least once to New York to peddle the product. Now he again concerned himself somewhat with the family business which continued to be operated throughout his life and of which, in time, he became nominally the manager. But his duties were not confining, he never devoted any considerable part of his energies to them, and he never, from the closing of the school onward, tied himself to any trade or profession. Three years after he ceased to be a schoolmaster he was called "the only man of leisure in the town."

Meanwhile, however, and beginning almost immediately after his return from college, he had set about that business of making the mental and spiritual settlements in life which seemed to him of such infinitely greater importance than any material settlements could be. In 1837, he had made the first entry in the *Journal* which he was to continue until six months before his death, and through that *Journal* he was to gain an entree into the Emerson household as well as the Emerson circle.

Sister Helen had read some of the early pages of the *Journal*. She told Emerson's sister-in-law, Mrs. Lucy Jackson Brown, that some of the thoughts resembled Emerson's own, and introductions were arranged. Soon Thoreau was frequently making one of the little company which gathered for conversation at the home of the older and already famous man; soon, also, Emerson was regarding him with respect and admiration. "I delight much in my young friend, who seems to have as free and erect a mind as any I have ever met," he wrote after a meeting in February 1838, and a week later he was entering more praise into his diary: "My good Henry Thoreau made this else solitary afternoon sunny with his simplicity and clear perception. . . . Everything that boy says makes merry with society, though nothing can be graver than his meaning."

Before this Thoreau had begun to take some part in the intellectual life of the village, for he was a member of the Lyceum, and during the course of one subsequent winter he secured for it twenty-five lectures for a total expenditure of one hundred dollars—which included the cost of rent, fuel, and lights! Before the members of this institution—

which obviously had to take what was available—he had given a talk on "Society" as early as 1838 when he was twenty-one years old and for a number of years he continued to try out on that audience observations and opinions which had previously been recorded in the ever-growing *Journal.* Presently he even—since conversation, lecturing, and publishing were, in that order, the almost inevitable activities of the group in which he found himself—managed to contribute (without pay) a few poems and some prose to *The Dial,* that famous though short-lived organ of the Transcendental movement of which first Margaret Fuller and then Emerson himself were editors.

But it is evident from both his letters and his *Journal* that Thoreau had by no means completely committed himself to the group or its activities. He had already (as he phrased it) "signed off" from the Concord church and he had no intention of "signing on" as member of any other institution. He was not sure that he wanted to assume the role of practicing prophet which came so naturally to Emerson, Margaret Fuller, and Bronson Alcott. Above all he was not sure that what seemed to them the good life of high-minded conversation and oracular instruction of the great public would be a good life for him, whose business seemed more with himself and with nature than with even the most select and educatable public. In what was perhaps his very first discourse before the Lyceum, he had observed that: "That which properly constitutes the life of every man is a profound secret," and had protested that society was made for man rather than man for society.

Nevertheless circumstances were to direct that his relationship with Emerson should become more intimate. He had no occupation, and when Emerson invited him to come and live in the house as handy man as well as member of the family, he came—on April 26, 1841—to stay for two years. In payment for his physical labor he received only his keep but he was brought inevitably into closer contact with the members of the Transcendentalist circle, who were puzzled by an aloofness and reserve which contrasted strangely enough with the expansiveness characteristic of at least the lesser disciples of Transcendentalism. Margaret Fuller thought him a bare hill still unwarmed by the breezes of spring, and though Emerson thought "we shall yet hear much more of him," even he objected to his brusqueness of manner, his penchant for contradiction, and his pugnaciousness about trifles. "He needs," Emerson thought, "to fall in love, to sweeten him and straighten him."

In July 1842, Nathaniel Hawthorne came with his bride to live in Concord, and he too soon came into contact with Thoreau—first, if the supposition of Sanborn is correct, not as a fellow intellectual but as the gardener lent by Emerson to prepare the grounds for the bride and groom. Probably the two men were disposed by a similar lack of social expansiveness to respect one another, and an entry in Hawthorne's notebook provides so much the best sketch of Thoreau at this period that a rather extended excerpt from it should be given.

Mr. Thoreau is a singular character; a young man with much of wild, original Nature still remaining in him; and so far as he is sophisticated, it is in a way and method of his own. He is as ugly as sin; long-nosed, queer-mouthed, and with uncouth and somewhat rustic manners . . . though courteous . . . corresponding with such an exterior. But his ugliness is of an honest and agreeable fashion, and becomes him much better than beauty . . . he has repudiated all regular means of getting a living, and seems inclined to lead a sort of Indian life. . . .

He is a keen and delicate observer of Nature . . . a *genuine* observer, which I suspect is almost as rare a character as even an original poet. And Nature, in return for his love, seems to adopt him as her especial child; and shows him secrets which few others are allowed to witness. He is familiar with beast, fish, fowl and reptile, and has strange stories to tell of adventures and friendly passages with these lower brethren of mortality. Herb and flower, likewise, wherever they grow, whether in garden or wildwood, are his familiar friends. He is on intimate terms with the clouds also, and can tell the portents of storms. He has a great regard for the memory of the Indian tribes, whose wild life would have suited him so well; and, strange to say, he seldom walks over a plowed field without picking up an arrow-point, spearhead, or other relic of the red man. With all this he has more than a tincture of literature; a deep and true taste for poetry, especially for the elder poets; and he is a good writer. At least he has written a good article,—a rambling disquisition on Natural History, in the last *Dial*, which, he says, was chiefly made up from journals of his own observations. Methinks this article gives a very fair image of mind and character . . . so true, so innate and literal in observation . . . yet giving the spirit as well as the letter of what he sees; even as a lake reflects its wooded banks, showing every leaf . . . yet giving the wild beauty of the whole scene.

Six months later Hawthorne felt compelled to add: "Mr. Emerson seems to have suffered some inconvenience from his experience of Mr. Thoreau as an inmate. It may well be that such a sturdy, uncompromising person is fitter to meet occasionally in the open air than as a permanent guest at table and fireside." Thoreau, on the whole, would have liked that.

The truth seems to be that he did not always find the high thinking which went on vocally at gatherings in the Emerson house so inspiring as it might have been. Even before going there he had declared himself a "transcendental brother," but his brethren could on occasion be silly enough—just how silly, at least when Emerson was not present, may be read in an account written to the latter by his wife in February 1843:

Last evening we had the "Conversation," though, owing to the bad weather, but few attended. The subjects were: What is Prophecy? Who is a Prophet? and The Love of Nature. Mr. Lane decided, as for all time and the race, that this same love of nature . . . of which Henry [Thoreau] was the champion, and Elizabeth Hoar and Lidian (though L. disclaimed possessing it herself) his faithful squiresses . . . that this love was the most subtle and dangerous of sins; a refined idolatry, much more to be dreaded than gross wickedness, because the gross sinner would be alarmed by the depth of his degradation, and come up from it in terror, but the unhappy idolaters of Nature were deceived by the refined quality of their sin, and would be the last to enter the kingdom. Henry frankly affirmed to both the wise men that they were wholly deficient in the faculty in question, and therefore could not judge of it. And Mr. Alcott as frankly answered that it was because they went beyond the mere material objects, and were filled with spiritual love and perception (as Mr. T. was not), that they seemed to Mr. Thoreau not to appreciate outward nature. I am very heavy, and have spoiled a most excellent story. I have given you no idea of the scene, which was ineffably comic, though it made no laugh at the time; I scarcely laughed at it myself . . . too deeply amused to give the usual sign. Henry was brave and noble; well as I have always liked him, he still grows upon me.

Physically Thoreau must have been at this time an agreeable if not especially elegant figure. Most readers no doubt tend to think of him in connection with the most frequently reproduced portrait, which presents a rather wooden face decorated with a set of not very becoming chin whiskers. But that daguerreotype was not taken until 1856, about the time when his health began to decline, and he was, during most of his life, clean shaved. Though of only average height, or even somewhat less, he gave an impression of abounding health, and both Emerson and Ellery Channing testify to something striking about his whole bearing as well as about the keen resoluteness of his expression. The gray-blue eyes were deep set, the nose was prominent and aquiline (like one of the portraits of Caesar, Channing called it), the mouth was prominent with full, often pursed, lips. His complexion was fair, his hair light brown and abundant. But it was the poised readiness of his body which must have been the most striking feature of his appearance. "His whole figure," says Channing, "had an active earnestness, as if he had no moment to waste. The clenched hand betokened purpose. In walking, he made a short cut if he could, and when sitting in the shade or by a wall side, seemed merely the clearer to look forward into the next piece of activity. Even in the boat he had a wary, transitory air, his eyes on the outlook—perhaps there might be ducks, or the Blanding turtle, or an otter or sparrow." More surprising to those who tend to think of him as earnest and solemn is the fact that he was full of humorous high spirits. He danced, not only vigorously but well. He sang popular songs. And no one, said Channing, laughed more or better.

Reading and writing, the most solitary of the intellectual pursuits, were naturally those which Thoreau found most congenial. The year before he went to live with Emerson he had written Sister Helen a letter in which he declared somewhat sportively that "an honest book's the noblest work of Man" and suggested that she also should write something. "If you cannot compose a volume, then try a tract. . . . You will not lack readers—here am I, for one." He himself was keeping on with the *Journal* which was to cover many hundreds of pages before he left the Emerson house and which, though it was intended in part as a storehouse for material later to be worked up for a public, no doubt did not please him the less for the fact that in the form then being set down it was addressed primarily to himself.

He had no intention of becoming so committed to authorship as to discover too late that it also was a profession. He had, so he admits in 1842, sometimes "felt mean enough" when asked by some earnest seeker "what errand I had to mankind"; but that was merely because he could not explain what the errand was, not at all because he did not think that he had as much of one as he, at least, needed to have.

At evening walked to see an old schoolmate who is going to help make the Welland Canal navigable for ships round Niagara. He cannot see any such motives and modes of living as I; professes not to look beyond the securing of certain "creature comforts." And so we go silently different ways, with all serenity, I in the still moonlight through the village this fair evening to write these thoughts in my journal, and he, forsooth, to mature his schemes to ends as good, maybe, but quite different. So are we two made, while the same stars shine quietly over us. If I or he be wrong, Nature yet consents placidly. She bites her lip and smiles to see how her children will agree. So does the Welland Canal get built, and other conveniences, while I live.

Meanwhile he was, so at least he professed to believe, serenely and indescribably happy. A few days before he met his industrious friend he had written for his own benefit: "I am startled that God can make me so rich even with my own cheap stores. It needs but a few wisps of straw in the sun, or some small word dropped, or that has long lain silent in some book." "My life at this moment," as he had somewhat earlier confessed to himself, "is like a summer morning when birds are singing," and about the same time he was assuring a correspondent: "I love my fate to the very core and rind, and could swallow it without paring it, I think."

In the household it was clearly to Lidian Emerson, his patron's second wife, that he was most drawn. She was fifteen years his senior, shy, melancholy, witty, and religious in a relatively conventional way; not much given to the new thoughts effervescing around her. Certainly the relations between her and her husband, though of course on a very high plane, were not warm and the philosopher lived with her what he himself called a "bachelor existence." But Thoreau, who had a tendency to hope that any shy reserved person was that ideal friend to whom friendship need not be revealed and with whom one could communicate without saying anything, seems, after Ellen Sewall's cool letter, to have made Lidian his "sister."

Unlike most young men, he feared most not that he would never be more than then he was, but only that he might come to be less; that getting ahead or even merely making a living might become his chief business. Already at twenty-three, before he had gone to live with Emerson and thirteen years before he was to proclaim the same thought to a large public in his only much-read book, he was entering in the *Journal* a warning: "Most who enter on any profession are doomed men. The world might as well sing a dirge over them forthwith." "The farmer's muscles," he added, "are rigid," and so, he might have gone on, are those of the professional writer or even prophet. "I am," he confessed in a letter to Mrs. Emerson's sister, "as unfit for any practical purpose—I mean for the furtherance of the world's ends—as gossamer for shiptimber; and I, who am going to be a pencilmaker tomorrow, can sympathize with God Apollo, who served King Admetus for a while on this earth." Apollo, he admits, found this to his advantage at last and so perhaps will he, "though I shall hold the nobler part at least out of the service."

Emerson, who complained about his young protégé's indulgence in a spirit of contradiction, seems to have complained also about his tendency to say nothing at all, for Emerson was probably the "friend" who "thinks I *keep* silence, who am only choked with letting it out so fast" and to whom Thoreau replies in the *Journal:* "I have been breaking silence these twenty-three years and have hardly made a rent in it. Silence has no end; speech is but the beginning of it."

Curiously enough, Thoreau, on his side, does not, during all this time, mention Emerson's name in his *Journal* where it does not occur before an undated passage belonging apparently to the Walden period. Here he wrote of him: "There is no such general critic of men and things, no such trustworthy and faithful man. More of the divine [is] realized in him than in any." Yet even this entry is elsewhere not without its qualifications and the qualifications became more and more important. Later, at least, Thoreau thought there was an alloy of patronage in Emerson's praise and that Emerson was one of those who "flatter you, but themselves more."

It has already been admitted that the reading of *Nature* probably first encouraged Thoreau to trust in his own originality. Certainly he later learned much from Emerson even though some of what he learned had to be unlearned again. But we can only guess just how completely he had ever regarded himself as a disciple and just how soon he became aware of a restiveness which certainly began presently to affect him whenever he felt that he was yielding too much to any man's influence. And in any case it is easy to see what some of the fundamental differences between the two men were. In the sage of Concord Thoreau soon began to suspect that there was too much of the merely genteel, too little of the genuine wildness which he valued so much in himself and which he cultivated by direct association with physical nature.

Being a man who felt impelled to lead a life of outward as well as of inward nonconformity, he was suspicious of those whose inner life was compatible with a decorous, genteel position in a community like Concord, and he may have been mentally including Emerson in his condemnation when he came, in the first chapter of *Walden*, to complain: "The success of great scholars and thinkers is commonly a courtier-like success, not kingly, not manly. They make shift to live merely by conformity, practically as their fathers did. . . . The philosopher is in advance of his age even in the outward form of his life. He is not fed, sheltered, clothed, warmed, like his contemporaries. How can a man be a philosopher and not maintain his vital heat by better methods than other men?"

Looking back he liked to believe that he had always been less a member of any group than an individual going about his own business, and that to describe "how I have desired to spend my life in years past" would somewhat surprise even those of his readers who were, like Emerson, acquainted with his actual history. "In any weather, at any hour of the day or night, I have," he goes on, "been anxious to improve the nick of time, and notch it on my stick too; to stand on the meeting of two eternities, the past and the future, which is precisely the present moment; to toe that line. . . . To anticipate, not the sunrise and the dawn merely, but, if possible, Nature herself!"

It must be remembered that Thoreau, though he wrote only one book now, or ever, very widely read, has managed to acquire three different reputations, and that of the three only one—his reputation as a member of the Transcendentalist group—obviously owes very much to Emerson's influence. Moreover, that reputation is now not much more than a fact of literary history since New England Transcendentalism, considered as a theory of knowledge and a special technique for attaining Truth, hardly interests very many today outside the group whose concern is chiefly with the historical study of a literary movement. His other two reputations, the two in which Emerson's influence is far less important, are, on the other hand, both very much alive since he is today both hailed as a prophet of social reform and cherished as the chosen spokesman of thousands who have resolved to turn their backs upon society and to seek, as he once did, salvation for the individual soul through solitary communion with all that part of nature which is not human.

The fact that the *Journal* begins after he had already made contact with Emerson, at least through the printed page, and only shortly before he felt Emerson's personal influence, tends to obscure the question of what native impulses first emerged and leads easily to the assumption that he was, chronologically, first of all a moralist of Transcendental leanings. Thus there is no doubt that the earlier portions of the *Journal* reveal a struggle after Emersonian profundities or that the young writer was trying to find expression for himself in a style of writing and of thinking which the mere physical propinquity of a great writer made it almost inevitable he should imitate. Even his first published work, *A Week on the Concord and Merrimack Rivers,* which ostensibly describes a journey made in the autumn of 1839, is a curious narrative frequently interrupted by long passages of sometimes rather callow mysticism. But the fact that he went not to the study but to the river for communion with the Oversoul is itself significant. It suggests the possibility that the philosophy is chiefly an attempt to justify an expedition which would earlier have been made without any such justification and that the boatman was antecedent to the philosopher—perhaps even that the first appeal of Transcendentalism was the fact that it seemed to invest with high moral purpose activities which to family and fellow townsmen seemed irresponsible when indulged in by a grown man without a profession.

What, then, if we may try to reconstruct the pre-Emersonian Thoreau, was the first thing he wanted, and what was the first eccentricity he was compelled to develop in order not to deprive himself of it?

He had, it must be remembered, been raised in genteel poverty. Recently the pencil business had prospered, and as it became more and more the manufacture of graphite for electrotypers rather than for pencils, it was to prosper still more. But his father had been long an unsuccessful man and his mother, among other things, took in boarders. The very first choice he had to make was, then, the choice between living and making a living, between sacrificing himself to the so-called necessities, and learning how to do well enough without them. The choice that he made was not the usual one and it testifies to a native originality of mind as well as of temperament. But a proper understanding of his thought and his life must begin with the realization that this particular choice had to be made.

It is true that he ultimately developed a moral philosophy in which doing without superfluities became a virtue in itself and he certainly implied that the richest and the most secure would do well to adopt what he called "voluntary poverty." But his own poverty was not, in the first instance, voluntary. His choice was not a choice among many possibilities but only between two narrowly defined alternatives—between doing without and paying the enormous price which must be paid for middle-class decencies by those who have neither inherited wealth nor an obvious talent for any well-paid activity.

To say this is not to say that his declared preference for living close to the bone was mere rationalization or that his wisdom is invalidated by the fact that he acquired it through a struggle with a personal problem. But he did make virtue of necessity, or rather of what had become necessity once he had resolved not to pay for the superficialities what he would have had to pay, and that fact helps us to understand at least the more extravagant of his self-denying ordinances.

When, for instance, he despises foreign travel or ridicules the man who thinks theaters or concerts necessary to cultivate the soul, it is well to remember that he was discounting what he could not have rather than what he could, and that, as a matter of fact, he traveled as much as he was able conveniently to travel—namely, to Cape Cod, Canada, and the Maine woods. In his own mind he probably did not always keep clear the distinction between what was not worth having and what was merely not worth the price which he would have had to pay for it, but the distinction is nevertheless a valid one. "It has not," he was to say later, "been my design to live cheaply, but only to live as I could, not devoting much time to getting a living."

Indeed when he came to write the first chapter of *Walden* he was to be perfectly explicit: "Finding that my fellow-citizens were not likely to offer me any room in the court house, or any curacy or living anywhere else, but I must shift for myself, I turned my face more exclusively than ever to the woods, where I was better known. . . . My purpose in going to Walden Pond was not to live cheaply nor to live dearly there, but to transact some private business with the fewest obstacles." By the time *Walden* was written he was ready to proclaim further (at least in a sort of parenthesis) that the art of doing without which he had discovered in the search for a possible means of living his own life might be equally useful even to those who had quite other lives to lead. He pointed out for instance that it required in his day about fifteen years for the average workman to earn the money to pay for the kind of house in which he usually lived, and he was sure that this was too large a portion of anyone's life to be expended merely to provide shelter, no matter what marginal activity seemed to the laborer most worth indulging. But in the beginning his scheme of life was developed merely to solve an individual problem.

If we can accept as accurate the memories he was later to set down, the life which was not to be sacrificed to making a living had been, up to the time he went to college, mostly an instinctive one, and when the time came for him to supply a sketch for the Class Book at the end of his college career, he wrote: "I shall ever pride myself on the place of my birth. . . . If I forget thee, O Concord, let my right hand forget her cunning. . . . To whatever quarter of the world I may wander, I shall deem it good fortune that I hail from Concord North Bridge." It may be that simple homesickness contributed more to produce that outburst of local patriotism than the composer of it cared to admit or was even conscious of, and when on other occasions he expatiated upon the delights of the region where it had been his good fortune to be born, it was not upon domesticity but upon wildness that he always dwelt. "I can easily walk ten, fifteen, twenty, any number of miles, commencing at my own door, without going by any house, without crossing a road except where the fox and the mink do. . . . There are square miles in my vicinity which have no inhabitant." Again: "Those resorts which I most love and frequent, numerous and vast as they are, are as it were given up to me, as much as if I were an autocrat or owner of the world, and by my edicts excluded men from my territories. . . . I find such ample space and verge, even miles of walking every day in which I do not meet nor see a human being, and often not very recent traces of them."

On occasion he can remember that he walks "as one possessing the advantages of human culture, fresh from society of men, but turned loose into the woods, the only man in nature, walking and meditating to a great extent as if man and his customs were not." More often, however, he resents or thinks that he resents the intrusion of civilization or of human society and congratulates himself that, though he can see civilization and the abodes of men from afar, "these farmers and their works are scarcely more obvious than woodchucks." More typical Americans might be looking forward to the day when the still spacious country would be teeming with an industrious population; Thoreau looked back to the very recent past when the wilderness, of which he felt he was catching the last glimpse, was undisturbed. In his latest and soberest years, after he had reluctantly consented, on occasion, to think socially, he became, to some extent, that very tame and civilized thing, a "conservationist," and he even made a plea for the establishment of national parks. But in youth and young manhood he was fiercely individualistic. "I am convinced," he wrote in *A Week on the Concord and Merrimack Rivers*, "that my genius dates from an older era than the agricultural. . . . There is in my nature, methinks, a singular yearning towards all wildness. . . . Gardening is civil and social, but it wants the vigor and freedom of the forest and the outlaw. . . . There are other, savager and more primeval aspects of nature than our poets have sung. It is only white man's poetry."

Even the farmers of Concord were too domestic for him. "The same thing which keeps the hen-hawk in the woods, away from the cities, keeps me here. That bird settles with confidence on a white pine top and not upon your weathercock. That bird will not be poultry of yours, lays no eggs for you, forever hides its nest." The plain living of New England was not plain enough, at least for his imagination, and its economy was too complicated as well as too utilitarian. It infuriated him to think that huckleberries should be *sold*. He argued with his father about the *use* of making maple sugar when he could have bought it cheaper at the store. "He said it took me from my studies. I said I made it my study; I felt as if I had been to a university." Neighbors who would not hesitate to shoot the last pair of hen hawks in the town to save a few of their chicks disgusted him by this "narrow and groveling economy." "I would rather never taste chickens' meat nor hens' eggs than never to see a hawk sailing through the upper air again. This sight is worth incomparably more than a chicken soup or a boiled egg." Even the wildness of the woods, as he now found them, was too tame for him. "When I consider that the nobler animals have been exterminated here—the cougar, the panther, lynx, wolverine, wolf, bear, moose, deer, the beaver, the turkey, etc., etc.—I cannot but feel as if I lived in a tamed, and, as it were, emasculated country. . . . Is it not a maimed and imperfect nature that I am conversant with? As if I were to study a tribe of Indians that had lost all its warriors. . . . I take infinite pains to know all the phenomena of the spring, for instance, thinking that I have here the entire poem, and then, to my chagrin, I hear that it is but an imperfect copy that I possess and have read, that my ancestors have torn out many of the first leaves and grandest passages, and mutilated it in many places. I should not like to think that some demigod had come before me and picked out some of the best of the stars. I wish to know an entire heaven and an entire earth."

Few of the poets and philosophers who have made nature their theme or have sought in her their God ever had, or ever desired to have, Thoreau's kind of experience with nature's least humanized aspects. In tastes as well as in feelings he was at least as much akin to the Audubons and the Muirs as he was to the Wordsworths or the Emersons, and he considered himself indescribably fortunate to have been born not quite too late to catch a glimpse of a country not yet all tamed. An English book which suggests that the Englishman's right to walk through now vanishing woodland paths might be defended by paving them with "asphalt laid upon a good foundation" filled him with mingled consternation and contempt. When a tree is cut down in Concord, he asks, "Does not the village bell sound a knell? . . . I see no procession of mourners in the streets, or the woodland aisles. The squirrel has leaped to another tree; the hawk has circled further off, and has settled now upon a new eyrie, but the woodman is preparing to lay his axe at at the root of that also." And it was in part at least this sense that increasing gentility as well as increasing tameness was cutting off even the new philosophers from the very nature they professed to be turning to, that is responsible for his soon-to-develop sense of alienation from Emerson. It was not that he was unwilling to make, with Emerson, the assumption that association with nature would communicate to man the profoundest truths; but he doubted if men like Emerson, busy only with their thoughts in quiet studies, actually had much contact with anything except these same thoughts, or that their occasional careful interviews with an emasculated nature could possibly give them more than an emasculated vision of the truths they sought.

In his friend and first master, Thoreau was later to discover something which he described as almost "cockney," and Emerson, in unconscious retaliation for an insult he had never heard, spoke with good-natured mockery of Henry's "edible religion"—for Thoreau, expecting no very favorable answer, nevertheless liked to put to nature the question how far she alone would support him and to put it practically, by eating in the woods whatever seemed even possibly edible. Refusing to stop, like other country boys, with such things as huckleberries and maple sugar, he once indeed went so far as to make an unsuccessful experiment with the seeds of skunk cabbage. Acorns he professed to find quite palatable, though better raw than cooked, and "From my experience with wild apples I can understand that there may be a reason for a savage preferring many kinds of food which the civilized man rejects." "It takes," he added, "a savage or wild taste to appreciate a wild apple."

No doubt he congratulated himself in being, unlike the cockney Emerson, close enough to the savage to retain some lingering kinship with the savage palate, just as he was getting some last glimpse of the savage's physical world. Farmers were lesser men than hunters, and Emerson was so little of a farmer, even, that Thoreau doubted if he would be willing to "trundle a wheelbarrow through the streets, because it would be out of character." "To get the value of the storm we must be out a long time and travel far in it. . . . Some men speak of having been wetted to the skin once as a memorable event in their lives, which, notwithstanding the croakers, they survived." Had most of the nature philosophers ever been, metaphorically, wet to the skin with her rain even once.

Thoreau was no Rousseauist. His noble savage, in so far as he *was* noble, was so not because he was assumed to have in perfection the finest qualities of the civilized man but rather because he possessed qualities quite different, and if the instinctive sympathy with wild nature was probably Thoreau's first distinguishing characteristic, it is also the one that persisted with least modification through life, so that in his latest writings it plays an even larger part than it had in the first, and *The Maine Woods*—far less transcendental than *A Week on the Concord and Merrimack Rivers*—becomes a sort of despairing protest against the final destruction of the one world in which he felt thoroughly at home. An Indian guide, pointing to a belt of dead trees near a lake, explained that all the caribou had left because "no likum stump, when he sees that he scared." So, in the same way, was Thoreau himself scared.

Sometimes he was exalted to think how much was left, as he was, for instance, when he reflected that much of America was still unsettled and unexplored: "Like the English in New Holland, we live only on the shores of a continent even yet. . . . The very timber and boards and shingles of which our houses are made grew but yesterday in a wilderness where the Indian still hunts and the moose runs wild. New York has her wilderness within her own borders; and though the sailors of Europe are familiar with the soundings of her Hudson, and Fulton long since invented the steamboat on its waters, an Indian is still necessary to guide her scientific men to its headwaters in the Adirondack country." More often, however, it was the inevitable and rapid destruction of wild nature which horrified him, and his realization that this necessarily went hand in hand with what his fellow citizens regarded as progress is probably the original source of his rationalized conviction that the so-called "development" of America was, in truth, its destruction, morally as well as physically.

"The Anglo-American," he wrote, "can indeed cut down, and grub up all this waving forest, and make a stump speech, and vote for Buchanan on its ruins, but he cannot converse with the spirit of the tree he fells, he cannot read the poetry and mythology which retire as he advances." "The very willow-rows lopped every three years for fuel or powder, and every sizable pine and oak, or other forest tree, cut down within the memory of man! As if individual spectators were to be allowed to export the clouds out of the sky, or the stars out of the firmament, one by one. We shall be reduced to gnaw the very crust of the earth for nutriment."

Most of those who long, or think that they long, for the simple life do so because they have turned with disgust from the spectacle of competitive society, and in desperation they are driven to the assumption that nature will comfort them. But from such passages as the above it is not difficult to conclude that the evolution of Thoreau's convictions follows the path in an opposite direction—not, that is to say, from hatred of human society to the supposition that nature will be lovable, but from a love of nature to the assumption that human society is hateful. He did not love trees because he despised stump speeches but despised stump speeches because only by cutting down trees could they be made.

In an environment more primitive than that of Concord, at the frontier or even beyond it, such a temperament as

Thoreau's might possibly have satisfied its instinctive needs without the concurrent development of a philosophy, and without the consciousness of any necessity for social protest. He might have been hunter, or trapper, or scout, or possibly no more than a merchant or surveyor to whom the recreations of the outdoors were inevitable and unremarked. But Thoreau had grown up in an intellectual environment, he had been to college and developed an intellectual life. In the society of which he was a part, man was assumed to be, first of all, a moral being whose activities required justification. What would have been on the frontier a merely normal, active life would be shiftlessness and animality in Concord.

Fortunately for him, some connection could be made between the new doctrine that man was to seek salvation through the contemplation of nature and what he himself had long delighted to do. Had the intellectual leaders of Concord been the New England theologians of the preceding century, he would no doubt have thrown in his lot with the scamps. Had they been Yankee philosophers of another stamp, preaching the gospel of commercial or industrial enterprise, he would have been a ne'er-do-well. As it was, he threw in his lot with the Transcendentalists, and he set about asking the nature which he knew in his own way the questions which they, from a considerably greater distance, tried to put to her.

Even before he went to live in Emerson's house he had been aware of his contempt for conventional Christian moralizing, for he had noted somewhat smugly that when reading, for instance, a book on agriculture, he made it his practice to "skip the author's moral reflections, and the words 'Providence' and 'He' scattered along the page, to come to the profitable level of what he has to say." Now he wondered if much that he heard from the Transcendental brothers was not the same sort of thing in different words, and if they were not contracting from their so-called nature the very disease he was trying to cure himself of. "I never met a man who cast a free and healthy glance over life, but the best live in a sort of Sabbath light, a Jewish gloom." "What offends me most in my compositions is the moral element in them. The repentant never say a brave word. . . . Strictly speaking, morality is not healthy. Those undeserved joys which come uncalled and make us more pleased than we are grateful are they that sing." "The moral aspect of Nature," he concluded, "is a jaundice reflected from man"; and it is difficult to imagine any thought less Emersonian. Whitman would have enthusiastically agreed. Coleridge may have been more gently implying the same thing when he warned his dear William that "in our life alone does Nature live." But from the standpoint of New England Transcendentalism it was sheer atheism.

For all his unworldliness, Emerson was in some respects more worldly than Thoreau, more ambitious for him than he was for himself, and disturbed by the fact that Thoreau's light was kept hidden under the bushel of his contented reserve. He evidently felt that life as handy-man-companion was proving all too acceptable, and at the end of two years he expelled Thoreau gently into the world. He suggested, and Henry agreed, that the latter should go to live for a time with Emerson's lawyer brother on Staten Island—ostensibly as a tutor for the brother's young son but actually to make contacts with those who might buy his literary goods.

When on May 1, 1843, Thoreau set off he was almost twenty-six years old and he had, so far, managed to avoid deep entanglement with any profession, even that of literature. What he really thought of his patron's plan to launch him on the world it is difficult to say, and it is at least possible that he was consistent enough to hope, secretly, that it would fail. But he consented, nevertheless, and undertook to peddle his genius in the same market where he had peddled his father's pencils some seven years before.

William Emerson was a sincere and kindly man but completely absorbed in his profession, and the impression produced on Thoreau by the metropolis itself is summed up in the statement: "I walked through New York yesterday —and met no real and living person." The city, he remarked dryly, "is large enough now, and they intend it shall be larger still." To Sister Sophia he wrote of the honeysuckle on Staten Island and of how it differed from that of Concord; to his mother about the seven-year locust which was having its year. Obviously he was homesick, though he interrupts a paragraph devoted to thoughts of home with the protestation that he is not.

Armed with a letter from Emerson, he called on the elder Henry James. He explained Transcendentalism to James in a three-hour conversation and came away liking the man very much. "He has naturalized and humanized New York for me," although (in the same letter): "I don't like the city better the more I see it, but worse. I am ashamed of my eyes that behold it. . . . When will the world learn that a million men are of no importance compared with *one* man." Horace Greeley he described as "cheerfully in earnest . . . a hearty New Hampshire boy as one would wish to meet," and Greeley was sufficiently impressed not only to act as a sort of agent for Thoreau in his never very large literary negotiations but also long to remain, next to Emerson, the warmest admirer he had among men of letters.

But despite politeness and sometimes something more from these and from lesser men, there was little indication that Thoreau's talents were salable. The *Democratic Review*, to whose editor Hawthorne had introduced him, bought an insignificant essay on "The Landlord" and also commissioned a review of the book by the German Utopian, Etzler, in whose scheme for a highly mechanized world Thoreau managed to work up the appearance of mild interest—not, as has already been said, because he approved of mechanization, but because Etzler predicted a society in which everybody would live in almost uninterrupted leisure. Many of the magazines paid nothing yet got all the contributions they could print at this price, even though Thoreau thought most of them were worth no more. Those that did pay showed little eagerness to employ Thoreau. He had pretended to Emerson that he hoped for success; to the members of his family he was presently writing in a tone of resignation, with which there was, quite possibly, mingled a good deal of relief. He called on the Harper firm but was told that since it was making fifty thousand a year there seemed no reason to experiment. "My bait will not tempt the rats—they are too well fed. . . . They say there is a 'Ladies' Companion' that pays,—but I could not write anything companionable."

As for the city, it continued to remain unattractive. "Seeing so many people from day to day, one comes to have less respect for flesh and bones, and thinks they must be more loosely joined, of less firm fiber, than the few he had known. It must have a very bad influence on children to see so many human beings at once,—mere herds of men." And so, before the end of November, he was back in Concord, after an absence of less than seven months. He returned, not to Emerson's house, but to pencil-making and the bosom of his own family.

Of the two fiascoes—that in New York and that in the Emerson household—the latter was much the more important. It apparently convinced him that his sympathy with even the most intellectually attractive group he had ever known was far from perfect, and that even to them he was not so closely akin as he had, no doubt, once liked to hope. They were protestant and aloof, so far as most Americans and most of America were concerned, but he was protestant and aloof even from them. For the time being, at least, he had had enough of influences, even of influences as important as he recognized that of Emerson to have been. He must withdraw far enough to sort out his own thoughts and convictions, to separate what was really his or had been made his from all that he had passively taken over from others. He must set into some sort of order the complex of convictions, sensibilities, tastes, and prejudices which would explain him and his way of life even if they were never systematic enough, or possibly even consistent enough, to be called a philosophy. And so the symbolic retirement to the hut near the edge of Walden pond was both inevitable and not far away.

It is possible that his relations with Lidian Emerson had also something to do with the closing of an epoch. She had been the first person outside his own family to whom he had written from Staten Island, and in the first of the three letters he wrote her from there, he is professing to think of her "as some elder sister of mine." Nearly a month later he thanks her rapturously for some communication which he calls "very noble"; but the next letter from him is dated nearly four months later and is in so merely chatty a vein as to suggest the possibility that Lidian may—quite unnecessarily—have shied away from his ardor. His letters to her had not, indeed, been very different from those written shortly before to her sister, Mrs. Lucy Jackson Brown, since to Mrs. Brown also he could say: "We always seem to be living just on the brink of a pure and lofty intercourse," and it does not seem safe to assume that in the case of either he was seeking anything more than someone to whom he could whisper: "Solitude is sweet."

Mr. Canby quotes from a torn manuscript in the Huntington Library part of a suppressed essay, or notes for an essay, called "A Sister" which he believes refers to Mrs. Emerson. Elsewhere in the same manuscript Thoreau wrote: "By turns my purity has inspired and my impurity has cast me down." He then goes on to declare that his most intimate acquaintance with woman has been a sister's relation, "or at most a Catholic's virgin mother relation—not that it has always been free from the suspicion of lower sympathy." But before these admissions are taken to mean too much, it should be remembered that his idea of what constituted "impurity" was, and always remained, more than monkish, and the succeeding fragment continues a self-examination which makes it sufficiently clear that whatever might have been found in the depths of his subconsciousness, he was, both on the conscious level and just below it, resolved to cultivate his aloofness rather than to seek any experience which would overcome it. "Woman is a nature older than I and commanding from me a vast amount of veneration—like Nature. She is my mother at the same time that she is my sister, so that she is at any rate an older sister. . . . I cannot imagine a woman no older than I."

What drove him toward Walden was, then, not what is ordinarily called disappointment in love nor anything much like it. Instead it was primarily the failure of sympathy between him and the only group with whom sympathy had seemed possible. There was no one except himself to whom he could turn, and he would go away—not far away because mere physical distance or mere physical propinquity meant nothing—but just far enough to symbolize his voluntary withdrawal from community life; just as far, that is to say, as Walden pond where he would still be surrounded by those particular manifestations of nature which had first awakened him to her charms, and yet reassuringly remote from the influence of men whose irrelevancies were all the more distracting because they just failed to be relevant.

What he found there was not new thoughts, for nearly every leading idea in the book which grew out of his stay had already been at least hinted in the *Journal* and sometimes expressed very well indeed. What he did discover was a new urgency, and that new urgency enabled him both to find a more personal utterance and to separate what was peculiarly his from most of what had merely been imbibed as part of the Transcendental atmosphere. As long as he had been only an earnest young man trying to live up to both himself and his high-minded friends, the effect of a given hundred pages of his manuscript is diluted with mystical meanderings which at times are distressingly pretentious. But by the time he came finally to put everything into the form of an account of his life in the woods, he had discovered not only that the form provided some sort of unity but also that the very fact that he was defending his eccentricity against the world, instead of apologizing to himself for not being exalted or ineffable enough, gave to his utterance a humor, a pungency, and a certain defiant finality which make it unforgettable.

Paradise Found

*T*HE RETIREMENT to Walden is the central feature in the legend of Thoreau. It is the one thing about him which everybody knows, and the prominence which must be given it in any account of his life is justified by the fact that the experience unquestionably served to release his creative powers. But even if it had not actually had any such demonstrable effect, it would still be so artistically right that it would assume, willy-nilly, a very prominent place in his story. A philosopher should pass his forty days in the wilderness, and Thoreau, to whom the enduring legends were the only interesting form of fiction, would have been pleased to realize—whether or not he ever actually did realize—that he was following a pattern consecrated by eternal repetition.

From 1840 on, good reasons for withdrawing from social life had begun to accumulate in the *Journal*. The "garret" motif recurs, along with the determination to wipe his hands of life; to see how mean it is and to have nothing to do with it. He was determined to "move away from public opinion, from government, from religion, from education, from society." "There are certain current expressions and blasphemous moods of viewing things, as when we say 'he is doing a good business' more profane than cursing and swearing. There is death and sin in such words. Let not the children hear them." And he was also willing to go even further. "No true and brave person will be content to live on such a footing with his fellows and himself as the laws of every household require. The house is the very haunt and lair of our vice. I am impatient to withdraw myself from under its roof as an unclean spot. There is no circulation there; it is full of stagnant and mephitic vapors." He determines "to meet myself face to face sooner or later" and on a visit to Cambridge he is suddenly overwhelmed with distaste for the collection of English poets he had come to seek. "When looking over dry and dusty volumes of the English poets, I cannot believe that those fresh and fair creations I had imagined are contained in them. English poetry from Gower down, collected into one alcove, and so from the library window compared with the commonest nature, seems very mean. Poetry cannot breathe in the scholar's atmosphere. I can hardly be serious with myself when I remember that I have come to Cambridge after poetry; and while I am running over the catalogue and selecting, I think it would be a shorter way to a complete volume to step at once into the field or wood, with a very low reverence to students and librarians. Milton did not see what company he was to fall into."

For all this, Thoreau did not—pleasant as it would be to imagine it so—go arrowlike from Staten Island and its fiasco to Walden pond. Instead he returned to his parents' home, and helped them in building the new house called "Texas" because of its remoteness from the Milldam which was regarded as the center of Concord. It may even have been about this time that he devised an improved method of producing graphite which was to lift the financial state of the family. But no discovery of Yankee ingenuity in himself was likely to divert him into the cultivation of so dubious a gift.

To Emerson he complained that he found it impossible to do more than one thing at a time and that, though his evenings were nominally free for study, "if he was in the day inventing machines for sawing his plumbago, he invents wheels all the evening and night also." The fear that he might develop into what his neighbors would call a useful citizen merely added urgency to a long-recognized desire to retire somehow from the village into the country. Once he had considered even the possibility of becoming a farmer, until he asked himself the all-sufficient question: "What have I to do with plows?" and made the proper comment: "I plow another furrow." And, as early as December 24, 1841, he had written: "I want to go soon and live away by the pond, where I shall hear only the wind whispering among the reeds. It will be a success if I shall have left myself behind."

Three years and a half were to elapse between the time when that last passage was written (presumably in Emerson's house) and the time when Thoreau actually took up his residence "by the pond." The whole of the Staten Island episode intervened and so did his unhappy concern with machines for sawing plumbago. But it is obvious that he had not really accepted any of the ways of living he had tried. There seemed no way of making a living—teaching, writing, or pencil-making—which did not take up more precious time than he was willing to give to it, and the solution of the problem, very obvious to him though few other men have ever been able to accept it, was simply to need less rather than to get more. Teetotaler though he was, he might have echoed Omar's wonder what the vintners buy one half so precious as the stuff they sell. The wine of life was ill exchanged for cake and he was sure that bread could be got for very little.

All the region round about Concord through which he had wandered as boy and as man seemed to him sacred through intimacy, but Walden pond had long had for him a special significance. At the age of five, when he was living with his parents in Boston during his father's schoolteaching period, and when he had, no doubt, all but forgot what the country was like, he was brought back to Concord for a visit and was taken to Walden pond. It became at once, so he said, somewhat incoherently, "one of the most ancient scenes stamped on the tablets of my memory, the oriental Asiatic valley of my world, whence so many races and inventions have gone forth in recent times. That woodland vision for a long time made a drapery of my dreams. That sweet solitude my spirit seemed so early to require that I might have room to entertain my thronging guests, and that speaking silence that my ears might distinguish the significant sounds. Somehow or other it at once gave the preference to this recess among the pines, where almost sunshine and shadow were the only inhabitants that varied the scene, over that tumultuous and varied city, as if it had found its proper nursery."

He had returned there many times, and fortunately for him Emerson now owned a most suitable spot on the pond side where a garret might be built without any troublesome house beneath it. In exchange for the privilege of putting up a hut there, Thoreau would clear the brier patch and be, besides, as grateful as an anarchist with scant respect for property rights was likely to be. In March 1845, he began to prepare his site and during the rest of the spring he was busy with the aid of several friends constructing the solidly built one-room cabin which Ellery Channing, whom Thoreau had met through Emerson a few years before, described as no more than "a larger coat and hat—a sentry box on the shore . . . ready to walk into in rain or snow or cold."

In an ecstasy of enthusiasm over his discovery of just how little one could get along with and just how absurd it was for a man to invest ten to fifteen years of his life earning shelter, Thoreau was later to suggest, somewhat less than seriously, that the large boxes for tools which he had seen by the railroad might serve the purpose. "Every man who was hard-pushed might get such a one for a dollar, and, having bored a few auger holes in it, to admit the air at least, get into it when it rained and at night, and hook down the lid, and so have freedom in his love, and in his soul be free. . . . You could sit up as late as you pleased, and, whenever you got up, go abroad without any landlord or house-lord dogging you for rent. Many a man is harassed to death to pay the rent of a larger and more luxurious box who would not have frozen to death in such a box as this."

The cabin by Walden pond went one step, if hardly more than one step, beyond this. It was, so he tells us, tight-shingled and plastered, ten feet wide by fifteen long, with a garret, a closet, two windows, two trap doors, one door to the outside, and one fireplace. It cost him in materials exactly twenty-eight dollars, twelve and one-half cents, and it was certainly worth the money, though the jocose Channing must have his little fun: "As for its being in the ordinary meaning a house, it was so superior to the common domestic contrivances that I do not associate it with them. By standing on a chair you could reach into the garret, and a corn broom fathomed the depth of the cellar. It had no lock to the door, no curtain to the window, and belonged to nature nearly as much as to man." When visitors came they got a chair outside, and no superfluous furniture was allowed to accumulate. There was, besides the simplest utensils, a bed, a table, a desk, and a looking-glass three inches in diameter. There were also three chairs—just to show, as Thoreau remarked, that there was no use going to extremes. "None is so poor that he need sit on a pumpkin." A lady once offered to present him with a mat for wiping his feet, but he preferred the sod before the door which would need no shaking. "It is best to avoid the beginnings of evil."

On July 4, 1845, he officially took up residence and within a few days he was not only recalling in the *Journal* his boyhood visit but also congratulating himself upon having found his way back again:

Now, to-night my flute awakes the echoes over this very water, but one generation of pines has fallen, and with their stumps I have cooked my supper, and a lusty growth of oaks and pines is rising all around its brim and preparing its wilder aspect for new infant eyes. Almost the same johnswort springs from the same perennial root in this pasture. Even I have at length helped to clothe that fabulous landscape of my imagination, and one result of my presence and influence is seen in these bean leaves and corn blades and potato vines.

Outwardly there was nothing sensational in what Thoreau had undertaken to do. In one of its aspects the enterprise was merely a practical, if somewhat eccentric, solution of the problem of a man already past the first flush of youth who had found no trade or profession which pleased him, and who wished to live as cheaply as possible. There was not, as there was in the Fruitlands or Brook Farm experiments, any element of the merely lunatic. If we can divest ourselves of the knowledge that the hero of the story is now—as indisputably as any American writer— a world figure, and if we can remember that to his fellow townsmen he was not even, as he was to Emerson, a promising if still unfruitful thinker, we can realize that to many who heard of his retirement to the near-by woods, it was hardly more than the mean shift of a ne'er-do-well.

It was also, outwardly, not an adventure, but a gesture, at most. The woods were not very wild and not very remote; Thoreau's hut was within easy walking distance of the village; friends or acquaintances often dropped in to see him, and he often walked into the village for a dinner with some townsman, or to collect a bit of gossip. Thousands now living in cities are more isolated from other human beings than he ever was; thousands of others in thinly populated regions of the earth are physically more alone without thinking of themselves as being especially isolated. In the account which he gave of his experience he notes derisively that conventional fellow townsmen asked "if I did not feel lonesome; if I was not afraid, and the like"; but physically his taking to the woods was less hazardous than a week-end camping expedition in Bear Mountain Park and his surroundings were considerably less wild. If the one-hundredth anniversary of his retirement was extensively noted in newspapers a few years ago and if it was appropriately celebrated by nature lovers and amateur woodsmen, this was not because Thoreau had exhibited any especially adventurous spirit so far as the facing of any physical hardships is concerned. He scarcely belongs among the adventurous explorers, for whom in truth he had little respect since he thought of them as men perversely unaware of the fact that undiscovered country enough to occupy any man lay both within and just around us all. Indeed, on one of the last pages of *Walden* he was to ask derisively about an adventurer and about a patron of adventurers then in the public eye: "Is Franklin the only man who is lost, that his wife should be so earnest to find him? Does Mr. Grinnell know where he himself is?" Already he felt, as he was much later to note in the *Journal:* "It is in vain to dream of a wildness distant from ourselves. . . . I shall never find in the wilds of Labrador any greater wildness than in some recess in Concord, *i.e.* than I import into it."

But if Thoreau's retirement was rather a gesture than an adventure, it was also what gestures at their most striking must become—namely, a symbol, and to his often very downright mind the importance of the symbol lay in part in the fact that it involved certain acts which, however unspectacular, were nevertheless visible and concrete attempts to put into some sort of actual practice theories which could not honorably be allowed to remain merely theories. Emerson might talk about plain living and about breaking with convention, but there was nothing in his outward way of life capable of shocking the most conventional. He did not *do* anything. He did not take even a first step. He was, as a matter of fact, always to hold himself aloof from the experiments in which other Transcendentalists, even finally Hawthorne, were to become involved. Thoreau wanted to begin to live some special kind of life, not merely to think about one. He was determined to take some step, and among the various attempts which he makes in *Walden* to imply or state what his life in the woods had accomplished for him, perhaps the most significant is: "I learned this, at least, by my experiment; that if one advances confidently in the direction of his dreams, and endeavors to live the life which he has imagined, he will meet with a success unexpected in common hours."

Undoubtedly Thoreau was conscious that he was making his contribution to the series of experiments with which so many New Englanders were, or were soon to be, busy. Being an individualist it was inevitable that he should set up a kind of one-man Brook Farm, and for him, the only one concerned, it was a success from the start. Something of that happy confidence, that sense of being right and of having found the true path which was to inform *Walden*, the book, begins immediately to inform the pages of the deeply contented *Journal* from which the book was quarried. He was to lose some of that confidence again in later years, perhaps inevitably to lose it as he endeavored to reconcile and to think out to the end various paradoxes, each one of which seemed by itself so absolute and incontrovertible a revelation. But for the moment each was sufficient unto itself as each, somewhat obscurely and almost irascibly perceived before, took on its clear outline now. It was, he had proved, possible to simplify, not merely to talk about simplifying; possible to renounce those errors which, as he wrote, had made men the slaves of their own tools. If a man could not ride everywhere in next to no time and for next to nothing, he could live somewhere for almost as little. "And the cost of a thing is the amount of life it requires to be exchanged for it, immediately or in the long run."

Some part of his delight was merely from the gratification of what some more recent psychologist might dub the Robinson Crusoe complex, and that complex, though no doubt more or less consciously present in every man's mental make-up, was very highly developed in Thoreau. "It is worth the while," he wrote while still at Walden, "to have lived a primitive wilderness life at some time, to know what are, after all, the necessaries of life and what methods society has taken to supply them. I have looked over the old day-books of the merchants with the same view—to see what it was shopmen bought. They are the grossest groceries. Salt is perhaps the most important article in such a list, and most commonly bought at the stores, of articles commonly thought to be necessaries . . . by the farmer. . . . Here's the rub then. I see how I could supply every other article I need, without using the shops, and to obtain this might be the fit occasion for a visit to the seashore. Yet even salt cannot strictly speaking be called a necessary of human life, since many tribes do not use it."

But simple, self-sustaining existence was not an end in itself. "I wish," he wrote, on his third day beside the pond, "to meet the facts of life—the vital facts which are the phenomena or actuality the Gods meant to show us—face to face, and so I came down here." But even that was not quite all. Thoreau was still, and always remained, enough of a Transcendentalist to believe that there was also some ultimate truth beyond "phenomena" and "actuality" which could be caught only, if at all, by grace of a direct, super-rational communication from nature to man. And one thing was certain: at Walden one saw more of the significant "phenomena" and "actualities" than one saw of them in a city or even in a village, and on the basis of that fact it was reasonable to suppose that, living more naturally, one was also more nearly attuned to the truth which might some day be communicated.

To a mouse which ran over his shoes and up the inside of his pantaloons he fed a bit of cheese from his fingers, feeling the comfortable assurance that "There is not much danger of the mouse tribe becoming extinct in hard winters, for their granary is a cheap and extensive one." "And then the frogs, bullfrogs; they are the more sturdy spirits of ancient wine-bibbers and wassailers, still unrepentant, trying to sing a catch in their Stygian lakes." He was sure that he was more nearly of the frogs' fellowship than he was of any fellowship gathered in towns; more a part of their ancient world than of that newer one which had created needs to which it was now enslaved. "If I am not quite right here," he wrote, "I am less wrong than before." And he was supremely happy. "Sometimes, when I compare myself with other men, methinks I am favored by the gods. They seem to whisper joy to me beyond my deserts, and that I do have a solid warrant and surety at their hands, which my fellows do not. I do not flatter myself, but if it were possible, they flatter me. I am especially guided and guarded." And again: "Every natural form—palm leaves and acorns, oak leaves and sumach and dodder—are [sic] untranslatable aphorisms."

Despite such sentiments as this last, Thoreau was nevertheless beginning to free himself from the naïve Transcendentalist assumption that the lessons of nature are merely little allegories confirming the prejudices of the human moralists. Ultimately, indeed, he was to go so far in the other direction as to be all but forced into a pantheism which left little place for merely human concerns. But at the perfect Walden moment he had gone to nature to learn a lesson which he thought would be new and which he still assumed would be humanly comprehensible. "Dictates," which seemed to carry the authority of divine suggestion, came to him from beyond himself. What, he asked, if we were to obey them? What if, for example, we were to refuse, as they seemed to suggest we ought, either to eat meat or to buy and sell? And for the moment he did not ask the question which was later to trouble him much even though he never quite put it into words—the question how the divine in man, which forbids him to eat his fellows, is related to the natural which bids other natural creatures eat their own kind.

Poetry, which had seemed so dusty in the library alcove, came to life again. "There are," he realized afresh, "no monuments of antiquity comparable to the classics for interest and importance. . . . Books, the oldest and the best, stand rightfully on the shelves of every cottage." But "Books must be read as deliberately and reservedly as they were written." Men, too, once one is out from under their roofs, once one can see them by choice rather than by necessity, once they stand on their own legs, once—above all —one can meet them without being entangled in what he called "their dirty institutions," were often interesting and, sometimes, in certain of their aspects, attractive creatures. Ten days after he had installed himself, Therien, the French Canadian wood chopper who had made his dinner on woodchuck the night before, passed by. He was, said Thoreau, a true Paphlagonian man though he too had heard of Homer. Soon Henry and he were fast, self-reliant

friends. Therien was a well of good humor and contentment. "By George!" he would say. "I can enjoy myself
well enough here chopping; I want no better sport." "In
him," Thoreau wrote, "the animal man chiefly was developed. In physical endurance and contentment he was
cousin to the pine and the rock." But, as Thoreau remembered when he came to give the wood chopper his due place
in the public record of the Walden adventure, "the intellectual and what is called the spiritual man in him were
slumbering as in an infant."

Perhaps the association with Therien helped to prevent
Thoreau from ever falling into the delusion that he wished
actually to return to the merely primitive man, or that wildness, for all that he cherished a strain of it in himself and
others, was sufficient in itself. It was not long after he had
first met Therien that he wrote into the *Journal:* "Though
the race is not so degenerated but a man might possibly live
in a cave to-day and keep himself warm by furs, yet, as
caves and wild beasts are not plenty enough to accommodate all at the present day, it were certainly better to accept
the advantages which the invention and industry of mankind offer." He never proposed, as flippant critics seem usually to assume, that we should dispense with all the material
inventions of civilization, much less with its intellectual re-
finements. Neither did he ever seriously believe that all the
latter could be maintained without any of the former. What
he did wish to find out was how many tools and conveniences were really necessary and at what point they began
to cost more in time and effort than they were worth—an
inquiry which, by the way, has never been satisfactorily
concluded by Thoreau or anyone else. Even at Walden,
where he was admittedly conducting a somewhat extreme

experiment, he was seeking not so much to get away from either men or the things they had surrounded themselves with as from the demands which they and their kind of society made upon him.

The summer passed, quickly no doubt, and he harvested his beans. Winter came, the pond froze, and Thoreau, who had watched and measured and tested it with fanatical attention, listened to it "crack and whoop" in the night. He ate his rice, his Indian meal, and exactly twenty-two cents' worth of meat—the total cost of the bought food for eight months being $8.74, a sum which he had earned quickly by his own labor and which was therefore not excessive. He and a cat surprised one another when they met at the pond side; the chickadees came in flocks to pick the crumbs by his door, and he remembered that "I once had a sparrow alight upon my shoulder for a moment while I was hoeing in a village garden, and I felt that I was more distinguished than I should have been by any epaulet I could have worn." These things were especially delightful because they realized Thoreau's own ideal of what "Nature's social union" ought to be—not too much union or too much sociability, but a good deal of benevolent minding of one's own business, be one chickadee or man. With the exception of cats, of whom he was extremely fond, he neither at this time nor at any other kept pets, partly no doubt because he himself wanted to be nobody's pet except in so far as he could be, like a cat, one who walked by himself.

During the winter evenings he wrote and he read the "heroic books," including probably the *Bhagavad-Gita* which he must have heard Emerson discuss about this time, and he found that his residence "was more favorable, not

only to thought, but serious reading, than a university."
Meanwhile, moreover, he kept open his ears, his mind, or
whatever it is one keeps open for transcendental communications, in the constant hope of glimpsing fragments of
those "higher laws" which were, after all, among the most
important, if also the most elusive, of the several things he
had come to Walden to seek.

Sometimes, as he returned through the woods in the dark
from some fishing expedition and caught, perhaps, sight of
a woodchuck stealing across his path, the universe seemed
to approve "a strange thrill of savage delight" which
tempted him to seize and devour the woodchuck raw. Thus
he recognized in himself, not only an instinct toward the
"higher, or, as it is named, a spiritual, life" but also another
toward "a primitive, rank and savage one." "Once or twice
. . . I found myself ranging the woods, like a half-starved
hound, with a strange abandonment, seeking some kind of
venison which I might devour, and no morsel could have
been too savage for me." "I love," he added, "the wild not
less than the good. . . . I like sometimes to take rank hold
on life and spend my day more as the animals do." Cynics
may be inclined to suspect that an almost exclusive diet of
rice, Indian meal, and molasses might reasonably be expected to make even woodchuck look strangely attractive
to any man, but the strain of wildness which Thoreau
found and respected in himself was discovered too early
and continued too long to be explained away so simply.

If the law which sometimes bade him range the woods
like a savage was higher or more a part of something eternally enduring than the law which bade his fellows barter
goods and speculate in real estate, it was, nevertheless, lower
than other laws which in good time could lead some men,

if not all, toward another kind of life—gentler, without being, like what passed for civilized life, artificial and un-justified by anything outside itself. Dimly, though not yet clearly enough to require complete obedience, he heard those "dictates" which forbade trade and the eating of meat. Before he went to the woods he had sold his gun. "No humane being, past the thoughtless age of boyhood, will wantonly murder any creature which holds its life by the same tenure that he does. The hare in its extremity cries like a child. I warn you, mothers, that my sympathies do not always make the usual phil-*anthropic* distinctions." How heavily the twenty-two cents' worth of meat (pork it was) lay upon his conscience he does not say, but the fishing in which he still indulged he thought nothing to be proud of. When he yielded to the impulse to fish he found, after repeated experiment, that he fell a little in self-respect. "It is a faint intimation, yet so are the first streaks of morn-ing." Perhaps man, like certain insects, will some day come to be able to give up eating entirely during the last and most glorious part of his life.

Asceticism, perhaps rather more Hindu than Christian, seemed to lie just ahead, but neither at this time nor later does Thoreau ever actually embrace it. He will not give up the life in nature for the life beyond nature until he is ready for it, and above all he will not be seduced into the life, neither in nor beyond but merely outside nature, which most men lead. At Walden existence was too inexpressibly sweet to be troubled even by the contradictions in it, and even the contradictions were justified by the fact that they were contradictions within himself, not contradictions forced upon him from without. The highest laws are glimpsed, but the law really grasped and lived by is the law which says: "Follow your own genius"—be what you are, whether you are by your own nature hunter, or wood chopper, or scholar. When you have become perfect you will be perfect; but only if you have learned to be, all along, what at each moment you were.

"I love," he said, "a broad margin to my life," and at Walden he had it. Though he was entirely self-supporting, there was plenty of time to chat with neighbors, observe the muskrat and the otter, keep appointments with certain especially admirable trees, and indulge in the meditations which convinced him that he knew what the Orientals meant by contemplation and the forsaking of works. "This was sheer idleness to my fellow-townsmen, no doubt; but if the birds and flowers had tried me by their standard, I should not have been found wanting." Even when engaged in the most humble and practical tasks, even when living on the lowest animal level, he had the satisfaction of knowing, from the pleasure such occupations gave him, that he was on the right track, and not, like his fellow citizens to whom life was all work, on the wrong one. Joy is a symptom by means of which right conduct may be recognized. The simple fundamental things are not in themselves enough to live for, but they do not, like the "penances" of an artificial civilization, dull the soul and thus render it deaf to the intimations of nature.

During the first summer Thoreau tended, according to his own calculations, some seven miles of bean rows. Calling himself a Pythagorean and therefore not very favorable to this particular vegetable, he sold most of his crop—at a net profit of eight dollars, seventy-one and one-half cents—to buy rice; and next year he planted less. But growing beans, even to sell, not to eat, was a labor upon which some god smiled. "What was the meaning of this so steady and self-respecting, this small Herculean labor, I knew not. I came to love my rows, my beans, though so many more than I wanted. They attached me to the earth, and so I got my strength like Antaeus. But why should I raise them? Only Heaven knows. . . . Making the earth say beans instead of grass—this was my daily work."

Neither during this first summer and winter nor during the time which followed was Thoreau cut off from other people, or even unsociable. Aunt Prudence Ward, writing a letter in January 1846, mentions rather casually the fact that he is living in a little house by the pond "in view of the public road," that "he has many visitors, whom he receives with pleasure" and that "we talk of passing the day with him soon." Joseph Hosmer, son of Edmund Hosmer, accepted an invitation to spend the day; Bronson Alcott was there; and so, of course, was Emerson. Ellery Channing goes so far as to say that Thoreau went home to his family every day; and, though this may be a considerable exaggeration so far as the period of his official residence at Walden is concerned, it does tend to show how far from being a natural hermit one of his intimates supposed him. Certainly he did not impose upon himself any rule of solitude or of continuous residence. During the summer of 1846 he made his first journey into the Maine woods to see a forest more nearly primeval than any he had seen before. From thence he came back to Walden and during the same summer spent his famous night in jail, of which more anon. Then, on September 6, 1847, he left Walden for good.

The reasons for leaving were as various as the reasons for going had been and they operated upon as many different levels. For his public, such as it was, he gave in the published account only a suitably "spiritual" and tantalizingly Orphic one. "I left the woods for as good a reason as I went there. Perhaps it seemed to me that I had several more lives to live, and could not spare any more time for that one. . . . I had not lived there a week before my feet wore a path from my door to the pond side. . . . I fear that others may have fallen into it, and so helped to keep it open. . . . How worn and dusty, then, must be the highways of the world, how deep the ruts of tradition and conformity!" Two years before that account was published but more than four after the cabin had been abandoned, he had put into the *Journal* a passage in similar vein which is more explicit and which was rewritten for publication rather more completely than many others were. "Why I left the woods? I do not think that I can tell. . . . Perhaps it is none of my business, even if it is yours. . . . There was a little stagnation, it may be. About two o'clock in the afternoon the world's axle creaked as if it needed greasing. . . . Perhaps if I lived there much longer, I might live there forever. One would think twice before he accepted heaven on such terms. A ticket to Heaven must include tickets to Limbo, Purgatory, and Hell." But in the same paragraph he confesses that he has often wished himself back.

Many who have heard of the experiment are inclined to doubt, as certain of his contemporaries did, that it "proved anything." After all, they say, not everybody could find a pond to go and live by, even if everybody wanted to. But Thoreau had never intended to suggest that they could. The two most easily stated of the many questions he went to ask were simply: (1) Can I, an individual with certain tastes who finds himself in certain circumstances, lead a happy and fruitful life if I simplify my needs to the point where the very little money I can readily earn will suffice? (2) Will the experience suggest that the minimum of comforts and luxuries compatible with an intellectual and spiritual existence is probably lower than even the people who talk much about plain living tend to assume? The soul, he was sure, could get along without the luxuries or the conveniences for which he was not willing to pay the price.

Even in theory he was not demanding or advocating that all men should live as simply as he had. Indeed the "simplicity" which he recommends is not an absolute but a relative thing; it means only that every man should refuse to pay a price for what is not essential *to him*. Doubtless some men needed things Thoreau did not. If a man really needed concerts, museums, and what not, he would pay for them what he must. Thoreau himself did not plan to give up everything but only those things which he found he did not need, and his scorn was reserved principally, not for those who needed more than he did, but for those who sacrificed themselves to get things they did not really want. Most of his contemporaries, he was sure, were doing just that. If they ceased their folly they would not thereupon all go to live by Walden ponds. But they would simplify nonetheless. A man with a family—and there is no evidence to suggest that Thoreau, like some New England reformers, would have advocated universal celibacy—would need more than he did. But such a man would also, and this was the important point, need less than he thought.

It is noticeable that both in *Walden* itself and in the whole six-thousand-page stretch of the *Journal*, Thoreau pretty consistently avoids explicit consideration of all middle grounds and all middling concerns. God gets in, and so do the beans he harvested; but family life does not, nor do any of the little practical arrangements, not primitive or fundamental on the one hand nor ineffable on the other, which even Thoreau had to make. He is, accordingly, silent about the dull, middle-class considerations which made it possible for him to leave Walden without the raising of inconvenient problems, and we must look elsewhere to discover that when the world's axle creaked, Emerson was preparing to go to England to lecture and that there was again a place for Thoreau in the household where he now became the temporary major-domo. By November 14th, a little more than two months after he left Walden, he is writing to his friend and employer a long letter which is, in part, a sort of steward's report. "Lidian and I make very good housekeepers. . . . Ellen and Edith and Eddy [the Emerson children] and Aunty Brown [Lidian's sister] keep up the tragedy and comedy and tragic-comedy of life as usual." He has helped Alcott build a summerhouse about whose elaborate peculiarities Alcott was a bit touchy, and he humbly hopes he is doing well. "I heartily wish I could be of good service to this household. . . . It is a little like joining a community, this life, to such a hermit as I am; and as I don't keep the accounts, I don't know whether the experiment will succeed or fail finally. At any rate, it is good for society, so I do not regret my transient nor my permanent share in it."

Another paragraph of the same letter is devoted to the simple, dignified statement of an extraordinary fact. "I have had a tragic correspondence, for the most part all on one side, with Miss ———. She did really wish to—I hesitate to write—marry me. That is the way they spell it. Of course I did not write a deliberate answer. How could I deliberate upon it? I sent back as distinct a *no* as I have learned to pronounce after considerable practice, and I trust this *no* has succeeded. . . . *There was no other way*. I really had anticipated no such foe as this in my career."

The original of the letter has been lost. The blank where the name should have been may have been left a blank by Thoreau himself, and Mr. Canby, who seems to be the first of Thoreau's biographers to speculate upon the subject of the lady's identity, admits that he can do no more than speculate. Presumably she was someone whom Emerson knew and there is a remote possibility that she may have been Margaret Fuller, since Margaret had certainly once written of Thoreau the somewhat alarming opinion that he was a bare hill, unwarmed by spring, and since she was soon to scandalize some of her friends by a marriage which they thought as unsuitable in a somewhat different way as one now thinks marriage with Thoreau would have been. On the other hand Emerson's reply to Thoreau's letter contains a significant passage omitted from the published version in which he speaks of "one odious circumstance, which we will dismiss from remembrance hence-forward," and Mr. Canby, who doubts that Emerson would have used the word "odious" in connection with Margaret, considers two other possible candidates, to both of whom, however, there are admittedly objections.

Neither would come into the story at all if Aunt Maria Thoreau, the abolitionist sister of Henry's father, had not, something more than a year after Thoreau's shocked confession, passed on to Prudence Ward a bit of gossip to the effect that "Miss F—— had committed or was going to commit suicide on account of H—— Thoreau," and if

Henry himself had not, in August 1852, written into his diary the following passage: "Hearing that one with whom I was acquainted had committed suicide, I said I did not know when I had planted the seed of that fact that I should hear of it." Now, nobody known to have had any connection with Thoreau is known to have committed suicide, and it is not even certain that Thoreau was referring in the passage just cited to a woman rather than to a man. But he had had some contact with two women besides Margaret Fuller, both of whose names began with F and either of whom might therefore conceivably have been the subject of Aunt Maria's inaccurate gossip.

One was Anne Frances Ford, a cousin of the Wards whom Thoreau had probably met, who died of tuberculosis in August 1847, and who thus might have been the person referred to in Aunt Maria's letter though she could not have been the maker of the proposal because she was already dead when Emerson left for England. The other was one Sophia Foord, an eccentric acquaintance of Lidian Emerson, whom—though she is not known to have committed suicide—Mr. Canby tends to regard as the most likely candidate. Perhaps, after all, it does not make much difference, so far as the story of Thoreau is concerned, who made what he undoubtedly regarded as an indecent proposal. His only reaction was shocked astonishment and any woman would have provoked that reaction.

It is also abundantly evident that Thoreau did not allow the "odious circumstance" to trouble him very much, for letters written during this period of the second residence in Emerson's household reveal him as not only still serenely happy but even exuberant. To Harrison Blake, a young man who had written admiringly to Thoreau and with whom Thoreau began an extensive correspondence, he wrote in a style suited to the mystical and exalted temperament of the recipient: "I love to live. I love reform better than its modes. . . . I know that I am. I know that another is who knows more than I, who takes interest in me, whose creature, and yet whose kindred, in one sense, I am. I know that the enterprise is worthy." In a subsequent letter, dated a few weeks later, he was, however, confessing to the same correspondent: "I am too easily contented with a slight and almost animal happiness. My happiness is a good deal like that of the woodchucks." And at almost the same time he could write to another correspondent, Horace Greeley, in a slightly more practical if not less confident manner. Greeley had just now, in May 1848, succeeded in extracting from Rufus Griswold, editor of *Graham's Magazine*, seventy-five dollars for an essay on Carlyle which Thoreau had submitted in August 1846 and which had been published in the spring of the following year. Thanking Greeley, Thoreau took occasion to explain just how much life at the pond had reassured him so far as any uneasiness regarding the mere making of a living was concerned: "I lived by myself in the forest, in a fairly good cabin, plastered and warmly covered, which I built myself. There I earned all I needed and kept to my own affairs. During that time my weekly outlay was but seven-and-twenty cents; and I had an abundance of all sorts. Unless the human race perspire more than I do, there is no occasion to live by the sweat of their brow. If men cannot get along without money (the smallest amount will suffice), the truest method of earning it is by working as a laborer at one dollar per day."

Thus fortified by a sense of economic security he began

again to offer himself—strictly on his own terms—to the public. After Emerson came back from England in July 1848, Thoreau returned to his own family in the "Texas" house, and then, in the autumn of 1849, helped make additions to another house—now known as the Thoreau-Alcott house—which his father had bought to provide space for the expanding graphite manufactory. Meanwhile, however, some of the fruits of his stay at Walden were beginning to be exhibited. He had previously been an occasional lecturer in Concord and he now went, at Hawthorne's invitation, to Salem and to Boston. Various references to him survive in letters and journals, and according to Aunt Maria Thoreau "they seem wonderfully taken with him" in Salem. Then in May 1849, less than three months after Aunt Maria's letter, his first, ill-starred book was published (or at least printed) and its absolute commercial failure probably long postponed the appearance of his masterpiece.

From all this it is evident that one of the reasons why he lived two years by the pond is an important one concerning which little has so far been said, for it would not be stretching a point very much to say that he went to Walden in order to write *Walden*. At least writing, some of which went without major change into that book, was one of the important activities carried on in the cabin, and writing had almost certainly been part of his plan. Wisely he did not hesitate to work into the final manuscript any suitable material which he had accumulated after the residence at Walden had been officially terminated, but much—perhaps most—of the substance of the book had been written out while he was still there. Just exactly how much, it is impossible to say since some of the *Journal* (said to contain a good deal of the material of the posthumous *Maine Woods* volume) is in the hands of a private collector. But there is enough in the published version to show that though some of *Walden* is passion recollected in tranquillity and some is tranquillity recollected in tranquillity, various key passages were written sometimes in a form quite close to that in which they were finally printed, while Thoreau was actually living the life he described.

But at Walden Thoreau was not only collecting materials for future use. He was also, with publication in mind, putting into some kind of shape *A Week on the Concord and Merrimack Rivers.* In March 1847, when Alcott visited him at Walden, he heard Thoreau read aloud from the manuscript, which was by then probably nearly complete, and immediately Alcott wrote into his diary (everybody, of course, kept one) an enthusiastic passage about Thoreau's "sufficiency and soundness," about his "aboriginal vigor" and about how the book was "fragrant with the life of New England woods and streams." To him Thoreau seemed to be "Virgil and White of Selborne and Izaak Walton and Yankee settler all in one." By November of the same year, Thoreau was writing to Emerson in England that "Wiley and Putnam, Munroe, the Harpers, and Crosby and Nichols have all declined printing it with the least risk to themselves," and it was not until May 1849 that the book was finally issued in an edition for which Thoreau made himself financially responsible.

It is odd and perhaps unfortunate that he should have gone back so far for the subject of his first book when he had at the moment of writing already moved on to much more mature thoughts and experiences which were already being recorded in the *Journal.* The river trip which furnishes the thread of his narrative had been made in August and September 1839, nearly six years before he went to Walden, ten years before the account actually got published, and when he was just past his twenty-second birthday. It is true that, as he was later to do in the case of *Walden*, he worked in much that he had not written, and probably had not thought, until long after the trip had been made. The original record of the expedition as published in the *Journal* is indeed rather brief; another version —probably that upon which he worked at Walden—seems to have been in existence about 1841, and the manuscript, as finally given to the printer, included a dissertation on Persius previously published in *The Dial*, several poems which had appeared in the same magazine, and also an essay on "Friendship" which, according to Alcott, was not written until 1848. Nevertheless, the fact that everything purports to be related somehow either to the long-past journey or at least to the man who made it seems to introduce a sort of cultural lag—if the phrase may be used in reference to the development of an individual—as well as an irresistible tendency to fragmentation.

It is true that the method of *Walden* seems similar. Here also a minor adventure is half-humorously expanded to nearly epic proportions and the narrative is made an occasion for introducing a great variety of thoughts which actually or pretendedly occurred to the hero in the course of his adventure. But the scheme which works astonishingly well in the later book hardly works at all in the earlier one. In the case of *Walden*, the structural units are topical, the whole is actually an exposition rather than a narrative, and some sort of unity is achieved. In the case of *A Week on the Concord and Merrimack Rivers* the chronological order has no relation to the disquisitions which constitute the most important part of the book, and the chronological thread of narrative breaks so often that the whole is little more than a notebook.

Even more important is the fact that the mind revealed in the earlier work is not so confidently original nor so rich as that revealed in *Walden*. Two of Thoreau's major themes—mysticism on the one hand and, on the other, sympathy with wildness in nature and in man—are both elaborately developed, but neither is as crisply presented as it was presently to be, and the first especially is still, in expression at least, too much something borrowed from Emerson and the Hindus, rather than something bearing the strong impress of Thoreau's own personality. Quite possibly this is less the result of his returning to an earlier period for material than simply of the fact that the maturity of *Walden* had actually not yet been fully achieved, for it is certain that the essay on "Friendship" which was apparently composed as late as 1848 is one of the most paradoxical of his writings and also one which, to some readers at least, seems to come closest to what Lowell (not in this instance referring to Thoreau) was to call "sheer fudge." In any case there is, along with much impressive writing—some sentences and some paragraphs as good almost as anything he ever wrote —also a good deal of what looks like straining after effect, especially after an effect of mystical profundity which sometimes suggests an author who had read not only Emerson and the other Transcendentalists but also Carlyle, and was determined to demonstrate that he too was among the prophets.

Most important of all, perhaps, is the fact that the third of his major themes—the conviction that practical steps might be taken by the men who compose society (if not by society itself) tending to lead mankind into the path of simpler and happier living—hardly gets a due share of the attention. There is, to be sure, in the middle of the long, laudatory discussion of the *Bhagavad-Gita*—beside which "even our Shakespeare seems sometimes youthfully green" —a curious passage which is at one point almost Marxian in its criticism of a moral absolute. "No sufficient reason," he remarks, "is given why Arjoon should fight. . . . The Brahman's virtue consists in doing, not right, but arbitrary things. What is that which a man 'hath to do'? What is 'action'? What are the 'settled functions'? What is 'a man's own religion,' which is so much better than another's? . . . It is a defense of the institution of castes, of what is called the 'natural duty' of the Kshetree, or soldier." But in general the Thoreau of *A Week on the Concord and Merrimack Rivers* is primarily the mystic and the lover of the primitive, not yet much the critic of society. And as a result the book does not present the complete man.

The three themes tend, even in *Walden*, always to remain three themes. They are never united into a tight system in such a way that to remove one would be logically to topple the whole. But the balance and wholeness of personality which Thoreau seems to achieve does, nevertheless, depend upon the balance maintained among the three themes and upon certain relations which he manages to establish between them. They are like the three sides of a triangle, or even, still more fantastically, like the three points of support on a stool. Together they form a design, together they constitute a personality if not a philosophy, which will stand up. Omit one, and the design is incomplete, the personality ineffectual. *A Week on the Concord and Merrimack Rivers* was, of course, except for *Walden* the only volume published during Thoreau's lifetime. It is probably more often read today than any of the posthumously published works and probably it deserves to be. But it is a pendant to his fame, and had it been his only book instead of the precursor of *Walden*, it is doubtful if his reputation would be very wide.

When the first book came out, Horace Greeley commissioned a laudatory notice for the *Tribune* from George Ripley who had come in contact with Thoreau at the Emersons', and Lowell discussed it at length in the *Massachusetts Quarterly Review*. The latter ridiculed what he called the "worsification" of Thoreau's poetry, praised the account of the actual journey, complained that the two rivers were too often made to "run Thoreau or Emerson or indeed anything but their own transparent element," and protested that "we were bid to a river-party—not to be preached at." But he ended with the sentence: "The style is compact, and the language has an antique purity like wine grown colorless with age."

On the whole the review was somewhat foppishly condescending, but it probably intended to recommend an unusual book. Unfortunately, however, neither Lowell nor Ripley could get Thoreau an audience. As has already been said, he had, by October 28, 1853, got back seven hundred and six copies out of the edition of one thousand. Seventy-five had been given away, two hundred and nineteen sold. The unwanted volumes were, he noted, "something more substantial than fame, as my back knows, which has borne them up two flights of stairs to a place similar to that to which they trace their origin." He also noted, with grim humor, that there was one and only one bit of luck in connection with the whole enterprise. The books had been wrapped up in packages of fifty each and labeled on the outside: "H. D. Thoreau's Concord River." To return them, his publisher had only to cross out "River" and substitute "Mass." to give the bundles, just as they were, to the expressman.

Thoreau had borrowed the money to pay for the printing and slowly paid it back out of what he earned peddling pencils and surveying. Once, while on a selling trip to New York and aware of being in debt, he was tempted to take a flyer into speculation by buying cranberries in Boston to sell in New York, but he was glad he had resisted the temptation when he discovered they were cheaper in New York. Finally, as he noted in his *Journal* under the date November 28, 1853, four and a half years after publication of the book: "Settled with J. Munroe & Co., and on a new account placed twelve of my books with him on sale. I have paid him directly out of pocket since the book was published two hundred and ninety dollars and taken his receipt for it. This does not include postage on proofsheets, etc., etc. I have received from other quarters about fifteen dollars. This has been the pecuniary value of the book."

Always prepared for the worst where any public was concerned, Thoreau was probably not too much discouraged by his failure, though he had certainly hoped for something better. It was after the volume had been turned down that he wrote Harrison Blake the summary statement, "I love to live," and at about the same time that he wrote concerning these same refusals to J. Elliot Cabot, a naturalist who was working with Agassiz and who had requested Thoreau to procure him some fishes from Concord: "I esteem it a rare happiness to be able to *write* anything, but there (if I ever get there) my concern for it is apt to end. Time & Co. are, after all, the only quite honest and trustworthy publishers that we know. I can sympathize, perhaps, with the barberry bush, whose business it is solely to *ripen* its fruit (though that may not be to sweeten it) and to protect it with thorns, so that it holds all winter, even, unless some hungry crows came to pluck it." But, for all this, it is probably just as well that his masterpiece had been written at least before he knew the full extent of his first fiasco.

The detailed history of the process by which *Walden* reached its final form cannot be completely traced with full assurance because, as has already been pointed out, certain important pages of the *Journal* are in private hands. There is, nevertheless, abundant material to illustrate the fact that it was put together out of materials previously written, some of which were composed during Thoreau's actual residence by the pond side, some of which were already in existence before he went there, and some of which were not put on paper until long after he had left. Thus, for instance, he had been by the pond for only a short while when he confided to the *Journal* the passage about the wood chopper Therien, which is copied with only a few omissions and verbal revisions into the sixth chapter of *Walden*. It was about this same time, too, that he wrote the sentence, "Books must be read as deliberately and reservedly as they were written," which was lifted out of its immediate context and incorporated in the third chapter of *Walden*. The paragraph about the bullfrogs that embody the spirits of "ancient wine-bibbers and wassailers" also was written during the Walden period and so, most important of all, was much of the powerful passage about the strange penance being performed by New Englanders, which begins with the third paragraph of *Walden*. A part of the passage beginning with the amusing description of Thoreau's difficulty in persuading tailors to make his clothes as he wants them, rather than as "they" are wearing them at the moment, does not appear in the *Journal* until early in 1854; and the suggestion that the hard-pressed might use toolboxes as residences, not until 1852.

Certain other sentences used in *Walden* had, on the other hand, been given almost their final form before the cabin was built. Thus the sentence, "The buckeye does not grow in New England, and the mocking-bird is rarely heard here," along with a number of the other sentences which introduce the dazzling last chapter had actually gone into the *Journal* in March 1840, when Thoreau was only twenty-two and had not yet gone to live with Emerson for the first time.

Obviously, then, *Walden* was a pastiche composed of bits which had, from the beginning, been set down in the hope that some use would eventually be found for them. The *Journal*, it must be remembered, was not a complete record of the events of his life (indeed, few of what are ordinarily called biographical facts get into it), and neither was it written exclusively for his own satisfaction. It was a storehouse, a gigantic notebook, and it continued to retain something of that character even through the later years when the author saw less and less likelihood that the materials still being accumulated would ever be used. While at Walden he himself wrote in it: "From all points of the compass, from the earth beneath and the heavens above, have come these inspirations and been entered duly in the order of their arrival in the journal. Thereafter, when the time arrived, they were winnowed into lectures, and again, in due time, from lectures into essays." But he was nevertheless aware that he was not really achieving consecutive coherence, for he goes on: "And at last they stand, like the cubes of Pythagoras, firmly on either basis; like statues on their pedestals, but the statues rarely take hold of hands. There is only such connection and series as is attainable in the galleries. And this affects their immediate practical and popular influence."

Long as it was to be delayed, *Walden*, the book, was already taking shape as a book at least as early as February 1849, for at that time Aunt Maria Thoreau wrote in a letter that her nephew was preparing a manuscript for the press and that the title would be "Waldien (I don't know how to spell it) or life in the Woods"; and she went on to express the opinion that "the title will take if the Book don't." She had read what was already written and she was by no means wholly favorable in her opinion. "You know I have said, there were parts of it that sounded to me very much like blasphemy, and I did not believe they would publish it, on reading it to Helen the other day Sophia told me, she made the same remark, and coming from her, Henry was much surprised, and said she did not understand it, but still I fear they will not persuade him to leave it out."

Curiously enough there is no single mention of the book in Thoreau's letters until after it had already been published and the fact suggests that he deliberately, perhaps because of some embarrassment concerning the fate of *A Week*, refrained from any attempt to enlist the interest of his friends. Few books actually sound more confident than *Walden* does and the fact contributes a good deal to its exhilarating effect, but Thoreau, being the kind of man he was, may have been able to achieve that confidence in the importance of what he had to say without having any confidence whatever that the importance would be publicly recognized. In any case, we have no record of when he first tried to place the book with a publisher or whether, as with the previous one, he approached several. We know only that before March 1854 Ticknor & Fields had accepted it, apparently at their own risk, and that after it was published (during the same year) two thousand copies were sold. It was not, however, reprinted until just after Thoreau's death.

Greeley, ever faithful, arranged with the publisher to present excerpts in advance of publication and it got reviewed elsewhere, but it was not more than a moderate success with the general public and by no means an unqualified one with either Thoreau's family or his friends. Channing did not like it and had not liked *A Week;* Emerson, whose posthumous essay remains the best thing ever written about Thoreau, declared with some exaggeration shortly after the publication of his friend's masterpiece: "All American kind are delighted with *Walden*." But even Emerson was never wholly satisfied with the course which Thoreau's genius took and probably would not have given the book so high a rank in American literature as it has since been given.

Something more will be said later about the growth of Thoreau's fame and of the part which *Walden* had in it both at the time when *Walden* was a new book and in after years, but it is difficult not to be surprised that it did not, merely as a piece of writing, create somewhat more of a stir. No doubt not even the members of the Transcendentalist group were quite prepared to understand the significance of his economic opinions. From their standpoint there was probably something off-center in his aim, though to us it appears directed towards the very center of the target. No doubt, also, the unmistakable anti- or at least non-Christian assumptions offended many even among those who would not be so downright as to call it, as Aunt Maria did, "very much like blasphemy." Yet, for all this, one might have expected the sheer verve and brilliance of the conception and of the writing to astonish more, even if they did not please more, than apparently they did.

Thoreau's mental processes did not stop when he had finished *Walden*. He remained a seeker until the end of his life and the *Journal* is evidence that he was exploring new suspicions and new hints. If he had lived another fifteen or twenty years, it is at least possible that he might have written a new and somewhat different book. But the new line on which he was working had not by the end of his short life yet led to anything he was capable of finding expression for as he had found expression for the illumination which preceded the writing of *Walden*. In the future there were always to be, as there had always been before until about 1845, more questions than answers, and one secret of the magistral confidence of *Walden* is simply the fact that at the moment he was for once rather a finder than seeker. The questions which the book raises are numerous if one stops to pursue them far enough. All answers have a way of thus provoking further questions. But the particular questions which Thoreau had been asking had found their particular answers. He knew quite specifically how he wanted to live and what he wanted to live for; he was also sure that his discoveries had general relevance—not that everybody should live as he did but that each should go about the solution of his own particular problem in the same radical way.

A Week on the Concord and Merrimack Rivers had been the account of a vacation, which is to say of an interlude, a truancy, or an escape. *Walden* was an account of a way of life, even of a permanent way of life if one considers that what it describes is not merely a way of living by a pond but a general attitude capable of making life so simple that there is, as Thoreau put it, no need for the brow to sweat. The finder can be, as the seeker seldom is, gay; and *Walden* is, among many other things, a gay book. In the *Journal* Thoreau speaks often of joy and even of ecstasy. He may at most periods of his life have known a good deal of both, although it is also evident that he had moments, especially as he grew older, when the transcendental voices remained stubbornly silent and even nature awoke only feeble response. But neither joy nor ecstasy is the same as gaiety, and in *Walden* there is much that can hardly be called by any other name. He is gay when he describes the routine of daily living, gay when he reports his interviews with visitors human or animal, and gay when he flings into the face of his fellow citizens his account of their preposterous, self-imposed labors—Herculean in their magnitude, Sisyphean in their endless futility. And he is gayest of all, perhaps, when he goads them with some blasphemy, some gently insinuated renunciation of stern duty.

I have traveled a good deal in Concord; and everywhere, in shops, offices and fields, the inhabitants have appeared to me to be doing penance in a thousand remarkable ways. . . . I see young men, my townsmen, whose misfortune it is to have inherited farms, houses, barns, cattle, and farming tools; for these are more easily acquired than got rid of.

. . . Who made them serfs of the soil? . . . Why should they begin digging their graves as soon as they are born? . . . How many a poor immortal soul have I met well nigh crushed and smothered under its load, creeping down the road of life, pushing before it a barn seventy-five feet by forty, its Augean stables never cleansed, and one hundred acres of land, tillage, mowing, pasture, and wood-lot. . . . I have no doubt that some of you who read this book are unable to pay for all the dinners which you have actually eaten, or for the coats and shoes which are fast wearing or are already worn out, and have come to this page to spend borrowed or stolen time, robbing your creditors of an hour. . . . The mass of men lead lives of quiet desperation. What is called resignation is confirmed desperation. From the desperate city you go into the desperate country, and have to console yourself with the bravery of minks and musk-rats. A stereotyped but unconscious despair is concealed even under what are called the games and amusements of mankind. There is no play in them, for this comes after work. But it is a characteristic of wisdom not to do desperate things.

"Deny this," he is saying, "deny any part of it if you can." Deny the details, or deny the general conclusion: that most men lead, though most men need not lead, lives of desperation, usually quiet and sometimes confirmed. Emerson never spoke with the same practical and homely directness, never with the same scornful urgency.

Alcott had asked Thoreau in 1848 if it were not true that the Transcendentalists seemed to have no positive and real existence "here in this world, in this nineteenth century"; if he and they had not failed inasmuch as neither had "as yet attracted some fine soul, some maid from the farmer's hearth or youth from farm or workshop to our houses." And Thoreau evidently agreed that they had so failed.

Walden was, among other things, an attempt to speak of matters simple and practical enough to be meaningful to those whom high abstractions left cold; and if on the whole the high abstraction did nevertheless in the end get more lip service at least than his practical counsels, that is merely another example of the fact that human beings, not wanting to be reformed, are very likely to prefer the high-sounding admonitions which they do not really have to do anything about to the simpler recommendations which must either be rejected or acted upon.

No doubt many of Thoreau's contemporaries asked, as many subsequent critics have asked: "What after all is so remarkable about having lived for two years in a cabin by a pond?" And the answer is simply that there is only one thing in the least remarkable about it—the fact, namely, that so few others have ever done the same, even though to do so would be to solve all the problems which many wretched men desperately accept as unsolvable. To Carlyle, Emerson had once written that though the rising generation of New Englanders "reject all the ways of living of other men" they "have none to offer in their stead." Thoreau had found one for himself and he wanted to suggest that others should at least feel as free as he did to consult only their own desires and their own needs.

It appears from a letter written to Channing that Thoreau continued or would have liked to continue to tinker with the text of *Walden* even after it was in proof, and this may have something to do with the fact that nothing else he ever wrote is so perfectly formed. Sometimes he could be, in his *Journal* especially, terribly diffuse; but from *Walden* hardly a word could be omitted which would not be in some way missed. Even more remarkable is the fashion in which what had once been a collection of fragments is made to seem a whole, not merely by the logical connection of one fragment to another but because of both a stylistic homogeneity and a unity of mood.

Walden is divided into eighteen chapters, each devoted to a topic. Some of them, like "The Bean-field," "The Ponds," "Brute Neighbours," etc., are largely descriptive. Others, like "Economy," which is the first, and "Higher Laws," which is the eleventh, are expository or argumentative, and nowhere is there an orderly presentation of the thesis from first things to last. In other words the over-all shape of the book preserves the main outlines of the thing it professes to be: not an argument, but an account of the somewhat eccentric experiment concerning which Thoreau's neighbors had expressed a curiosity. The theses and the adjurations which actually constitute a considerable part of its bulk are, formally, to be considered as obiter dicta or, at most, digressions, which the author permits himself in the course of his report on life at Walden. Actually, however, there are four related but distinct "matters" with which the book concerns itself, and they might be enumerated as follows: (1) The life of quiet desperation which most men lead. (2) The economic fallacy which is responsible for the situation in which they find themselves. (3) What the life close to nature is and what rewards it offers. (4) The "higher laws" which man begins, through some transcendental process, to perceive if he faithfully climbs the stepladder of nature whose first rung is "wildness," whose second is some such gentle and austere but not artificial life as Thoreau himself was leading, and whose third is the transcendental insight he only occasionally reached.

The elements of an inclusive system are present, scattered here and there through the logically (though not artistically) fragmentary discourse. Thoreau has, for instance, a theory of wages and costs ("the cost of a thing is the amount of what I will call life which is required to be exchanged for it, immediately or in the long run") and a somewhat Marxian—and Carlylesque—conception of production for use ("I cannot believe that our factory system is the best mode by which men get clothing . . . since, as far as I have heard or observed, the principal object is, not that mankind may be well and honestly clad, but, unquestionably, that the corporations may be enriched"). He has also, however, a theory of ultimate value which is metaphysical rather than economic. That theory of ultimate value, together with the distrust of mass action which goes with it, leads him away from any concern with social reforms other than those which every man can achieve for himself. It also leads him in the direction of a solitary life in nature to which he was temperamentally inclined and which can be justified on mystical grounds. It is a bridge across which he may go toward those ultimate ends the Transcendentalists and the wise Orientals are seeking.

The fact that he never attempts to schematize these various convictions has, moreover, the effect of making *Walden* more persuasive, or at least more difficult to controvert, than would otherwise be the case, because it makes it less easy for the reader to get hold of any link in a chain of reasoning which he is tempted to try to break. Thoreau does not so much argue that it is possible and desirable to live in a certain way as tell us how he lived and what rewards he discovered. He presents us, as it were, with a *fait accompli,* and, like Captain Shotover in Shaw's *Heartbreak*

House, he will not abide our question. He discharges a shaft, and is gone again before we can object or challenge.

For all his seeming directness he is extremely difficult to corner. No writer was ever, at dangerous moments, more elusive, and no proponent of fundamental paradoxes ever more skillfully provided himself with avenues of escape. His residence at Walden is, when he wishes to make it so, an experiment whose results have universal significance; but it can, on convenient occasion, shrink to the status of a merely personal expedient. It is alternately, as a point is to be made or an objection to be met, a universal nostrum or the whim of an individual eccentric. In the second paragraph he pretends that he writes the account only because his neighbors have expressed curiosity concerning such matters as are implied in their questions concerning what he got to eat and whether or not he felt lonesome. He will, he says, talk principally about himself because there is no one else whom he knows so well. But the very next paragraph begins: "I would fain say something . . . concerning . . . you who read these pages, who are said to live in New England; something about your condition . . . in this world, in this town, what it is, whether it is necessary that it be as bad as it is, whether it cannot be improved as well as not." And he is off for many pages which are not about himself or how he lived at Walden, but about how others live elsewhere. He did not come into the world, he had previously protested, to make it better; and yet, until you catch him at it, this is exactly what he is trying to do. When you do catch him at it, he retreats again into the extremest possible individualism. In some sense he is certainly suggesting that others imitate him; but he also protests that he would like to have as many different kinds of men in the world as possible. If you ask him what would happen if all tried to find a pond to live beside, he answers that he never suggested they should; that in fact he himself lived there for only two years; and that he left, perhaps, because he had some other lives to lead.

"All this is very selfish, I have heard some of my townsmen say. . . . There are those who have used all their arts to persuade me to undertake the support of some poor family in the town; and if I had nothing to do—for the devil finds employment for the idle—I might try my hand at some such pastime as that. However, when I have thought to indulge myself in this respect, and lay their Heaven under an obligation by maintaining certain poor persons in all respect as comfortably as I maintain myself, and have even ventured so far as to make them the offer, they have one and all unhesitatingly preferred to remain poor." Thoreau makes, if you like, a foray into sociology, but it is a raid, not a plan of conquest, and its aim is to harass and disturb the enemy—not to impose the will of a benevolent conqueror upon it. The impregnable fortress into which he retreats is the fortress of absolute individualism, the declaration that he is not responsible for anything except his own soul. "I, on my side, require of every writer, first or last, a simple and sincere account of his own life . . . some such account as he would send to his kindred from a distant land; for if he has lived sincerely, it must have been in a distant land to me." Nonconformity and uniqueness are the ideals. "If a man does not keep pace with his companions, perhaps it is because he hears a different drummer. Let him step to the music which he hears, however measured or far away." The very most he can pretend ultimately to teach by being himself is that other men should also be themselves. "As for Doing-good . . . I have tried it fairly, and strange as it may seem, am satisfied that it does not agree with my constitution. Probably I should not consciously and deliberately forsake my particular calling to do the good which society demands of me, to save the universe from annihilation; and I believe that a like but infinitely greater steadfastness elsewhere is all that now preserves it. But I would not stand between any man and his genius; and to him who does this work, which I decline, with his whole heart and soul and life, I would say, Persevere, even if the world call it doing evil, as it is most likely they will."

Thoreau's cabin at Walden has already been likened to the poet's symbolical garret, to Robinson Crusoe's island, and to a one-man Brook Farm. It was also Diogenes' tub and, during the philosopher's moments of asceticism, St. Simeon's pillar. Like each of these it helped dramatize a personality and from each at least one chapter of the book might appropriately have been dated. Nor is it meaningful to ask in which the real Thoreau dwelt. The real Thoreau was to some extent at home in all of them though he dwelt no more steadily in any than he did on his Crusoe's island.

The original Robinson was a solitary by force of circumstances and not at all by choice. Ostensibly his adventure was not an adventure but a misfortune, and, at face value, the book which describes his singlehanded conquest of nature ought to be read with the most sympathy by philosophical cockneys. But, if we are right in assuming that making Crusoe so unappreciative of the meaning of his predicament is only a shrewd literary device and that he is remembered because his adventure translates into realistic terms the old daydream of life in the golden age when nature sufficed to satisfy all man's needs without the inter-vention of any social machinery, then Crusoeism is not too inappropriate a name to serve for that part of the Walden experiment, and for those sections of *Walden*, the book, which are not concerned either with unmistakably Trans-cendental notions or explicit social lessons. Such Crusoeism was certainly the thing that Thoreau first became aware of in himself, and the most nearly unique part of his writing is that which describes the ecstasies and contentments of a life which he felt was as little dependent upon any resources other than his own and nature's as Robinson's ever was, and in the leading of which he accepted the few manufactured articles which he used as casually and as uncritically as Robinson took those that were washed ashore or fetched from the wreck. Thoreau the "nature writer" seems to owe less to any predecessors than Thoreau the mystic owes to Emerson and others, or than Thoreau the economist owes to Carlyle and, directly or indirectly, to the other radicals who were inspiring all New England to Utopian experi-ments. But if it is the Transcendentalist who is most often discussed by literary historians and the social protestant who is most often cited with respect by the leaders in world affairs, it is probably the Thoreau who turns his back upon mankind who has the most devoted readers. Probably he has sent more men into the woods (though few have actually lived as he did) than into either asceticism on the one hand, or political activity on the other.

One of the most important aspects of *Walden* as a classic must, then, be its success as a work of the imagination rather than as a work of moral or social criticism. That many of its ideas were seminal may turn out to be, ulti-mately, the most significant thing about it, but its apparently ever-increasing popularity with readers who cherish it as a precious and sometimes almost secret possession is probably due principally to the fact that it has become a locus for the presentation of certain emotional attitudes, the classic record of one kind of life and one kind of sensibility, just as, let us say, the *Confessions* of Rousseau became the classic account of a different kind of life and a different set of sensibilities. Many men have found themselves, or some dream of themselves, in his pages. Pilgrimages are made to Concord in the same way—and for the same reasons—that they are made to Stoke Poges or to Assisi.

None of this would have been possible if Thoreau had not lived at Walden or rather if he had not seized upon and dramatized the fact. If, for instance, all the leading themes of his masterpiece had been expounded equally well in his earlier book, that book could never have achieved equal acceptance for the simple reason that a man cannot be remembered for having spent a week on a river as he can be remembered in association with a place—especially with a place as well named as Thoreau's pond was. His act, or at least his dramatization of it, was a stroke of the creative imagination and so successful that Thoreau is the man who lived at Walden in somewhat the same way that Dante was the man who visited Hell. And the fact that the adventure was in itself so unspectacular is but another aspect of perfect artistic appropriateness because it emphasized so dramatically one of the points which he wished to make. Let others seek the North Pole or the sources of the Nile. Walden is just as far away if measured in terms of the only distance that counts. It is an Ultima Thule which no man can say that he is prevented by any circumstances from visiting.

Ellery Channing, not always a very perceptive interpreter of his friend's character or aims, did once remark that it was Thoreau's task to show the *multum* in the *parvo* —or, as he put it on another occasion, to maximize the minimum. One of the earliest surviving entries in Thoreau's diary, made when he was twenty, is the sentence, "Hell itself may be contained within the compass of a spark," and a few years later he was noting that cowbells had meant more to him than any bells which had ever swung in a belfry. He thanked whatever gods might be that lack of wealth had nailed him down to his native region, for "What would signify in comparison a thin and diffused love and knowledge of the whole earth instead, got by wandering?" And the year after *Walden* was published he was noting in the *Journal:* "I wish so to live ever as to derive my satisfactions and inspirations from the commonest events, everyday phenomena, so that what my senses hourly perceive, my daily walk, the conversation of my neighbors, may inspire me, and I may dream of no heaven but that which lies about me. A man may acquire a taste for wine or brandy, and so lose his love for water, but should we not pity him? . . . That man is the richest whose pleasures are the cheapest." Later still he was burying in that same *Journal* one of the many characteristically written sentences which needed no more than to be lifted into some new work (as many previous sentences had been lifted in *Walden*): "I read the story of one voyageress round the world, who, it seemed to me, having started, had no other object but to get home again, only she took the longest way round."

The retreat to Walden was, therefore, not an escape toward the strange, but a digging into the familiar, and thus it could become a symbol of that form of adventure for which the only necessary equipment is spiritual.

In *A Week on the Concord and Merrimack Rivers* there is a minor element of burlesque. The setting sail is described in deliberately grandiose terms, as though the author had in mind at the moment the classical genre which Pope illustrated in *The Rape of the Lock*. An even fainter suggestion of the same thing is present in the scheme of *Walden*. Thoreau was not unaware of the comic element involved in a flight from civilization which took him only a mile from the edge of his native village, only one field away from the highroad, and only half a mile from his nearest neighbor. Indeed, as he himself tells us in the *Journal*, at least one reader thought the whole book a joke and relished the map of the pond as a caricature of the Coast Surveys. But Thoreau's jokes are almost always serious—*i.e.*, revelations of truths which are commonly overlooked, and that form of burlesque which consists in finding *multum* in *parvo* is not for him merely burlesque. As he himself said, any place is as wild as the wildness one can bring to it, and Walden pond was a solitude for the simple reason that he could be alone there.

All his previous life had been, and all his subsequent life was going to be, equally unspectacular. When one of the world's great—a Count Tolstoi, for instance—embraces poverty, the gesture naturally attracts attention. Even Ruskin, a college professor, will draw spectators when he undertakes to work with his hands. But when a poor man lives simply, that is not, ordinarily, news. Yet Thoreau made it something more than news—which he despised. He made it the basis of a legend, and legends were among the very few human creations which he wholeheartedly admired.

The question, "Does Mr. Grinnell know where he himself is?" carries more than one suggestion. It reminds us, among other things, that Thoreau was an explorer who became famous, not because he was lost, but because he had found himself.

Different classes of readers inevitably find different portions of *Walden* the most meaningful. Comparatively few are, as Thoreau himself was, almost equally interested in the aspects of external nature, in mystical intimations, and in sociological deductions. But if one leaves aside the question which sections are the most engaging and the most valuable, there can be little doubt that the first chapter and the last are the most unforgettably vigorous pieces of writing, the most astonishing demonstrations of virtuosity. In the sections which lie between, Thoreau is often discursive, picturesque, and engaging, often humorous, persuasive, and charming; but he is also relaxed and almost conversational. It is chiefly in the first chapter and the last that he undertakes to hit hard and speak with the fiery earnestness of the man formally assuming the prophet's robe and determined that, willy-nilly, he will be heard.

Yet these two sections are too unlike in both substance and style to compete with one another or even to be compared. The first, called "Economics," concerns itself with the most practical and homely aspects of his subject and hits hard with prose, earnestly describing the "penances" which drive men to quiet desperation and suggesting immediate, concrete remedies. The other is spoken from the tripod by a prophet whom the divine fumes have intoxicated and who, in his vision, sees things not quite utterable. Emerson would never have wished to be so down-to-earth as Thoreau was in the chapter on Economy; it is doubtful, on the other hand, if he ever succeeded in sustaining through an equal number of connected pages so original an Orphic strain as that which makes the chapter called merely "Conclusion" a succession of lightning flashes.

Thank Heaven, here is not all the world. . . . Yet we think that if rail fences are pulled down, and stone walls piled up on our farms, bounds are henceforth set to our lives and our fates decided. If you are chosen town clerk, forsooth, you cannot go to Tierra del Fuego this summer: but you may go to the land of infernal fire nevertheless. . . . What does Africa, what does the West stand for? Is not our own interior white on the chart? black though it may prove, like the coast, when discovered. Is it the source of the Nile, or the Niger, or the Mississippi, or a North-west Passage around this continent, that we would find? . . . Be rather the Mungo Park, the Lewis and Clark and Frobisher, of your own streams and oceans; explore your own higher latitudes, with shiploads of preserved meats to support you, if they be necessary; and pile the empty cans sky-high for a sign. . . . Every man is the lord of a realm beside which the earthly empire of the Czar is but a petty state, a hummock left by the ice. . . . There are continents and seas in the moral world to which every man is an isthmus or an inlet, yet unexplored by him. . . . It is easier to sail many thousand miles through cold and storm and cannibals, in a government ship, with five hundred men and boys to assist one, than it is to explore the private sea, the Atlantic and Pacific Ocean of one's being alone.

Throughout whole paragraphs almost every sentence is a metaphor and the metaphors range all the way from those readily translatable into prose to those genuinely Orphic in their tantalizingly elusive implications. At the same time almost every sentence is illuminated by a grotesque humor which juxtaposes the homely to the ineffable, and is pointed by scorn for those who tamely prefer what is to what might be. Thoreau's mind seems to leap from subject to subject as though, in a moment of insight, truth had been revealed and the only danger was that no utterance could be found sufficiently elliptic to communicate it all before the moment passed.

I fear chiefly lest my expression may not be *extra-vagant* enough, may not wander far enough beyond the narrow limits of my daily experience, so as to be adequate to the truth of which I have been convinced. *Extra vagance!* it depends on how you are yarded. The migrating buffalo, which seeks new pastures in another latitude, is not extravagant like the cow which kicks over the pail, leaps the cow-yard fence, and runs after her calf, in milking time. I desire to speak somewhere *without* bounds; like a man in a waking moment, to men in their waking moments; for I am convinced that I cannot exaggerate enough even to lay the foundation of a true expression. Who that has heard a strain of music feared then lest he should speak extravagantly any more forever?

A moment later he is surveying in a few brief sentences his experience at Walden and what it had taught him and he sums it up in the triumphant thesis: "Superfluous wealth can buy superfluities only. Money is not required to buy one necessary of the soul." What is left but to conclude with a final burst of Emersonian optimism: "There is more day to dawn. The sun is but a morning star."

The brilliance of that final chapter is pyrotechnic in its effect; one seems to be present at the birth of a whole galaxy of dancing stars. How, the reader is likely to find himself asking, can any writer have been at any given time so sustainedly incandescent? And the answer—which is of course that Thoreau was not, and that perhaps no writer could be—is an answer which helps to explain why no other such masterpiece as *Walden* was ever to come from its author. The book as a whole was a crystallization and the last chapter was a mosaic of crystals. The moment of sustained and inclusive illumination never existed, and the Orphic profundities never fell as they seem to fall, one after another, from the lips of a prophet in the grip of a divine seizure. They had been written down as fragments, neither successive nor connected, and they were then, sometimes years later, carefully selected and carefully fitted together in such a way that what looks like explosive brilliance was actually the result of a patient craftsmanship carefully matching and arranging brilliants which had been hoarded one by one over the years. The reader of the *Journal* comes across them here and there, imbedded, often, in a matrix not in itself gleaming, and they leap out at his eye as they evidently leaped out at their author when he went searching through his own pages. In *Walden* we pass in a few minutes from the sentence about the wild goose who is more cosmopolite than we to the sentence about the necessity of speaking extravagantly. Actually twelve years lay between the time when the first was written down (1840) and the time when, nearly seven years after Walden had been abandoned, the second appears in the *Journal*.

It is customary to say that the later *Journal* is the record of a man who had lost his road and from whom the tide of joy, of purpose, of inspiration was slowly ebbing away. To what extent that is true we shall presently have occasion to inquire, though to at least one reader it seems obvious that Thoreau was not at any time merely a man gesticulating in a vacuum, and that though the Finder who had so triumphantly proclaimed himself in *Walden* was become merely a Seeker again, his new search was not one necessarily doomed to failure. He evolved slowly and no long stretch of time was granted him. One reason that we have from him no other finished masterpiece comparable to the one which he did manage to achieve may be simply that he did not live long enough. When *Walden* was published, he still had, to be sure, some eight years yet to live. But that was little more than half the time during which his one great book was actually being written, even though a somewhat briefer period had served to assemble it.

Before we consider the Thoreau who attempted to express himself in the several thousand pages which he never had opportunity to use in the manner he at least dimly hoped he might some day use them, we must notice events which occurred before *Walden* was published. Deliberately, perhaps, he excluded or all but excluded them from consideration in that book, but they were nevertheless probably in part responsible for the new directions his thought was already beginning to take.

Inspector of Snowstorms

THE PUBLICATION of *Walden* had little outward effect upon either the position or the daily life of Thoreau as a humble and sporadically useful citizen of Concord. It will be remembered that at the end of his stay by the pond side he had gone back into the Emerson household, and that in 1848 he had gone from there to live again with his own family, whom he again sometimes helped with the prospering business of graphite-making though he took no responsibility for its management until after his father's death in 1859 when his own existence was almost over. His way of life during this period had none of the obvious dramatic value of life by the pond side, but both his pursuits and the disposition of his time were actually much the same. What he lived for was still communion with nature whom he interviewed unremittingly in the course of his long walks and whose communications he set down in his journal, while he remained, as always, resolved that too much life should not be wasted in making a living.

Whatever hopes he may have had for the new book, which was probably in something not too far from its final form as early as 1849, the financial failure of *A Week on the Concord and Merrimack Rivers* had certainly warned him against assuming that even his modest wants could be supplied by his writings. While living at Walden, he had, as the *Journal* reminds us, done various odd jobs about the town, "some fence-building, painting, gardening, carpentering, etc., etc." and had even, as he goes on to say, once built a fireplace for a villager who had not been frightened off by Thoreau's confession that he was not a mason. Now he turned more definitely to the practice of surveying as an occupation which was in itself not unpleasant, which involved no commitment to a routine, and which would support him in exchange for a comparatively small part of his time He had known something of the art back in the days when he had kept school with his brother, for they had given lessons to their pupils, and some time in the late 'forties he had invested in an expensive set of instruments with which to set himself up as a professional. Various farmers employed him since he was a more than satisfactory workman, and indeed he was later to become the township's official surveyor.

He continued, of course, to lecture occasionally both to his fellow townsmen and to 6thers elsewhere, and reference has already been made to the little flurry which he enjoyed about the time when *A Week on the Concord and Merrimack Rivers* was published. But he was not, in general, very popular; he at least persuaded himself that he did not want to be, and his distaste for the occupation increased as he grew older. The year before *Walden* was published he was alarmed lest he might become committed to wasting too much time writing lectures and delivering them. "I realized," he wrote, "how incomparably great [are] the advantages of obscurity and poverty which I have enjoyed so long (and may still perhaps enjoy). I thought with what more than princely, with what poetical, leisure I had spent my years hitherto, without care or engagement, fancy-free. I have given myself up to nature; I have lived so many springs and summers and autumns and winters as if I had nothing else to do but *live* them, and imbibe whatever nutriment they had for me; I have spent a couple of years, for instance, with the flowers chiefly, having none other so binding engagement as to observe when they opened; I could have afforded to spend a whole fall observing the changing tints of the foliage. Ah, how I have thriven on solitude and poverty! I cannot overstate this advantage. I do not see how I could have enjoyed it, if the public had been expecting as much of me as there is danger now that they will. If I go abroad lecturing, how shall I ever recover the lost winter?"

Two years later he was describing thus how an audience received him and, more important, what his attitude was toward it:

At my lecture, the audience attended to me closely, and I was satisfied; that is all I ask or expect generally. Not one spoke to me afterward, nor needed they. I have no doubt that they liked it, in the main, though few of them would have dared say so, provided they were conscious of it. Generally, if I can only get the ears of an audience, I do not care whether they say they like my lecture or not. I think I know as well as they can tell. At any rate, it is none of my business, and it would be impertinent for me to inquire. The stupidity of most of these country towns, not to include the cities, is in its innocence infantile. Lectured in basement (vestry) of the orthodox church, and I trust helped to undermine it.

To most of his fellow townsmen he was not a teacher and writer who did surveying on the side but a surveyor who unaccountably sometimes lectured and wrote. Surveying was the nearest thing to a respectable calling he had ever had and it was surveying which redeemed him (in so far as he was redeemed at all) from the reproach of being an eccentric idler. In 1850 he was writing in his journal a defiantly defensive account of the forest fire which he and a companion had accidentally set six years before, was still remembering how he had been called "damned rascal" behind his back, and how one or two aggrieved citizens "shouted some reminiscences of 'burnt woods' from safe recesses for some years after." Indeed, more than one reference in the *Journal* testifies to Thoreau's awareness that he was by no means exempt from the familiar rudeness of his fellow townsmen and that he reacted to it sometimes with indignation, sometimes with wry humor.

From a post-office loafer he learned that he, Emerson, Channing, and others were known in mild derision as "the walkers." "Do you miss any of your wood?" Thoreau asked, and got rustic humor in reply: "No, I hain't worried any yet. I believe you're a pretty clever set, as good as the average, etc., etc." That was more than two years after *Walden* was published, but it revealed no attitude very different from that of Sam the jailer who had some years before called out one evening: "Thoreau, are you going up the street pretty soon? Well, just take a couple of these handbills along and drop one in at the Hoars' piazza and one at Holbrook's, and I'll do as much for you another time." "There is," he convinced himself, "some advantage in being the humblest, cheapest, least dignified man in the village, so that the very stable boys shall damn you," and he meant it at least to the extent that he found the position of surveyor or even odd-job man less humiliating than the attempt to lecture to audiences who, even when polite, did not follow him very far. That was, as he wrote his friend, Harrison Blake, "an irreparable injury done to my modesty." "The lecturer," he added, "gets fifty dollars a night; but what becomes of his winter? . . . I should like not to exchange *any* of my life for money."

Up to 1854, the year when *Walden* at last appeared, he had, it must be remembered, published outside the few early pieces in *The Dial* nothing of any conceivable importance except the unsalable *A Week on the Concord and Merrimack Rivers,* a review of Etzler's Utopian scheme, an article on Carlyle (1847) in *Graham's Magazine,* and the essay on "Civil Disobedience" (of which more later), printed in an apparently unread volume of essays by former contributors to *The Dial.* After *Walden* had appeared, he was still, as he was destined to remain, without a profession, since he was certainly not a professional writer or lecturer and hardly a professional surveyor or odd-job man. Traveling in Concord remained his chief occupation, but he was not averse to jaunts farther afield. It will be remembered that he had made one trip to the Maine woods during the summer of 1846 when he was, so to speak, officially in residence at Walden. He was to make two others to the same general region in 1853 and 1857; four jaunts to Cape Cod, sometimes alone and sometimes in the company of Ellery Channing; and also a brief visit to Canada with the same companion in 1850. These furnished the materials for the "travel books" which did not appear as books until after his death.

It is obvious that he had at least vaguely in his mind the

possibility that he might some day write another book and that, if he did so, the expanding *Journal* might furnish the materials. But it is equally obvious that he regarded long preparation for some new start a requisite, and it may very well be that in his case, as seems to have been the case with other great journal writers, the book that was thus being written with himself as its only reader served actually to supply the need for expression which otherwise might have driven him to direct writing for publication.

In any case no inconsiderable part of his time must have been spent in writing this *Journal*. When one considers the fact that more than six thousand printed pages were composed in twenty-three years, it is obvious that, had he thought of himself simply as a writer, he might be classed as a reasonably industrious one. He was, after all, producing at the rate of about one medium-sized volume per year and no inconsiderable part of what he wrote was composed with obvious care. But of this no public was aware, and he himself seems to have regarded it, not as his chief occupation, but merely as a record of the really fruitful hours spent in the open air.

To read it is to receive a very rich and detailed account of his private—one might almost say his secret—life; but it is also to remain almost completely unenlightened concerning the personality or the activities of which his fellow citizens took note. One would never guess that Thoreau was, during most of that time, living on terms of affectionate intimacy in a family presided over by a father whom he respected and a mother whom he loved. Neither would one suspect, if one did not have Ellery Channing's account, that he was the one upon whom the other members of the household depended in all minor domestic crises.

Nor is one more than occasionally reminded of the fact that for all his impatience with the machinery of formal sociability, he got on very well with simple, unassuming people.

Despite his personal austerity (again, this is according to Channing) he was never in too much of a hurry to stop for a bit of gossip, and he was delighted with the company of the disreputable, "those who love grog and are never to be seen abroad without a fishpole or a gun in their hands." "To those in need of information—to the farmer-botanist naming the new flower, the boy with his puzzle of birds or roads, or the young woman seeking for books—he was always ready to give what he had."

The "captain of a huckleberry party" needs social gifts of a certain sort, and Thoreau obviously had them. Most days he kept the afternoon sacred for the three- or four-hour walk usually taken alone, but in general his aloofness must have been a spiritual quality of which he was himself rather more vividly aware than were many of those with whom he talked. He also carried on some correspondence with several persons outside the Concord circle—notably with Harrison Blake, the Harvard graduate already mentioned; with Thomas Cholmondeley, an Englishman who had visited Concord in the fifties; and with Daniel Ricketson, a New Bedford Quaker whom Thoreau met at about the same time.

Once while living at Walden, however, he had come into formal conflict with his fellow citizens, or at least with the government which represented them. For some years before that he had paid no poll tax (though other taxes he did pay) on the ground that it was exclusively for the benefit of a government he did not approve of. His dereliction had been allowed to pass unquestioned; but one day, when he went into the village to get a shoe he had left with the cobbler, he was put under arrest and clapped into the village jail. Perhaps the fact that the Mexican War had broken out a few months previously had something to do with the tax collector's zeal, and it certainly predisposed Thoreau to stubborn resistance. A few years before, when the ever-serious Alcott had gone to jail for exactly the same offense, Thoreau had reported the affair to Emerson as though it were a good deal of a joke, climaxed by the opinion of the tax collector when the latter was asked by Helen Thoreau what he thought of the business: "I vum, I believe it was nothing but principle, for I never heerd a man talk honester." In the meantime, however, Thoreau's own indignation against a government which protected the institution of slavery had been mounting, and he was suddenly stubborn.

He spent one night in a cell with an alleged barn burner and next morning he was released when one of the female members of his household paid the tax. That, as he said derisively, "is the whole history of 'My Prisons.'" In *Walden* he reduced the whole thing to one seriocomic paragraph intended to illustrate the fact that "wherever a man goes, men will pursue and paw him with their dirty institutions, and, if they can, constrain him to belong to their desperate odd-fellow society."

Considered merely as drama, the incident was not one of his most successful efforts to reveal the *multum* in the *parvo*. Unfortunately there is no contemporary evidence to support the often told story that Emerson came to see him at the jail and that when he asked, "Henry, why are you there?" he got for answer the question, "Why are *you* not *here?*" According to the account given many years later by the man who had been his jailer, Thoreau was "mad as the devil"—possibly because he saw the danger that the joke might be thought to be on him. Alcott, naturally, approved; but at the time, at least, Emerson professed to find Thoreau's conduct "mean and skulking," and one may take it for granted that many of his fellow townsmen saw the exploit not as something heroic, but quite what one might expect of the "rascal" who had set the woods on fire.

One interesting aspect of the incident is the extent to which it illustrates how completely Thoreau took for granted the fact that he was operating in a fundamentally stable and reasonable society which could be defied without consequences more serious than a purely symbolic confinement in jail. Dissenter and rebel though he was, he still retained—indeed he could hardly have escaped from—his relatively humble but clearly defined position in that recognized New England hierarchy which had managed the affairs and set the tone of society for two centuries. There was not, at the moment, any possibility that rebelliousness would release against him any such savage retaliations as we today take for granted in most parts of the world. Probably he could not, in 1846, have imagined John Brown.

Not many years later, by the time the Civil War was imminent, the situation had changed considerably and there were already signs that the old order was breaking up. The Concord of even the 'forties already included elements not compatible with that cool, decorous, peacefully stratified, town-meeting sort of democracy of which one is most aware when one studies the lives of the official worthies. Industrialization and mechanization were beginning to have their effects. The Irish, who had been brought in to build the railroads, had stayed on to supply both servants and farm hands, now scarce because of the exodus of natives toward the West. Some feared them, others urged that they be educated and accepted; but they must have contributed to the growing importance of the social forces tending to produce a different and rougher kind of democracy than that which had been traditional in New England. Concord had, for example, recently had a taste of what presidential campaigning could become, for it had been the scene of rowdy meetings preceding the election of Harrison and Tyler. Webster spoke. Rival banquets offered barbecued pigs and hogsheads of cider. Ten thousand persons were said to have attended one rally.

Thoreau was, then, not without some experience of the "stump speeches" of which he spoke with such contempt. But it may be doubted, nevertheless, whether even he realized just how rapidly the old order was passing away. It was being disintegrated not only by such new thinkers as Emerson and himself but, perhaps more rapidly and more radically, by a new and more disorderly class of people. Indeed some would, no doubt, be inclined to interpret the withdrawing and mystical aspects of Transcendentalism as a sort of failure of nerve, and see a parallel between the Transcendental moralists and, let us say, a Marcus Aurelius, despairing of a world becoming too disorderly to be understood.

For all this, Thoreau's night in jail was not without its important consequences for him. According to *Walden*, the incident occurred in the summer of 1845; but references in the journals of both Emerson and Alcott seem to make it plain that this is an error—perhaps a deliberate one, since

Walden professes to deal only with the first year by the pond side—and that it was really during the summer of 1846 that Thoreau went to jail. In any case he discussed the adventure in a lecture before the Concord Lyceum in January 1848, and it was presumably this lecture which became the essay "Civil Disobedience," published the following year in a volume of papers by former contributors to *The Dial*. At the time it seems to have attracted no attention; but this is the essay which Mahatma Gandhi made a sort of bible of nonresistance and upon which Thoreau's reputation as a prophet of revolution largely rests.

Indignation against the institution of slavery, and especially against the support which the state of Massachusetts continued to lend it through the government at Washington, was from that moment onward to burn more and more fiercely in the soul of Thoreau. It was later to reach an intensity capable of driving him to a defense of John Brown's violent methods, which he could not consistently have defended at the time when "Civil Disobedience" was written. Indeed, throughout the rest of his life the need to reconcile his defiant individualism with his concern over a public matter was to trouble him more and more. His failure ever really to reconcile the two is one of the several factors which disturbed the happy confidence of *Walden* and to some extent poisoned the paradise which he thought he had found. It helped transform him from a Finder back into a Seeker again.

It is nevertheless a mistake to suppose, as present-day radicals are always tempted to assume, that he ever gave up one philosophy for another or ever became converted heart and soul to any religion of social responsibility. Above all it is a mistake to suppose that the essay on "Civil Disobedience" either in itself or at that time signalizes any such change. In a proper place consideration will be given to those of its aspects which anticipate the somewhat different attitude he was later to take and the greater responsibility for action which he was willing to admit, but the pages of his *Journal* are sufficient evidence that during most of the years still remaining to him his usual activities and his most characteristic meditations were only occasionally influenced by any consciously admitted concern over slavery or any other public question. When the essay is thus examined—not in connection with his ultimate attitude, and especially not in connection with the convictions of our own day, but rather in the light of Thoreau's own beliefs and actions at the time when it was written—it is seen to be less a declaration of any intention to become a social reformer than a reaffirmation of his defiant individualism even when faced with a social wrong as monstrous as he believes slavery to be.

It is true that he calls upon all honest men to do what he has done and to refuse active or even symbolical support to the state which countenances the nefarious institution of slavery. He excoriates those who think that they have done their duty when they have merely voted right and who then take refuge in that kind of good citizenship which consists in bowing to the will of the majority. But he also insists that, though this far he will go, he will go no further. "The government does not concern me much," he writes, "and I shall bestow the fewest possible thoughts on it." And again: "It is not a man's duty, as a matter of course, to devote himself to the eradication of any, even the most enormous wrong; he may still properly have other concerns to engage him; but it is his duty, at least, to wash his hands of it, and, if he gives it no thought longer, not to give it practically his support." Obviously he thought of himself as one with "other concerns to engage him"; obviously he hoped, at least, that he might be able to give the subject "no thought longer"; and if the present-day revolutionists were anxious to repudiate rather than to claim him they would certainly call attention to the usual associations of that phrase: "wash his hands of it."

When "Civil Disobedience" was being written out as a lecture, the publication of *Walden* was still some years away and the book had not yet received its final form; may, indeed, have been still pretty far from complete. Yet *Walden* was to take for granted a certain relationship between man and the state which any assumption of social responsibility would jeopardize, and the kind of life it celebrates assumes the pre-existence of certain necessary conditions which any man who acknowledged an inclusive social responsibility could not claim a right to take for granted. Thus it assumes, for example, that the spiritual Crusoe who lives this happy life may draw to some extent upon the resources of a functioning system of industry and commerce, even as the original Crusoe got his nails and his tools from the convenient wreck. It even assumes, for that matter, the existence of libraries, for Thoreau, as has already been pointed out, never proposed that man should return to savagery and never supposed that civilization represented nothing but a regression from the life formerly led by some noble savage. Neither did he have any scruples about demanding that the existing social order should confer upon him whatever small benefits it was capable of conferring. Thus when the Harvard library refused him permission to take out books because he lived too far away, he went to the president of the university with the argument that the railroad made Concord as close as Boston had once been, and he won his point. More important, perhaps, is the fact that *Walden* also presupposes a government which will permit an errant individualist to go his own way and, if he so chooses, "stand or sit thoughtfully" while his century goes by.

Thoreau was not unaware of the fact that he assumed the existence of these conditions, and it certainly did not seem to him, as it has seemed to certain of his critics, that the assumptions invalidated the argument. The necessary conditions were actually present and it was one of the peculiarities of his Utopia that it was realizable in the here and now. If he did not, like most reformers, first demand that everything be made different before any good life could begin, he had the right, in exchange, to accept conditions as they actually were. There is no evidence that he had ever heard of the Kantian rule which insists that the rightness or wrongness of any act must be judged by the answer to the question, "Would the performer be willing to have everybody else do the same thing?" But it is not likely that he would have been very favorably impressed if he had heard of it. Living on rice and molasses by a pond side did not seem to be one of the comparatively few things that everyone would want to do and if it should ultimately turn out that everyone wanted to do it, the problem could be dealt with at the time. There was no reason why he should not, meanwhile, find his happiness as he could.

His encounter with the tax collector had reminded him that the existing government did, nevertheless, make certain demands upon him and that they might become, not merely inconvenient, but morally intolerable. Yet for the moment at least his reaction was not a determination to abandon the life he had chosen and to devote himself to the task of reforming the society which intruded upon him. To have done so would have been to violate the first principle of his philosophy and to imitate on the grandest possible scale the conduct of the poet whom he was to ridicule in *Walden* for determining to get rich so that he might have leisure to write, when he should (as Thoreau said) "have gone up to the garret at once." A postponement of living was the thing which, above all others, he would not tolerate, and so it is in "Civil Disobedience" itself that he declares: "I came into this world, not chiefly to make this a good place to live in, but to live in it, be it good or bad." He has, he said, "signed off" the church, and he adds that he would have signed off all the other societies which he never signed on to, if only he had known where to find a complete list. From the standpoint not only of *Walden* but of the life which he was for the next ten years to attempt to lead, the most significant words in "Civil Disobedience" are, then, those which make the careful qualifications in the following sentence: "I quietly declare war with the State, after my fashion, though I will still make what use and get what advantage of her I can, as is usual in such cases." To do any more or to accept any less would be necessarily to lose again the Paradise Found at Walden.

What, one must now ask, was the "private business" he had to transact, what the use he made of that "wide margin" which, so he said, he must have around his life? To some extent the question is answered in those portions of *Walden* which describe his activities in bean field and in woods. But there is a fuller account in the *Journal*, the great bulk of which, as now published, covers the years after he had left the pond side and when he was attempting quietly to practice the art of life as he had discovered it there. How much of the earlier *Journal* disappeared after it had been used in *Walden* and *A Week* can only be guessed, but most of the rest has been preserved—possibly because he himself never got around to rearranging its materials—and of the fourteen large published volumes, only the first is dated before 1850. Our own generation has seen two admirable books: Odell Shepard's *The Heart of Thoreau's Journals* and Francis H. Allen's *Men of Concord*, quarried out of it; but hundreds of pages of sometimes brilliant, sometimes touching, passages still remain buried among many more of the routine record. It is still necessary to go to the complete text to get any complete answer to the question how Thoreau spent his time and (as he himself put it) what he "lived for."

The external features of this life as they appeared to a friendly observer have been described by Ellery Channing with whom Thoreau sometimes walked and sometimes talked. "His habit was to go abroad a portion of each day, to field or woods or the Concord River. . . . During many years he used the afternoon for walking, and usually set forth about half-past two, returning at half-past five." In his pocket was a "spy-glass" and the notebook into which went the brief notes to be used in his *Journal*. His purpose, so he told Channing, was "to see what I have caught in my traps which I set for facts," and three hours was about the time required to visit the various spots which interested him most.

He was not always a solitary, for he skated and otherwise diverted himself with Emerson, Alcott, and others. Sometimes he took a companion even on his walks, but it is obvious that the somewhat mercurial Channing often annoyed him and that there was no one whose presence was not, on the whole, less desirable than his absence would have been when serious business was afoot. There were moments when gossip intrigued him enough to get even into the sacred pages of the *Journal*, and a man who had no appreciation of it could hardly have written the delightfully humorous description of the village gossip mills which enlivens one chapter of *Walden*. People, then, were not outside the range of his interest, since some of the most pungent pages of the *Journal* are devoted to character sketches.

But the usual emphasis was, with him, reversed, and it was the solitary rather than the social aspects of life which seemed to him the more important, the nonhuman rather than the human part of the universe the more significant. The proper study of mankind, he seems to say, is not man but nature, and as the editor of his *Journal* has put it: "to have said that one of Thoreau's human neighbours was as interesting to him as a woodchuck would have been to pay that neighbour a rather handsome compliment. None of the brute animals, so-called—we have it on his own authority— ever vexed his ears with pomposity or nonsense." By 1851, he was proposing to himself that he should "have my friends and relations altogether in nature, only my acquaintances among the villagers," and less than two years later he was remarking that echoes "are almost the only kindred voices that I hear." No wonder that he preferred to take his walks without having present a mere acquaintance who could only disturb the intimate intercourse with his real friends or that, as he told Channing, he carried no stick because even that would be too much company.

For some kind of business in the woods he had a superb physical equipment provided by a body which was not only tireless but quick and sure in its reactions. "There was," Emerson said, "a wonderful fitness of body and mind. He could pace sixteen rods more accurately than another man could measure them with rod and chain. He could find his path in the woods at night, he said, better by his feet than his eyes. He could estimate the measure of a tree very well by his eye; he could estimate the weight of a calf or a pig, like a dealer. From a box containing a bushel or more of loose pencils, he could take up with his hands fast enough just a dozen pencils at every grasp. He was a good swimmer, runner, skater, boatman, and would probably outwalk most countrymen in a day's journey. And the relation of body to mind was still finer than we have indicated. He said he wanted every stride his legs made."

But what was it that nature said to him and that he said to nature? What were the immediate delights furnished by the apparently routine walks, and so precious that he could attempt to silence even the voice of conscience when it whispered to him about the horrors of slavery and by so doing threatened to deprive him of them? What, beyond these immediate delights, were the ultimate rewards he hoped some day to win, the ultimate truths he for so long hoped to find? Thoreau's solitariness was not merely churlish; he was not merely running away from human society but attempting to run forward into something, and it was not a sense of emptiness but a sense of richness which his solitude brought him. Even Emerson was so far from being able to answer the question that Thoreau seems to him to be only wasting his time, and almost at the very moment when the latter is determining to "have only acquaintances among the villagers," Emerson is writing into his journal: "Thoreau wants a little ambition in his mixture. Fault of this, instead of being the head of American engineers, he is captain of a huckleberry party." Nor can Channing, ready though he is to assume that Thoreau knows his own business, give more than a very partial and misleading answer: "The idea he conceived was, that he might, upon a small territory,—such a space as that filled by the town of Concord,—construct a chart or calendar which should chronicle the phenomena of the season in their order, and give their general average for the year. This was only one of the various plans he had in view during his walks; but his habit of mind demanded complete accuracy, the utmost finish, and that nothing should be taken on hearsay. . . . His calendar embraced cold and heat, rain and snow, ice and water; he had his gauges on the river, which he consulted winter and summer; he knew the temperature of all the springs in the town; he measured the snows when remarkable. All unusual changes of weather, with novel skies, storms, views, find place in his notes."

All this is true enough as far as it goes. Even while living at Walden Thoreau had begun, in very amateurish fashion, to try out the scientist's technique of record and measurement. This was for him a blind alley except so far as it did involve contact with phenomena, and it is the dead record of this sort of thing which sometimes needlessly swells the bulk of the latest volumes of the *Journal* until one is tempted to remind him, as in the last chapter of *Walden* he had reminded others: "It is not worth the while to go round the world to count the cats in Zanzibar." His answer would have been the sentence which follows, "Yet do this even till you can do better, and you may perhaps find some

'Symmes' Hole' by which to get at the inside at last," for it was only in the moments when he could find nothing better to do that he counted cats. It was not primarily to take nature's temperature with a pocket thermometer that he signed off all human institutions and confessed to the very audience which was listening to his own denunciation of slavery: "However, the government does not concern me much, and I shall bestow the fewest possible thoughts on it."

It is true that a few men knew of him chiefly as an untrained but willing naturalist in the then conventional meaning of the term. While he was still living at Walden, J. Elliot Cabot, one of Agassiz's coworkers at Harvard, arranged for him to send specimens of fishes from the pond, and apparently he proved to be a successful collector. His own library included a number of technical books to which he sometimes refers, and occasionally we find him interesting himself in such a question as that concerning the identity of a certain species of glowworm which he had found in the Maine woods. Botany interested him also—rather more indeed than zoology did. In youth he had acquired the habit of looking up the names of plants in a handbook, and this mild interest in nomenclature tended to grow. In his will he left his collection of plants and Indian relics to the Boston Society of Natural History, and in one of his last surviving letters he remarks that he would like, if he lives longer, to write a "report on Natural History generally." But his pursuits as well as his interests were less scientific in the then accepted sense of the term than these facts would suggest. In Linnæus he found a classification of the various kinds of interest which men may take in plants and correctly classified himself among the *Miscellaneous Bota-*

nophilists—either, that is to say, as one of the "Poetae" or of those "Biologi" of whom Linnæus says "Panegyrica plerumque exclamarunt."

His knowledge about plants and animals as distinguished from his familiarity with them was, indeed, both elementary and random. That was partly, of course, because popular handbooks were not so readily available as they are now, but the fact remains that at the present day there are hundreds of men who would hardly describe themselves as even amateur naturalists who can call by name five times as many plants, birds, and animals as he could. Reading the *Journal*, it is almost disconcerting to discover that at thirty-four he was not sure of the identity of the common thalictrum of the fields and that a year later he had to have help in naming a Luna moth! As Mr. Bradford Torrey, editor of the *Journal*, remarks: "The truth appears to be that even of the commoner sorts of birds that breed in eastern Massachusetts or migrate through it, Thoreau—during the greater part of his life, at least—knew by sight and name only a small proportion, wonderful as his knowledge seemed to those who, like Emerson, knew practically nothing." To this day the curious have been unable to decide what the "night-warbler" he talked a good deal about really was, and some are inclined to suspect that it was not one bird but several.

The paraphernalia of the professional (like professionalism itself) he tended to distrust. Curiosity led him to look through a telescope bought by a neighbor, and very shortly thereafter he visited the Harvard Observatory, but he defended himself against his interest by getting the Harvard man to admit that even to astronomers the naked eye still had its importance. He was proud of the fact that until

1854 he got along without owning a "spy-glass" for his ornithological observations, and he has a characteristic passage extolling the merits of his own especially contrived hat which he believed better than a botany box for transporting plant specimens, since "there is something in the darkness and the vapors that arise from the head—at least if you take a bath—which preserves flowers through a long walk." But these eccentricities were the by-products of a sound instinct which warned him that for all one might say, and all he might accept, concerning the utility of classifications, his own aims were fundamentally different from those of even the most renowned scientists.

What the difference was may be easily suggested by a convenient contrast. When the first cask of Concord fish arrived in Cambridge, Agassiz was (so Mr. Cabot wrote) delighted, and began immediately to prepare them for his draughtsmen. "Some of the species he had seen before, but never in so fresh condition; others, as the breams and the pout, he had seen only in spirits, and the little tortoise he knew only from the books." Of the perch Agassiz remarked that it was almost identical with that of Europe, but distinguishable, on close examination, by the tubercules on the suboperculum. Some years later Thoreau was describing his own methods of studying plants. Often, so he said, he visited a particular plant four or five miles distant from his home as much as a dozen times in a fortnight in order to know exactly when it opened, and at other times he followed the whole course of some specimen which interested him, from leaf to fruit. "I wanted," he said, "to know my neighbors, if possible—to get a little nearer to them"; and that last phrase is the key to understanding his purpose. It is true enough that such observations, laborious though they seem, were too random to have much scientific value and are not usable even by the ecologists whom, in some degree, Thoreau was anticipating. But his primary purpose was not scientific. It was what he himself would have been inclined to call, rather vaguely, "poetic," and it aimed at familiarity with, rather than knowledge about, living things. Agassiz wanted to know about the "tubercules on the suboperculum" which distinguished the European perch from the American, Thoreau to know his neighbors and "get a little nearer to them" if possible. "A man has not seen a thing," he once wrote, "who has not felt it."

The *Journal* is, after all, the most important part of the residuum of his life. It is his account of his stewardship, the chief record of the fact that Henry Thoreau was granted a certain number of years on this earth. More sincerely perhaps than Rousseau, he could present its pages to the recording angel and say, "Such I was." Here is a record of the use which he made of his time, of his sensibilities, and of his intelligence. And whatever the recording angel may think, whatever the posterity which remembers him may think, there seems to be no reasonable doubt that he himself regarded his life as a private success, however much it may have been a public failure. One of the very last of his recorded utterances was the calm assertion of his conviction that whatever God might be, God had found him acceptable, and there is no evidence that he had any regrets or that, if he had had his life to live over again, he would have wished it any different. Whatever others might think, he had been, in his own opinion, very much more than the captain of a huckleberry party.

Only the entire record as he himself left it can supply adequate material for any attempt to judge him. The concrete detail concerning what he did and saw and felt is indispensable, for without it one cannot give due weight to the richness or the variety of the things which he found to interest and to stimulate him. In his own mind it was certainly the continuous sense of being alive in a continuously beautiful and wonderful world of phenomena which, even more than any thoughts or conclusions concerning that world, made living a precious boon. Though he became more and more a kind of scientist and though he remained also—despite growing doubts—a kind of Transcendentalist, he never neglected the visible or the tangible merely because he believed that he had occasionally caught a glimpse of something beyond either. Probably none of his sayings is more widely known than the "One world at a time" which he whispered near his end to a pious visitor who wished to discuss a future life. But the injunction includes more than its religious or antireligious meaning. Thoreau, unlike many other mystics and transcendentalists, had accepted the one world of external reality—a world not to be neglected while the search for the other world beyond it was still on. The phenomena of nature, animate and inanimate, furnished his indispensable daily bread, and daily bread, like all homely things, was to him tremendously important. The sight of trees in winter, a happy encounter with a woodchuck, or even a conversation with some sturdy farmer might furnish the occasion for one of the most elaborately worked-up of the *Journal* pages, and it was undoubtedly because the Emersons and the Margaret Fullers had no adequate appreciation of such things that both his sympathy with such persons and their understanding of him were imperfect.

The reader who wishes to go to the journals themselves

in order to judge the delights which Thoreau enjoyed and the truths he thought he had discovered, or at least glimpsed, had perhaps best be advised that the matters of which it treats are of several kinds and that, if we leave aside the quasi-scientific records, the bulk is concerned with an account of Thoreau's association with visible nature—which means not meditations, mystical or otherwise, for which nature affords an excuse, but an actual description of what his ears heard and his eyes fell upon. Undoubtedly he is, among other things, gratifying that purely instinctive delight in physical activity, that native wildness, of which he himself made so much. At the opposite extreme, this sensual wildness fades away into the mere recording of quasi-scientific fact; but between the two lies the most important area of all—that in which Thoreau is enjoying a genuinely social intercourse with the friends of the fields and woods whom he had resolved to know so much more intimately than the mere acquaintances of the village. And there is a very real sense in which these memoirs of his are more closely analogous than might at first be thought to the more familiar sort of memoirs in which men, often not otherwise very distinguished, have gained immortality by recording their association with their human fellows. The delight which Thoreau took in nature is no more explicable to those who cannot share his pleasure in this kind of association than the delight of a Pepys or a Boswell is explicable to those who do not share their interest in a different sort of social intercourse. But to him it was of vast importance.

Among the other matters included are fragments of a still-developing social, moral, and economic philosophy as well as transcendental "whisperings" concerning those "higher laws" he still hoped to see more clearly. Nor are still other matters lacking. One catches some very significant glimpses of several never quite resolved conflicts, including a conflict between the transcendental moralist and a kind of scientific pantheism which threatens to undermine the serene mysticism of the orthodox transcendentalist as alarmingly as that transcendentalism had undermined orthodox Christian faith. And of that more anon. But the reader who does not respond to Thoreau's account of his social life in nature will not understand the solidest of the reasons why he found his life richly worth the living.

If a week was interrupted by too many human beings, it took him, he said, another week to get over it, and he laughed at those who warned him against the danger of solitude as the Eskimos of north Greenland, cut off on all sides by the ice, had laughed at the explorer Kane when he warned them of extermination unless they crossed the glacier to the south and rejoined the other members of their race. "It is here that the walrus and the seal, and the white bear, and the eider ducks and auks on which I batten, most abound." "I had no idea," he said on another occasion, "that there was so much going on in Heywood's meadow."

Most men, it seemed to him, had got the necessary introduction to nature as boys for they had hunted and fished. But few, for some reason, ever followed up the acquaintance. They continued, he said scornfully, to suppose that the fish were themselves important. Even most Concorders might visit his sacred pond a thousand times "before the sediment of fishing would sink to the bottom and leave their purpose pure,—before they began to angle for the pond itself." His own response still had, to be sure, its rich sensual element: "My body is all sentient." But sensuality passed on into interest, and interest into sympathy, or oneness. Few others, it seemed to him, had ever achieved this perfect relationship. The Indian is "somewhat of a stranger in nature" but "the gardener is too much a familiar." Neither enjoys as he does a reverent communion—nor even, for that matter, the mere sense of fellowship.

I saw a muskrat come out of a hole in the ice. He is a man wilder than Ray or Melvin. While I am looking at him, I am thinking what he is thinking of me. He is a different sort of a man, that is all. He would dive when I went nearer, then reappear again, and had kept open a place five or six feet square so that it had not frozen, by swimming about in it. Then he would sit on the edge of the ice and busy himself about something, I could not see whether it was a clam or not. What a cold-blooded fellow! thoughts at a low temperature, sitting perfectly still so long on ice covered with water, mumbling a cold, wet clam in its shell. What safe, low, moderate thoughts it must have! It does not get on to stilts. The generations of muskrats do not fail. They are not preserved by the legislature of Massachusetts.

And to think that there are men, most men indeed, to whom getting rich or getting elected is more important! "Much more is a-doing than Congress wots of in the winter season. What journal do the persimmon and buckeye keep, or the sharp-skinned hawk?" Fifteen years after this last sentence was written he is still congratulating himself that he should have had the good fortune to be born into a world not yet all despoiled and that, while enjoying none of what are commonly called "advantages," he has discovered the true secret of life. "While you are pleased to get knowledge and culture in many ways, I am delighted to think that I am getting rid of them. I have never got over my surprise that I should have been born into the most estimable place in the world, and in the very nick of time too." He does not know, he says elsewhere, in any litera- ture, ancient or modern, "any adequate account of that Nature with which I am acquainted."

In the light of such convictions as these one begins to perceive that his gibe in the first chapter of *Walden* against those "who can be so frivolous" as to concern themselves with the gross servitude known as Negro slavery is not itself so frivolous—whatever else it may be—as some would suppose. To him it seemed that all the aims and values cher- ished by organized society were radically wrong; that what was needed was not the correction of this or that recognized injustice or recognized failure but the correc- tion of its whole conception of what men should live for; and he felt, no doubt, that to concern himself actively with abolitionism would be tacitly to agree that society as a whole was right—right enough at least to make such tinker- ing with the details the most useful thing a man could de- vote himself to. Was the freedom his fellow townsmen en- joyed itself so noble and so happy that Negroes should be promised ultimately something like it? Would it not be better if the New Englanders should first heal themselves?

Whether slavery were abolished or continued, all Amer- ica had embarked upon an adventure of which he thor- oughly disapproved. Its conception of what constituted success, whether for an individual or for a nation, was vulgar and vicious. It was committed to the conviction that getting and spending are the whole duty of man. Our "manifest destiny"—he uses the phrase—was something which he would have liked to be able to repudiate utterly, and to his friend Harrison Blake he wrote in 1853: "The whole enterprise of this nation, which is not an upward, but a westward one, toward Oregon, California, Japan, etc., is totally devoid of interest to me, whether performed on foot, or by a Pacific railroad. It is not illustrated by a thought; it is not warmed by a sentiment; there is nothing in it which one should lay down his life for, nor even his gloves—hardly which one should take up a newspaper for. . . . What end do they propose to themselves beyond Japan? What aims more lofty have they than the prairie dogs?"

The Gold Rush to California was important because it was the nakedest of all the manifestations of the essential vulgarity of the American ambition. "I know of no more startling development of the morality of trade and all the modes of getting a living than the rush to California affords. Of what significance is . . . a world that will rush to the lottery of California gold-digging—to live by luck, to get the means of commanding the labor of others less lucky, *i.e.* slaveholding, without contributing any value to society? And that is called enterprise, and the devil is only a little more enterprizing! . . . The hog that *roots* his own living and so makes manure, would be ashamed of such company. . . . Going to California. It is only three thousand miles nearer to hell. . . . What a comment, what a satire, on our institutions! The conclusion will be that mankind will hang itself upon a tree. And who would interfere to cut it down?"

But the Gold Rush is, after all, only the most startlingly barefaced development of the "morality of trade" which Thoreau had hated from the early days of his developing philosophy. It was in itself unproductive; it could not be, as genuinely useful work usually is, joy-giving, and therefore also an end in itself. "A man had better starve at once

than lose his innocence in the process of getting his bread";
and lose his innocence, *i.e.*, his capacity for joy, he must, if
he lives by any process not productive and natural.

Thus in the end it seems all to come back to the fundamental error of supposing that the true business of life is
not living but making a living, or that the two can ever be
healthily separated. At Walden they had been perfectly
united and in the main they continued to be so after
Thoreau had completed his experiment of living outside
society and embarked on another which was, if you like, an
experiment tending to prove that the essential Walden technique could be applied even by one who did not physically
withdraw from the village community. Gathering wood
for one's fire was a typical example of useful labor which
was also a reward in itself, for, as he wrote to Harrison
Blake in a letter wishing that his transcendental friend
might sit for a while by his chimney: "Talk of burning
your smoke after the wood has been consumed! There is
far more important and warming heat, commonly lost,
which precedes the burning of the wood. It is the smoke of
industry, which is incense. I had been so thoroughly
warmed in body and spirit, that when at length my fuel
was housed, I came near selling it to the ash-man, as if I
had extracted all its heat."

"Most men," he wrote in "Life Without Principle,"
"would feel insulted, if it were proposed to employ them in
throwing stones over a wall, and then in throwing them
back, merely that they might earn their wages. But many
are no more worthily employed now. . . . The ways by
which you may get money almost without exception lead
downward. To have done anything by which you earned
money *merely* is to have been truly idle or worse. If the

laborer gets no more than the wages his employer pays him, he is cheated, he cheats himself." It was a subject with which he could never finish and the pages of the *Journal* also are sprinkled with references to it. "There is little or nothing to be remembered written on the subject of getting an honest living. Neither the New Testament nor Poor Richard speaks to our condition. . . . How to make the getting of our living poetic! for if it is not poetic, it is not life but death that we get. Is it that men are too disgusted with their experience to speak of it? or that commonly they do not question the common modes?"

Obviously Thoreau approached the whole subject of economics from a very unusual angle. His "Man" is the perfect antithesis of that abstraction called The Economic Man. The latter is a creature who exists only as producer and consumer, whereas Thoreau's man is, or at least ought to be, everything else. His final ideal was not full employment but something which he suggested when he exclaimed: "It would be glorious to see mankind at leisure for once,"—as mankind might be if man were content with necessaries, not obsessed with the determination to increase the number of things called "necessaries" until the whole waking day is hardly sufficient to supply them. "Most men are so taken up with the cares and rude practice of life that its finer fruits cannot be plucked by them. Literally, the laboring man has not leisure for a strict and lofty integrity day by day." Thus to Thoreau the solution is, of course, not "increased production" but simpler living, and even the division of labor is suspect since it tends to deprive the individual of the satisfaction of performing essential tasks for himself. In *Walden* he had asked: "Shall we forever resign the pleasure of construction to the carpenter?

. . . I never in all my walks came across a man engaged in so simple and natural an occupation as building his house. . . . Where is this division of labor to end? and what object does it finally serve? No doubt another man *may* also think for me; but it is not therefore desirable that he should do so to the exclusion of my thinking for myself." Almost at the very end of his life he was writing with bitter humor of where all division of labor was actually leading.

To such a pass our civilization and division of labor has come that A, a professional huckleberry-picker, has hired B's field and, we will suppose, is now gathering the crop, perhaps with the aid of a patented machine; C, a professed cook, is superintending the cooking of a pudding made of some of the berries; while Professor D, for whom the pudding is intended, sits in his library writing a book . . . a work on the Vacciniex, of course. And now the result of this downward course will be seen in that book, which should be the ultimate fruit of the huckleberry-field and account for the existence of the two professors who come between D and A. It will be worthless. There will be none of the spirit of the huckleberry in it. The reading of it will be a weariness to the flesh. To use a homely illustration, this is to save at the spile but waste at the bung. I believe in a different kind of division of labor, and that Professor D should divide himself between the library and the huckle-berry-field.

No wonder, then, that Thoreau should have refused to countenance the assumption that slavery was a blemish on an otherwise noble commonwealth or that, when he turned from woodchuck or chickadee to study his fellow man, he should have preferred simple men to cultured—not because he idealized them, but because they seemed, to him at least, creatures who had not yet gone far astray and were still, so to speak, firmly footed on a low but solid ground from which it might be possible to go sanely forward. Most farmers were not, to be sure, what the poets had painted them. Of most, it could only be said—as he said of Isaiah Green, who had lived nearly eighty years—that "their long life was mere duration"; that though they were as respectable as woodchucks, they were hardly more. Sometimes he is touched, as he was, for instance, when he met Cyrus Hubbard, "a man of a certain New England probity and worth" out again in the snow with his sled for the five thousandth time and "superior to the faith he professes" for "it is a great encouragement that an honest man makes this world his abode." Here and there, moreover, one might find a farmer like George Minott, "perhaps the most poetical farmer—who most realizes to me the poetry of the farmer's life—that I know." Minott does nothing with haste or drudgery, he makes the most of his labor and "takes infinite satisfaction in every part of it." He knows every pin and nail of his barn and he has not too much land to trouble him, merely enough "to amuse himself and live."

How superior is even the mediocre farmer, self-reliant and productive, to such monsters as the three reformers who called uninvited upon Thoreau one day and were immortalized in one of the few pages of pure disgust he ever wrote:

Here have been three ultra-reformers, lecturers on Slavery, Temperance, the Church, etc., in and about our house and Mrs. Brooks's the last three or four days—A. D. Foss, once a Baptist minister in Hopkinton, N. H.; Loring Moody, a sort of travelling pattern-working chaplain; and H. C. Wright, who shocks all the old women with his infidel writings. Though Foss was a stranger to the others, you would have thought them old and familiar cronies. (They happened here together by accident.) They addressed each other constantly by their Christian names, and rubbed you continually with the greasy cheeks of their kindness. They would not keep their distance, but cuddle up and lie spoon-fashion with you, no matter how hot the weather nor how narrow the bed . . . chiefly. . . . I was awfully pestered with his benignity; feared I should get greased all over with it past restoration; tried to keep some starch in my clothes. He wrote a book called "A Kiss for a Blow," and he behaved as if there were no alternative between these, or as if I had given him a blow. I would have preferred the blow, but he was bent on giving me the kiss, when there was neither quarrel nor agreement between us. I wanted that he should straighten his back, smooth out those ogling wrinkles of benignity about his eyes, and, with a healthy reserve, pronounce something in a downright manner. It was difficult to keep clear of his slimy benignity, with which he sought to cover you before he swallowed you and took you fairly into his bowels. It would have been far worse than the fate of Jonah. I do not wish to get any nearer to a man's bowels than usual. They lick you as a cow her calf. They would fain wrap you about with their bowels. . . . addressed me as "Henry" within one minute from the time I first laid eyes on him, and when I spoke, he said with drawling, sultry sympathy, "Henry, I know all you would say; I understand you perfectly; you need not explain anything to me"; and to another, "I am going to dive into Henry's inmost depths." I said, "I trust you will not strike your head against the bottom."

Once his first youth had passed Thoreau did, then, hear occasionally, as Wordsworth had, the still sad music of humanity. At the very beginning of the Walden period it had intruded itself upon him when he paid four dollars and twenty-five cents for the lumber in an Irishman's shanty and at six next morning met the owner and his family on the road: "One large bundle held their all—bed, coffee-mill, looking-glass, hens—all but the cat; she took to the woods and became a wild cat, and, as I learned afterward, trod in a trap set for woodchucks, and so became a dead cat at last." The incident was perhaps the real beginning of his persistent interest in Irish immigrants as a class—alien, despised, "thinking to live by some derivative, old-country mode in this primitive new country," and yet, like the most stolid of the native farmers, primitive rather than corrupt, close to nature even if only to her most brutish part. More than one of the shanties he visited and more than one of the children who lived in them he came to know in that reserved but honorable fashion in which he knew the woodchucks. Early in the first summer at Walden he had taken refuge from a thunderstorm in a shack and observed that even the Irish were bedeviled by the complexity of the machinery necessary to live the only kind of life they knew how to live.

There dwelt a shiftless Irishman, John Field, and his wife, and many children, from the broad-faced boy that ran by his father's side to escape the rain to the wrinkled and sibyl-like, crone-like infant, not knowing whether to take the part of age or infancy, that sat upon its father's knee as in the palaces of nobles, and looked out from its home in the midst of wet and hunger inquisitively upon the stranger, with the privilege of infancy; the young creature not knowing but it might be the last of a line of kings instead of John Field's poor starveling brat, or, I should rather say, still knowing that it was the last of a noble line and the hope and cynosure of the world. An honest, hard-working, but shiftless man plainly was John Field; and his wife, she too was brave to cook so many succeeding dinners in the recesses of that lofty stove; with round, greasy face and bare breast, still thinking to improve her condition one day; with the never absent mop in hand, and yet no effects of it visible anywhere. The chickens, like members of the family, stalked about the room, too much humanized to roast well. They stood and looked in my eye or pecked at my shoe. He told me his story, how hard he worked bogging for a neighbor, at ten dollars an acre and the use of the land with manure for one year, and the little broad-faced son worked cheerfully at his father's side the while, not knowing, alas! how poor a bargain he had made. Living, John Field, alas! without arithmetic; failing to live.

But at least they had the advantage of being "beneath charity" and "many degrees below the almshouse." At least, also, they never knew the squalor of town-bred children, and sometimes it seemed as though they were not doing so badly after all when little Johnny Riordan went gladly to school and did not love it when deep snows kept him at home. When Thoreau asked another Irishman how many potatoes he could dig in a day, he was well enough pleased with the reply: "Well, I don't keep any account. I scratch away, and let the day's work praise itself." Next day Thoreau reminded himself that a man who went one step further would have asked if the day's work had not reason to blame itself, but the answer he had got to his inquiry was good as far as it went. "There's the difference between the Irishman and the Yankee; the Yankee keeps an account. The simple honesty of the Irish pleases me." How life— almost any life—was sweetened when it was simple and direct, when men got what they needed from nature directly enough to know from whom they were getting it and left the divine origin still plainly marked upon the things with which they surrounded themselves.

Passed a very little boy in the street today, who had on a home-made cap of a woodchuck-skin, which his father or elder brother had killed and cured, and his mother or elder sister had fashioned into a nice warm cap. I was interested by the sight of it, it suggested so much of family history, adventure with the chuck, story told about it, not without exaggeration, the human parents' care of their young these hard times. Johnny was promised many times, and now the work has been completed . . . a perfect little idyl, as they say. The cap was large and round, big enough, you would say, for the boy's father, and had some kind of cloth visor stitched to it. The top of the cap was evidently the back of the woodchuck as it were expanded in breadth, contracted in length, and it was as fresh and handsome as if the woodchuck wore it himself. The great gray-tipped wind hairs were all preserved, and stood out above the brown only a little more loosely than in life. As if he put his head into the belly of a woodchuck, having cut off his tail and legs and substituted a visor for the head. The little fellow wore it innocently enough, not knowing what he had on, forsooth, going about his small business pit-a-pat; and his black eyes sparkled beneath it when I remarked on its warmth, even as the woodchuck's might have done. Such should be the history of every piece of clothing that we wear.

Thoreau never wrote a passage more charming than this one (set down almost at the end of his life), and it is perhaps worth remarking that it is an almost perfect example of a style which is the exact opposite of his other, better-known manner. Its secret—in so far as the secret of such quiet, unspectacular perfection can ever be revealed—seems to be that it is an expression of love as purely as the passage on the three reformers is an expression of disgust. Thoreau saw the little boy as he seldom saw human beings, but often saw the other manifestations of animate nature, and his heart went out to him in phrases usually reserved for the creatures who, for him, were more truly fellow creatures than men could be. The desperation and the meannesses of the latter, even the stolid nobility he sometimes perceived in them, were remote. When occasionally he recorded, with grim humor, some such extraordinary example of New England avariciousness as his account of the work required from an Irish hired girl or the story of Billings and Prichard who, when dividing the stock of a store, broke a cracked bowl in two so that each might have his half, he is as detached as most men are detached when some cruelty of nature, for which they assume no responsibility, comes to their attention. Society, red in tooth and claw, was the world *he* never made and was usually detached from. But the little boy in the woodchuck cap was something human which, for once, brought out the intimate love he could seldom feel for anything in that part of the universe he did not wish to belong to.

Most men, especially if they were prosperous and respected citizens, were already too far gone on the wrong road to seem other than hopeless. He regarded them as Westerners sometimes regard the members of some highly complex but totally alien Oriental civilization whose problems they can never understand. From the point which they had reached, it was hopeless to think one might ever argue back to a promising starting place, and only the improbable miracle of a sudden change of heart could furnish the basis for a reform. If even the Irish were already too far gone in civilization to understand real simplicity, with whom could one begin? One day at Walden a half-witted pauper from the almshouse stopped to talk. Thoreau had often seen him with others "used as fencing stuff, standing or sitting on a bushel in the fields to keep cattle and himself from stray-ing" and he turned out to be the only man who ever ex-pressed the desire to live as Thoreau did. "He told me, with the utmost simplicity and truth, quite superior, or rather *inferior*, to anything that is called humility, that he was 'de-ficient in intellect.' . . . 'I have always been so,' said he, 'from my childhood; I never had much mind; I was not like other children; I am weak in the head. It was the Lord's will, I suppose.' And there he was to prove the truth of his words. . . . I have rarely met a fellow-man on such promising ground—it was so simple and sincere and so true all that he said. . . . It seemed that from such a basis of truth and frankness as the poor weak-headed pauper had laid, our intercourse might go forward to something better than the intercourse of sages."

Thoreau's sometimes sympathetic awareness of the farmer and the immigrant is a significant part of both his literary and his actual personality. When the most im-portant of the *Journal* passages which reveal it are col-lected, as they have been, into a separate volume, they are extensive and arresting—sufficient indeed to have formed by themselves the basis of a minor reputation had they happened to be the only things we knew by their author. But neither in extent nor in emphasis do they seem of more than tertiary importance when the *Journal* is read as a whole. They are relatively brief and widely scattered; ob-viously incidental, almost irrelevant, to its principal con-cerns. And hence they tend to confirm rather than to qual-ify the general impression that in his conscious scheme of life, man as he existed in contemporary society interested Thoreau hardly more than the other aspects of animate nature interest most present-day dwellers in either town or country. He was occasionally aware of and interested in the life history or habits of Irishmen or paupers just as the average citizen is occasionally interested in the habits or life history of some animal which happens to come to his attention.

To say this is not to say that man's *potentialities* did not interest him. In a sense, of course, his whole enterprise was an attempt to discover, through the cultivation of himself, what these potentialities were. In the beginning, indeed, he readily enough assumed that the meaning of nature could not be anything except her meaning for man; and though, as we shall see, he tended to become less and less sure that any such assumption was justified, the fact remains that to the end, man's life in nature inevitably continues to be the subject of his meditations. But for him the proper study of mankind is man, only if "man" be taken to mean the ultimate human potentialities, and the study of either the manners or the psychology of the existing population of Concord was hardly more than a trivial amusement—sometimes as entertaining as gossip sometimes is, but essentially no more than gossip.

Unless this fact is accepted, it becomes almost impossible not to miss, in any interpretation of his career, the emphasis which he himself would have put upon its different aspects. His notions concerning economics and sociology are the notions of one who assumes that the ultimate business of man is some such business as he himself engaged in and that the ultimate rewards of living are some such rewards as he himself won. His thoughts may furnish—in fact, they have furnished—hints and inspirations to reformers who, seeking other ends, have found it possible by modification to adopt

some of his means to their ends. But even the most fundamental of his injunctions, the recurrent "Simplify, Simplify," means "Simplify in order that you may lead a certain kind of life and enjoy certain kinds of happiness."

A man's importance to the world is not always what he
thinks it is, but in his own mind Thoreau was not, as our
own prejudices lead us to assume, a reformer and sociologist
who happened to have a taste for contemplating nature and
dealing directly with the fundamental necessities of life. He
was, on the contrary, a man who developed certain sociological ideas because society as it existed in his time tended
to make difficult the kind of life which he thought most
worth living. Inevitably it follows that an attempt to understand him—as contrasted with an attempt to understand
the nature of his influence or so-called "importance"—cannot stop with either the presentation or the criticism of the
merely economic or sociological aspects of his teaching but
must go on to consider both the daily life which has just
been described and also the intellectual as well as the emotional problems which sometimes heightened and sometimes interfered with the sheer joy of living freely in the
presence of the visible and tangible world which he so much
loved.

Here the reader must again be reminded that of
Thoreau's voluminous writings only a very small portion
was published before his death, that the only one of his
longer works often read today was at least ostensibly concerned only with an adventure which came to its end when
he was thirty years old, and that even "Civil Disobedience"
was composed at about the same time. He was, after that,
to write far more than he had already written up to and
including those two works, and what he wrote makes it

clear that his principal concern was neither the slavery question—though that troubled him more than he was for long willing to admit even to himself—nor the problem of getting a living, which he had satisfactorily solved, but quite simply the attempt to make as rewarding as possible the life which he had won for himself the means of leading.

Quite obviously he believed, as the present chapter of this book has attempted to show, that this life was both happy and meaningful. Many pages of the *Journal* are filled with vivid accounts of things done and sights seen which the author records with what is plainly a deep, unquestioning satisfaction. One might, for example, easily compile an "Animals of Concord" to serve as a bulkier companion to the already existing "Men of Concord"; and one might, for that matter, go on to compile others on "Forests in Winter" or even, of smaller compass, on "Turtles I have Known" or "Village Cats." But Thoreau was not continuously immersed in direct experience with concrete things. Abstract questions concerning the meaning of human life and the meaning of nature continued not only to absorb him frequently but sometimes to trouble him. There were conflicts never resolved, conceptions never quite grasped. And though less obviously sensational than his economic and sociological paradoxes, some of the questions he was asking himself are still, and probably eternally, hardly less interesting to a speculative mind.

We shall, then, now pass on to some consideration of the emotional and intellectual aspects of his life in nature and attempt to answer some of the questions which the description of his ordinary activities is likely to raise. What, if the question may be put in so abstract a form, was his "theory of knowledge" and his conception of the *summum bonum?*

What is the relation between man and nature? What is the meaning of the delight which association with her affords him, what lessons does he learn, what challenging problems does he meet? How, in a word, is the instinctive pleasure which he had always taken in the out-of-doors to be rationalized and intellectualized?

Pantheist and Puritan

ANATOLE FRANCE—one of the many recent writers of repute whom Thoreau would have admired as little as he admired most of his literary contemporaries—tells the story of a nearly blind aesthetician who found that his inability to contemplate any actual works of art greatly facilitated the process of forming theories concerning art in general. Had this fortunate philosopher turned his attention to nature he would doubtless have discovered, as others certainly have, that here also it is in proportion to the actual richness of one's experience with the subject that the difficulty of either describing that experience or generalizing from it tends to increase. Those to whom nature is merely an abstraction and to whom her delights are largely theoretical have relatively little difficulty in defining what she means to them, and it was—somewhat unfairly perhaps—to this class that Thoreau consigned Emerson. But those who, to repeat Thoreau's own metaphor, have been more than once drenched to the skin often find that the very intimacy of their association defies adequate description.

From the standpoint of the mere metaphysician Thoreau

began, it must therefore be remembered, at the wrong end —not with a thought but with an experience. Nature was not something which he had heard about from scientist or poet or philosopher and which he decided, thereupon, to investigate either theoretically or practically. Nature was something of which he became aware, to which he felt himself drawn, as soon as he became aware of anything. She made herself known to him in walking and fishing and boating; she taught him an instinctive, primitive, perhaps animal, delight in bodily functioning. She had done all these things before he sought any explanation or planned any defense. In his case there was no "I think, therefore I am" but rather an "I am, and, therefore, sooner or later, I must think."

So far as the existing record informs us, it does not appear that he had even begun to *think* about nature until he read Emerson's essay. During his first years at Harvard he was, as has already been pointed out, bookish, first of all, and the essays which he wrote there tempt one to guess that at the time he had not yet realized that his passion for the woods and the fields was a suitable subject for intellectual consideration and that he set rural amusements aside as proper only for holiday relaxation while he devoted himself to the more conventional subjects of literary treatment. Certainly, so far as the record goes, there is no evidence that his original intellectual life began until Emerson's epoch-making essay fell into his hand and it is at least possible that actually it did not begin until then.

Almost inevitably, therefore, Thoreau commences philosopher by swallowing Emerson whole; by taking over something of Emerson's literary manner as well as his general intellectual approach; and also, no doubt, by reading between Emerson's lines whatever was necessary to make the statement completely satisfactory to him. Only later was he to discover how exclusively intellectual Emerson's approach was; how little, by comparison with Thoreau himself, Emerson was acquainted with the actual phenomena of nature, and how little susceptible he was to the delights which she spread before one who, like Thoreau, had a streak of wildness in him. "The world," Emerson had written, "is emblematic. Parts of speech are metaphors, because the whole of nature is a metaphor of the human mind. The laws of moral nature answer to those of matter as face to face in a glass." To the end of his life Thoreau was, in one way or another, asking himself from time to time if this statement was true, and much of his originality is dependent upon the fact that he often saw beyond its merely anthropocentric implications. But for the moment he seized upon it because it was, at least, one way of justifying the activities to which he was drawn. One man, as he was later to realize, goes fishing for the sake of the fish as edible objects and another man goes in order to get on with the counting of cats in Zanzibar. But neither the economic nor the purely scientific motives seemed to him quite adequate or quite noble. What if one may, as Emerson seemed to suggest, fish for truth, and what if, all along, this had been what he had unknowingly sought to do?

One of his scientific contemporaries is said to have remarked that Thoreau was a very good potential entomologist whom Emerson had spoiled. That is, of course, a false statement, not merely a wildly exaggerated one. Even if we leave aside all question of the extent of Emerson's influence, the fact remains that Thoreau was not "spoiled" but "made" by himself and by all the influences which came to bear upon him. It is, however, true that a large part of his thinking about the meaning of his life in nature —as distinguished on the one hand from his economic paradoxes and on the other from his descriptions of what he felt or saw—does operate between two poles, one of which is established by the Emersonian conception of nature as something with a purely human meaning, while the other (never more than tentatively located even by Thoreau himself) lies at the center of some opposing conception which humbles man more than it exalts him and poses the problem, not of discovering how nature reflects him, but how from her he may learn sometimes frightening truths he would never otherwise have suspected. Emerson's nature is arranged in a sort of Ptolemaic system with man at the center. Thoreau came ultimately to suspect something Copernican in her plan and more and more he found himself somewhat unwillingly cultivating a kind of objectivity which rejects all the too facile interpretations of natural metaphors. But he never for long completely renounced one attitude for the other, and the fact that he did not makes his profoundest thinking dialectic rather than consistent.

To call these doubts and these questionings "problems" is to suggest that they troubled him more than they did. The happy serenity of his mind as well as of his temperament was not seriously disturbed, for he was a happy seeker and he loved to push his thoughts about his experiences with nature as far as he could push them. But the fact remains that certain questions did remain unanswered, that he alternated between certain convictions, and that if the problems raised did not actually produce such a discord as was finally produced by his conflicting attitudes toward the antislavery agitation, they nevertheless did serve to provide a continuing intellectual accompaniment to his routine life and they help to account for the fact that this way of life did not become, as it might have, empty of all content except the emotional and the sensual.

In the preceding chapter of this book an attempt was made to illustrate by quotation certain characteristic aspects of his experiences with nature and with man. Some of these quotations were descriptive, others narrative, and still others analytical. But Thoreau thought of himself as a philosopher as well as a man of letters, and while, of course, the two cannot be separated, there is some excuse for considering by themselves the metaphysical ideas which seemed to him to afford justification, on the metaphysical level, for his determination to have his friendships in the woods and fields, rather than in the village, and to observe not the behavior of men, but the ways of nature.

As time went on, certain changes took place in what may be called the technique of his intercourse with the visible and invisible world. Inevitably, of course, he moved farther and farther away from the unthinking, almost unconscious activity which, so he tells us, was the source of his earliest ecstasies. But that is not all. As the mature man grew older, the mystic communion which had replaced thoughtless activity itself gave way more and more to deliberate observation, and threatened at times to transform him completely from a transcendentalist into some sort of quasi-scientific observer. "Once," so he was already complaining in 1852, "I was part and parcel of Nature; now I am observant of her"; and there were moments, at least, when the change seemed pure loss. Yet it was not, perhaps, merely the result of that inexplicable fading of mystical illumination into the light of common day of which mystics commonly complain. It was the result also of a growing objectivity which had its positive aspects and which was leading him not so much in the direction of the intellectually as well as emotionally arid attitudes which sometimes dominate the professional students of botany and zoology, as toward a pantheism less different in its emotional quality from his earlier faith than perhaps he himself realized.

What Thoreau had always sought in his intercourse with living things and even with the very hills and fields themselves was that warm and sympathetic sense of oneness, that escape from the self into the All, to which psychologists have given the chilly name "empathy." As far back as the time when he was writing *A Week on the Concord and Merrimack Rivers* empathy had enabled him to write:

Shad are still taken in the basin of Concord River, at Lowell, where they are said to be a month earlier than the Merrimack shad, on account of the warmth of the water. Still patiently, almost pathetically, with instinct not to be discouraged, not to be *reasoned* with, revisiting their old haunts, as if their stern fates would relent, and still met by the Corporation with its dam. Poor shad! where is thy redress? When Nature gave thee instinct, gave she thee the heart to bear thy fate? Still wandering the sea in thy scaly armor to inquire humbly at the mouths of rivers if man has perchance left them free for thee to enter. By countless shoals loitering uncertain meanwhile, merely stemming the tide there, in danger from sea foes in spite of thy bright armor, awaiting new instructions, until the sands, until the water itself, tell thee if it be so or not. Thus by whole migrating nations, full of instinct, which is thy faith, in this backward spring, turned adrift, and perchance knowest not where men do *not* dwell, where there are *not* factories, in these days. Armed with no sword, no electric shock, but mere shad, armed only with innocence and a just cause, with tender dumb mouth only forward, and scales easy to be detached. I for one am with thee, and who knows what may avail a crowbar against that Billerica dam? . . . Not despairing when whole myriads have gone to feed those sea monsters during thy suspense, but still brave, indifferent, on easy fin there, like shad reserved for higher destinies. Willing to be decimated for man's behoof after the spawning season. Away with the superficial and selfish phil-*anthropy* of men . . . who knows what admirable virtue of fishes may be below low-water-mark, bearing up against a hard destiny, not admired by that fellow-creature who alone can appreciate it! Who hears the fishes when they cry? It will not be forgotten by some memory that we were contemporaries. Thou shalt ere long have thy way up the rivers, up all the rivers of the globe, if I am not mistaken. Yea, even thy dull watery dream shall be more than realized. If it were not so, but thou wert to be overlooked at first and at last, then would not I take their heaven. Yes, I say so, who think I know better than thou canst. Keep a stiff fin, then, and stem all the tides thou mayst meet.

And whatever changes had taken place in either his metaphysics or his technique, one need only compare that passage with another written many years later—written indeed more than two years after his complaint that he was become, now, no more than a mere observer—to see that it expresses the same emotional state and needs only the reworking, which the later pages of the *Journal* never got, to be set beside what he had written so long before.

How much lies quietly buried in the ground that we wot not of! We unconsciously step over the eggs of snapping turtles slowly hatching the summer through. Not only was the surface perfectly dry and trackless there, but blackberry vines had run over the spot where these eggs were buried and weeds had sprung up above. If Iliads are not composed in our day, snapping turtles are hatched and arrive at maturity. It already thrusts forth its tremendous head . . . for the first time in this sphere . . . and slowly moves from side to side . . . opening its small glistening eyes for the first time to the light . . . expressive of dull rage, as if it had endured the trials of this world for a century. When I behold this monster thus steadily advancing toward maturity, all nature abetting, I am convinced that there must be an irresistible necessity for mud turtles. With what tenacity Nature sticks to her idea! These eggs, not warm to the touch, buried in the ground, so slow to hatch, are like the seeds of vegetable life.

It is true that after about 1855 more and more of the *Journal* pages are filled with mere facts dryly set down. Many of them seem to support Channing's previously quoted account of Thoreau's determination to catalogue exhaustively the phenomena of his little section of this earth, and many of these passages make dry reading, seem indeed almost as pointless scientifically as they are devoid of literary quality. Obviously the moments of happy insight did come less frequently. But at least they never ceased entirely and there is no evidence that Thoreau ever found his life other than rewarding and sweet. In March of 1860—less than two years before the beginnings of his last illness put an end to the *Journal*—he was admiring the flight of a hen hawk, wondering about the colors of its underwings, and regretting that men different from himself would shoot it down to answer an idle question. "Some, seeing and admiring the neat figure of the hawk sailing at two or three hundred feet above their heads, wish to get nearer and hold it in their hands . . . What is an eagle in captivity!—screaming in a courtyard! I am not the wiser respecting eagles for having seen one there. I do not wish to know the length of its entrails." One of the best pages from the *Journal's* last years is devoted to the eloquence of a cat's tail, another to the expertness of the squirrel stripping a pine cone, and the very last page of all to pebbles recently washed by rain. These are, to be sure, observations more detailed and exact than most he would have taken time to make in the days when intuition sprang forth more quickly and seemed more nearly all-sufficient. Yet the end sought is the same. Observation has become a new, more laborious technique, but neither it nor the facts it collects are ends in themselves, for the end sought remains the same—an emotional as well as an intellectual participation in natural processes.

What did to some extent change was not only the technique by means of which such participation was sought but also the moral drawn and the conclusions reached concerning the relationship between the human and the nonhuman. Though he had once explicitly called himself "a transcendental brother" and though he never ceased to reject, as in one of the just-quoted passages, what he took to be an inevitable part of the scientific method, he was nevertheless moving, in conviction as well as in technique, away from the transcendental assumption that the meaning of nature can be reached by intuition and toward what is the fundamental scientific assumption—namely, that only through observation may one ultimately reach not merely dead facts but also those which understanding can make live.

"It is more proper for a spiritual fact to have suggested an analogous natural one, than for the natural fact to have preceded the spiritual in our minds." Thus he wrote in the *Journal* on January 24, 1841, a few months before he first went to live with the Emersons, and no statement would seem to commit a man more absolutely to the intuitional as opposed to the scientific point of view. Yet it was later in the same year that he was proclaiming, "The moral aspect of nature is a jaundice reflected from man"; and only a few months after that, he could write, "What offends me most in my compositions is the moral element in them." Nor are the conflicts implicit in these statements ever wholly resolved. In 1852 he is proclaiming that "The constant inquiry which nature puts is: 'Are you virtuous?' "; and later in the same year, "The perception of beauty is a moral test." Only thirteen months before the *Journal* finally ends he is similarly noting that "A fact barely stated is dry. . . . It must be the vehicle of some humanity in order to interest us. . . . Ultimately the moral is all in all."

Perhaps these last two sentences will serve better than any others to indicate that the conflict was in part less conflict than confusion; that Thoreau seems never to have perceived quite clearly the difference between saying that nature confirms man's moral notions and saying, as he himself seems to become more and more inclined to say by implication, that what nature teaches *is* morality even when it conflicts with what either the individual or society has assumed.

In any event, however, a similar vacillation persists between the tendency to make man the center of any conceivable universe and the tendency to belittle his importance in the scheme of nature. "I do not," he was writing in 1852, "value any view of the universe into which man and the institutions of man enter very largely or absorb much attention. Man is but the place where I stand, and the prospect hence is infinite. . . . The universe is larger than enough for man's abode. Some rarely go outdoors, most are always at home at night, very few indeed have stayed out all night once in their lives, fewer still have gone behind the world of humanity, seen its institutions like toadstools by the wayside." Yet repeatedly thereafter he could, seemingly at least, contradict himself. "Nature must be viewed humanly to be viewed at all; that is, her scenes must be associated with human affections, such as are associated with one's native place, for instance. A lover of Nature is pre-eminently a lover of man" (1852). "There is no such thing as pure *objective* observation. . . . If it is possible to conceive of an event outside of humanity, it is not of the slightest significance, though it were the explosion of a planet" (1854). Indeed he had, not long before, done hardly more than rephrase Emerson's assertion that all nature is a metaphor when he wrote: "He is richest who has most use for nature as raw material of tropes and symbols with which to describe his life. . . . All nature will *fable*, and every natural phenomenon be a myth."

Here again there is perhaps more a conflict of statement than a conflict of thought. Thoreau himself once makes the distinction between Man and men, and to some extent it is of the first which he is speaking when he puts a stress upon the human meaning of nature, and of the latter when he describes all things human as irrelevant or trivial. But despite the growing objectivity of his own relation to nature and despite his growing alienation from the spirit of the transcendentalist, he also persistently remains a mystic. In 1853 he received a circular from the Association for the Advancement of Science and he filled in as requested the answers to certain factual questions, but "The fact is," he notes for his own information, "I am a mystic, a Transcendentalist, and a natural philosopher to boot." "What," he had asked himself the year before, "are these rivers and hills, these hieroglyphics which my eyes behold?" And hieroglyphics, in something at least akin to the Emersonian sense, he always wanted to continue to believe in.

He was aware enough of—perhaps he exaggerated—the fact that he observed more and more, and he feared that he communicated directly less and less. "I fear that the character of my knowledge is from year to year becoming more distinct and scientific. . . . I see details, not wholes nor the shadow of the whole" (1851). "I suspect that the child plucks its first flower with an insight into its beauty and significance which the subsequent botanist never retains." "I find myself inspecting little granules, as it were, on the bark of trees, little shields or apothecia springing from a thallus, such is the mood of my mind, and I call it studying lichens. . . . Surely I might take wider views" (1852). Bringing home in that same year two little frogs for study, he reminds himself, nevertheless, that he would "Obtain insight, avoid anatomy," and a few months later: "Carlyle said that how to observe was to look, but I say that it is rather to see, and the more you look the less you will observe. . . . Go not to the object; let it come to you." "My desire for knowledge," he had noted on still another occasion, "is intermittent; but my desire to commune with the spirit of the universe, to be intoxicated with the fumes . . . is perennial and constant."

Yet for all his fears and despite the indisputable fact that the *Journal* does tend to become more and more largely given over to a factual record, there seems to be no reason to suppose that his sense of intimate communion ever left him completely. Certainly purely mystical convictions did not, and neither did an at least recurrent faith in the valid-

ity of intuition. Walking in the winter woods in 1858, seeing, as he thought, very little evidence of God or man, and
feeling, so he said, that life was not as rich or inviting
an enterprise as it ought to be, he saw a perfect snowflake
fall upon his coat sleeve and it reminded him that nature
had not lost her pristine vigor yet. The snowflake, he
thought, came as the dewdrop did also, straight down from
the maker of the world. "We think that the one mechan-
ically coheres and that the other simply flows together and
falls, but in truth they are the product of *enthusiasm*, the
children of an ecstasy, finished with the artist's utmost
skill." And less than a year before he made the last entry in
the *Journal*, he was still enough of an intuitionist to describe
his surprise at the way in which thoughts sometimes seem
to come "ready-made . . . as if we only thought by sympathy with the universal mind, which thought while we
were asleep."

To set all these conflicting statements down one after
another is to create an impression of absolute confusion, of
irreconcilable conflict. On the one hand, nature is a moral
hieroglyphic; but on the other, morality is merely a jaundice reflected from man. The human race is no more important to the universe than a mushroom is to a forest, but
the lover of nature is inevitably a lover of man. We must
see rather than look because the universal mind thinks for
us, but at the same time we fill endless pages with detailed
observation and persistently interrogate even the lichens
which mottle the tree trunk and the rock. Moreover, the
chronology of these various pronouncements absolutely
forbids us to suppose that one point of view was definitely
abandoned in favor of the other. The intuitionist and the
observer, the humanist and the pantheist persist, if not side

by side, then at least alternately, as the mood of the thinker changes from day to day. The one unchanging thing is the endless pursuit of those moments of empathy which might be achieved less frequently as time went on but which were never entirely absent for long. They might arrive unexpectedly in what seemed like an intuition; or they might, on the other hand, seem to be generated by some observation which grew suddenly luminous. One such moment might seem to suggest that nature was revealing the correspondence between herself and man; another, that everything human was false and artificial. Yet neither the occasion nor the interpretation was so important as the moment itself. Whatever it might mean and however it might be captured, it was a final end. This was what, as he himself put it, "he lived for." "I hear," he writes once in the *Journal*, "the unspeakable rain, mingled with rattling snow against the windows, preparing the ground for spring."

To say, as we have said, that Thoreau never abandoned one intellectual position for another is not to say that a certain drift is not perceptible or that observation on the one hand, and a kind of pantheism much less humanistic than Emerson's on the other, did not tend to become, respectively, more and more important parts of his activity and of his thought. Just as surely as he tended more and more to "look," no matter how much he might persist in reminding himself that it was better to "see," so too he tended more and more to discover in nature not confirmations of humanity's moral prejudices but a scheme in which these prejudices seemed to be accorded a sometimes frighteningly scant consideration. Much of the characteristic transcendental doctrine persisted, but it no longer, as it once had, dominated his thinking, and some of the characteristic transcendental pronouncements which were quoted in the paragraphs just preceding may be interpreted as protests against other attitudes which were threatening them, just as the expressed doubts concerning the value of observation are provoked by the realization that it was toward observation that he was being more and more drawn.

There is, also, an obviously causal connection between the growing habit of observation and the growing dissatisfaction with the easier and more complacent aspects of the Emersonian view of nature. The less intimately acquainted one is with nature, the more readily one may assume that she is what one wants to assume her to be. The more closely one studies her "hieroglyphs," the more carefully one attempts to decipher rather than merely intuit their meaning, the more likely one is to doubt that optimistic human guesses contain all of the truth. And if Thoreau resisted, as he undoubtedly did, the direction in which he was being drawn, it was not only because John Locke, whom he read in college, had obviously sunk less deep into his mind than either Emerson or the Oriental philosophers whom he had read in the very crucial period just before the Walden episode. It was also because the only official science of which he had any knowledge was of the sort least likely to stimulate philosophical thought.

Something has already been said of his rather remote connection with the disciples of Agassiz. He had also read some science including the earlier Darwin, but the very word "science" was associated in his mind with the mere collection of facts—largely because, no doubt, he was living toward the end of the heyday of the anatomist and the taxonomist, when natural history did not mean primarily either the study of habits and life histories (which would, of course, have interested him) or, still less, those attempts to understand man as part of nature, which were soon to occupy not only Darwin but also the Huxleys and Haeckels. The completely unsystematic, almost desperately pointless character of his own quasi-scientific recordings is evidence enough that he did not really grasp what slight philosophical implications the vast enterprise of collecting and cataloguing did have; and it is quite obvious, from his various derogatory references to science, that in his mind it stood, not (as it might have) for an attempt to penetrate the secrets of life, but for the mere assembling of meaningless details. Its "objectivity" was not merely that freedom from humanistic prejudgments which he himself sometimes strove to obtain, but a complete denial of the legitimacy of any emotional attitude toward the world of nature and something therefore as far from "communion" as it was from philosophical thought.

As early as 1838, when he probably thought himself as near to Emerson, whom he had just met, as he was ever to think himself, he was already observing that "The fact will one day flower out into a truth"; but he was also already assuming that the "mere accumulators of fact" had no conception of what facts were good for. They were the makers of museums which, at about the same time, he was calling "the catacombs of nature—dead nature collected by dead men." "One green bud of spring, one willow catkin, one faint trill from a migrating sparrow would set the world on its legs again. . . . Where is the proper herbarium, the true cabinet of shells, and the museum of skeletons, but in the meadow where the flower bloomed, by the seaside where the tide cast up the fish, and on the hills and in the valleys where the beast laid down its life and the skeleton of the traveler reposes on the grass? What right have mortals to parade these things on their legs again, with their wires, and, when heaven has decreed that they shall return to dust again, to return them to sawdust. . . . Embalming is a sin against heaven and earth—against heaven, who has recalled the soul and set free the servile elements, and against the earth, which is thus robbed of her dust."

Thoreau, it will be remembered, sent "specimens" to the zoologists at Harvard, but his conscience was not easy. When, in 1854, he had killed a turtle "for the sake of science" he felt that he had "a murderer's experience in a degree" and that however his specimen might serve science, he himself and his own observations would be the worse for what he had done. "I pray," he wrote, "that I may walk more innocently and serenely through nature. No reasoning whatever reconciles me to this act." And what if the scientist, for whose benefits this murder was committed, made no real use of the so-called facts he might learn; what if that scientist actually neither knew nor ever could know anything about turtles? Ellery Channing describes Thoreau's disgust with a great folio about just these creatures. Thoreau himself, he says, had spent days and nights in watching them. He had caught them, hatched them, and noted down on the spot the process by which they laid their eggs. He probably knew, Channing goes on, more about turtles as they lived their lives than all the naturalists in Massachusetts. But in the whole folio, Thoreau said, he found no hint as to the habits of one single species and no indication that the author had ever seen a living specimen. When in 1858 he sent to the Boston Natural History Society some fishes from Walden pond, the pundits of the society puzzled much over the question whether they were or were not hitherto described species, but to Thoreau the names were not important. "What is the amount of my discovery to me? It is not that I have got one in a bottle, that it has got a name in a book, but that I have a little fishy friend in the pond."

Science itself was soon to recognize almost as clearly as Thoreau did that to rest content with dissection and classification was to shut both the mind and the heart to the nature which one pretended to study. Even Agassiz came to realize that the age of mere collecting was almost over. By 1860—too late for the fact to be very significant—Thoreau had read, or at least knew something about, *The Origin of Species* and corresponded with his English friend, Thomas Cholmondeley, on the subject. His letter does not survive and Cholmondeley's remark in reply—that Darwin's book "may be fanciful, but it is a move in the right direction"— might be taken to mean that Thoreau had been unfavorably impressed. At least once in the late *Journal*, however, he refers to the "development theory," which he cites as implying "a greater vital force in nature" and as being the equivalent of "a sort of constant *new* creation." Thus though there is no clear evidence that he fully accepted, or, for that matter, really understood, the theory of evolution, he must at least have recognized that here was something more than dissection and nomenclature. He himself was helping forge a link between a Gilbert White (whom he repeatedly quotes) and such more recent writers as Burroughs and Muir, even such as Julian Huxley and William Beebe, who, however diverse they may be, combine, as Thoreau himself would have liked to combine, scientific knowledge with both philosophical interest and an emotionally charged attitude toward nature. But he was never to read even Thomas Henry Huxley, much less still later writers, whose spirit would have been closer to his own; and among his near contemporaries the choice was merely a choice between, on the one hand, the authors of books like the folio on turtles which had so depressed him, and, on the other, *The Book of the Seasons* by that William Howitt whose facile, sentimentalized descriptions he first took as a model and then despised. In the pretentious dilettantism of his own friend Channing—who fretted while Thoreau was making notes and who protested, "I am universal; I have nothing to do with the particular and definite"—he recognized precisely the sort of mere vaporing he wished to escape. But official science gave him no help or encouragement and continued to represent in his mind the antithesis both of any genuine familiarity with even the living facts of nature, and of any emotional participation in her mysteries.

At the very moments when he himself was calling knowledge to the aid of wonder, he persisted in girding at detailed knowledge as though any close familiarity with facts betrayed him into the hands of the unimaginative and the blind. Thus once, during the third and last of his trips to the Maine woods, he dug out from beneath the bark of a tree the phosphorescent wood which had attracted his attention and he "let science slide" while he "rejoiced in that light as if it had been a fellow creature." "Science . . . would have put me to sleep; it was the opportunity to be ignorant that I improved." He exulted, so he thought, like a pagan suckled in a creed which was not outworn but "bran-new," never worn at all. "I believed that the woods were not tenantless, but choke-full of honest spirits as good as myself any day. . . . Your so-called wise man goes trying to persuade himself that there is no entity there but himself and his traps, but it is a good deal easier to believe the truth. . . . I have much to learn of the Indian, nothing of the missionary." And yet what could be more scientific, in one of the best senses of that term, than so characteristic an exclamation as this: "How sweet is the perception of a new natural fact! suggesting what worlds remain to be unveiled."

Nothing could, of course, be less congenial to Thoreau's mind than "science" of the sort beloved by the village atheist. The "scientific morality" of the positivist would have disgusted him more, if that is possible, than institutional Christianity. Never for a moment could he have believed that the world was merely mechanical. Arguing like Fabre rather than like Darwin, he was sure that if a moth attaches its cocoon to the leaves of the black willow and if the black willow is one of the few trees whose leaves hang on all winter, it is because: "It was long ago in a full senate of all intellects determined how cocoons had best be suspended." These minds which decided were, he was sure, kindred to the mind which admires the arrangement, for the mind of the universe is a mind "which we share." But the more his observation took in and the longer he brooded over the facts he had observed, the more obvious it became that man was a part of nature, not nature a part of man; that man reflected her, not she him; that her purposes and her standards might include some of his, but that they included much more also, so that the merely human was swallowed up in the natural.

"What is the relation between a bird and the ear that appreciates its melody, to whom, perchance, it is more charming and significant than to any else?" Asking himself that question in 1857, he permits himself to answer in an almost Emersonian manner: "Certainly they are intimately related, and the one was made for the other. It is a natural fact. . . . I see that one could not be completely described without describing the other." But actually he had been growing less and less inclined to accept a teleology which assigns so important a role to man. Observing a snowfall the year before and, incidentally, recording its phenomena with the minuteness which has led some critics to dismiss the later *Journal* as the work of a man who had abandoned himself to the observation of meaningless detail because he no longer felt or thought, he is struck once more by the microscopic beauty of the flakes. "A divinity must have stirred within them before the crystals did thus shoot and set." But they can, he realizes, hardly be *intended* for the human eye, however much that human eye may be fitted to delight in them, just as the human ear was fitted to delight in the song of the bird. "On the Saskatchewan, when no man of science is there to behold, still down they come, and not the less fulfill their destiny, perchance melt at once on the Indian's face. What a world we live in! where myriads of these little disks, so beautiful to the most prying eye, are whirled down on some traveller's coat. . . . Meanwhile the meadow mouse shoves them aside in his gallery, the schoolboy casts them in his snowball, or the woodman's sled glides smoothly over them, these glorious spangles, the sweeping of heaven's floor. And they all sing, melting as they sing of the mysteries of the number six—six, six, six." A year later the hooting of an owl was reminding him that the owl had been in the world before him. "There is no whisper in it of the Buckleys, the Flints, the Hosmers who recently squatted here, nor of the first parish, nor of

Concord Fight, nor of the last town meeting." Nor was such detachment—the spiritual counterpart of his physical and social detachment from the life of the village—any new thing. For all that he had once said, for all he was on occasion to say again, about the necessity of relating nature to man, he was nevertheless confessing in 1853 that he loved nature partly "*because* [italics his] she is not man but a retreat from him." "None of his institutions control or pervade her. There a different kind of right prevails. In her midst I can be glad with an entire gladness. . . . He is constraint, she is freedom to me. . . . None of the joys she supplies is subject to his rules and definitions. What he touches he taints. In thought he moralizes. One would think that no free, joyful labor was possible to him."

All life, he feels, is one, and it is to the All, not merely to the small human segment, that he wishes to belong. "The simplest and most lumpish fungus" is, so he reminds himself in 1858—again during that period when it is sometimes said he had ceased to feel—"related to ourselves" because it is matter not merely raw but "appropriated by spirit." Having signed off all human institutions, he wants to sign on to the universe; to know its laws and its purposes, not man's. "Think of cats, for instance. They are neither Chinese nor Tartars. They do not go to school, nor read the Testament. . . . What sort of philosophers are we, who know absolutely nothing of the origin and destiny of cats?" Finding a supposedly new species of bream in Walden pond, he did not, he said, want either to eat it or to study its anatomy. He wanted to know it as his contemporary, and would like, if he could, to "think like a bream for a moment." Most men profess to despise gossip. But what, Thoreau seems to be asking, is all history, and religion, and sociology but gossip when it is seen from the perspective of the maker of snowflakes and the creator of bream? Perhaps the turtle is the philosopher from whom man could learn most, for the turtle most perfectly exemplifies the slow, confident persistence of living things. "How many worthy men have died and had their funeral sermons preached since I saw the mother turtle bury her eggs here!" Kansas, he recalls, has lived an age of suspense since then. You may go to India and back while the turtles are still waiting to hatch. French empires may rise and fall in a hurry, but the turtle lasts longer. "One turtle knows several Napoleons." In the shell they have not yet seen a berry and they have known no cares, "yet has not the great world existed for them as much as for you?"

In the passage last quoted, the reference to Napoleon is almost purely conventional, but the reference to Kansas is topical enough to indicate that Thoreau was not actually so unaware of what was going on in the world of men as he would perhaps have liked to be. During the following year he was to meet John Brown for the first time, and some two years after that he was pouring onto the pages of the *Journal* the indignant sentences which were to be reworked into the fiery speech he made to his fellow Concordians a few weeks later. Nothing could well be either more inconsistent or more understandable; and these pages of the *Journal* themselves furnish the most vivid illustration of just how divided his mind was. The entry for October 19, 1859, begins with a diatribe against a government which kills the liberators of the slave, and then, after two printed pages of moral indignation, breaks off to note: "C. says that he saw a loon at Walden the 15th," after which it goes on painstakingly to record the phenomena Thoreau himself had observed on the walk from which he had apparently just recently returned. "See a black and rusty hedgehog(?) caterpillar in the path." Then, immediately after the caterpillar, come six and a half printed pages more about John Brown. A year later, when John Brown's body lay a-moldering in its grave, Thoreau could write to his friend, Harrison Blake, in a strain as purely, as ferociously, detached from all merely human concerns as any he ever achieved, and could proclaim a transvaluation of values which might have got a nod of approval from Nietzsche. "How wholesome winter is, seen far or near; how good, above all the mere sentimental, warm-blooded, short-lived, soft-hearted, *moral* goodness, commonly so-called. . . . Whatever is, and is not ashamed to be, is good. I value no moral goodness or greatness unless it is good or great, even as that snowy peak is. Pray, how could thirty feet of bowels improve it? Nature is goodness crystallized. . . . It is better to warm ourselves with ice than with fire."

Ably assisted by Carlyle, Margaret Fuller achieved whatever enduring fame is hers by that notorious pronouncement: "I accept the Universe." All transcendentalists inevitably aspire to some such statement, but the universe with all its multiplicity has always proved rather too large an order for either the human intellect to comprehend or the emotional constitution of man to reconcile himself to. At best, most of the New England Transcendentalists accepted a carefully edited version of the universe from which many phenomena were expunged with all the fussy fastidiousness of any other proponent of Victorian propriety. At worst they complacently read into the universe whatever they liked to think they had found there and they gave authority to whatever prejudices they most cherished by calling them "higher laws." Thus, though few objected to Margaret Fuller's accepting the universe, a great many, it appears, objected to her accepting Count Ossoli —on the assumption, apparently, that neither Italians nor Catholics were part of the universe as New England had chosen to define it. Few, if any, went as far as Thoreau attempted to go in understanding what it would mean actually to accept, intellectually as well as emotionally, that universe outside of man which an intimate acquaintance with the phenomena of nature seems to reveal, and—more importantly—what it would mean to try to identify one's self with nature herself rather than with man or anything exclusively human.

Perhaps no man could and perhaps no man should completely succeed in maintaining any such attitude. Perhaps the most man dare permit himself is an occasional moment like that in which Thoreau wrote the letter just quoted above; and even during such moments the sense of being as close to mountains as to human beings is at least in part an illusion. A creature who could continuously and consistently live by the light of any such convictions would be neither a man nor an animal but some sort of monster. And Thoreau, for all the relentless drive of his peculiar genius, for all the almost unparalleled steadfastness of purpose which enabled him to "sign off" the institutions of his age more resolutely than any but a mere handful of other men have ever done, was nevertheless a human being who trailed after him, into whatever airy regions he might climb, habits of thought and even prejudices, some of which were not even universally human but very characteristic of the society in which he grew up. Let us look for a moment at these habits and at their effect upon him.

Like many of his contemporaries Thoreau had cast off institutional Christianity easily enough and, indeed, he cast off Christianity itself almost as easily—so far at least as it was specifically distinguished from the Oriental religions which he would put above it. Why, he had asked in *A Week on the Concord and Merrimack Rivers*, should the humble life of a Jewish peasant make a New York bishop so bigoted, why should he continue to preach Christianity with such "snappish tenacity"? No doubt the New Testament is an invaluable book ("though I confess to having been slightly prejudiced against it in my very early days by the church and the Sabbath School"), but even Christ "had his scheme, his conformity to tradition. . . . He had not swallowed all formulas. . . . He preached some mere doctrines." Like other peoples we have our own "family history" of our God, but why should even the grandest imagining of some old poet be "imposed on us as adamantine everlasting truth?" The Hindus, so he told himself in the *Journal*, were more serenely and thoughtfully religious than the Hebrews, less corrupted by that "repentance" which is "not a free and fair highway to God." "Men talk about Bible miracles because there is no miracle in their lives." Otherworldliness he professes elsewhere to find no less perverse. He will not be "put off" with Christianity and be forced to hope because he cannot realize that "instant life on which we stand" and one moment of which, so he says, is worth acres of hope. Nearly eight years later he returned again to the same thought as he gibes at the "festivals" of the church now kept out of mere habit when the annual phenomena of a man's own life should be sacred to him and the signs of the zodiac are "not nearly of that significance to me that the sight of a dead sucker in spring is."

Thoreau could hardly have failed to be aware of the fact that the sermon which he spent his whole life preaching was on a text from that Bible, a book he professed to believe too exclusively emphasized, if not exactly overrated. "What is a man profited, if he shall gain the whole world, and lose his own soul?" That was the warning he issued not only to those who refused to live simply but also to those who, however simply they might live, were blind and deaf to the delights and the lessons of nature. Indeed the first chapter of *Walden* is built around the fact that most men spend their lives laying up treasures where moth and rust will corrupt—"as it says in an old book." But obviously he refused to admit that in this wisdom there was anything specifically or exclusively Christian. It was the common property of all wise teachers and it was also exactly what official Christianity tended either to leave out or to explain away—as it was compelled to do once it had made the fatal decision to co-operate with the evil society from which it drew its support. That old writer on heraldry who is alleged to have proved to his own satisfaction that Christ was a gentleman on his mother's side of the family and that He might have legitimately borne coat armor, was, Thoreau said, the real transmitter of the tradition represented by the modern church with its exclusive emphasis upon what he called "respectable Christianity." Only death and funerals, so he said on another occasion, only the necessity that men be decently buried, had preserved the institution until his day. You could not imagine a church without a burying ground, could not imagine the two kept at opposite ends of the town, "without any carrion beneath or beside" the first and "all the dead regularly carried to the bone-mill."

The cry that comes up from the churches in all the great cities in the world is, he concluded, " 'How they stink!' " On still another occasion he was castigating the church members who not only served false gods but were completely oblivious to the real worth and beauty of the world. Christianity, he says, is preached chiefly to the house-bred, to those to whom the woods mean only the ten cords they burn per winter and who are not, Thoreau thinks, worth the trees they destroy. "Let us religiously burn stumps and worship in groves, while Christian vandals lay waste the forest temples to build miles of meeting-houses and horse-sheds and feed their box-stoves." But of all Christians, the worst and the most futile were, he thought, the chosen ministers who preach to the wood-wasters. In *Cape Cod* he compares these ministers to windmills, and a little farther on he speaks of their "profaning the Sabbath by preaching."

Thoreau seldom mentioned names in writing. It is indeed a curious feature of the *Journal*, and one which adds to his characteristic air of detachment from concern with the affairs of men, that even his intimates are rather rarely definitely identified when some reference is made to them, so that sometimes one must deduce that some person he knew as well as Emerson or Channing or Alcott is intended. But one of the few individuals singled out for the dishonor of appearing without disguise was the most famous preacher of his time when, in 1859, Thoreau demanded that, "If Henry Ward Beecher knows so much more about God than another, if he has made some discovery of truth in this direction, I would thank him to publish it in *Silliman's Journal*, with as few flourishes as possible."

Undoubtedly Thoreau's growing indignation over the workings of the Fugitive Slave Law tended to exacerbate his contempt, if not for Beecher, then at least for the ministerial profession as a whole, since so many of its members preached the mealy-mouthed doctrine that it is our duty to obey the law rather than righteously to refuse our support to injustice. But his inclusive conviction that Christian ministers were the chosen instruments of a conspiracy to suppress that heart of the Christian doctrine which was identical with the heart of all great religious doctrines and diametrically opposed to everything by which or for which civilization lived was a conviction which he had long cherished. Indeed, it is in his first published book that one finds the best-known, or at least most often quoted, of his outbursts on the subject.

It is remarkable that, notwithstanding the universal favor with which the New Testament is outwardly received . . . there is no hospitality shown to it, there is no appreciation of the order of truth with which it deals. I know of no book that has so few readers. There is none so truly strange, and heretical, and unpopular. . . . There are, indeed, severe things in it which no man should read aloud more than once. "Seek first the kingdom of heaven." "Lay not up for yourselves treasures on earth." "If thou wilt be perfect, go and sell that thou hast, and give to the poor, and thou shalt have treasure in heaven." "For what is a man profited, if he shall gain the whole world, and lose his own soul?" . . . Think of repeating these things to a New England audience! . . . Who, without cant, can read them aloud? Who, without cant, can hear them, and not go out of the meeting house? They never *were* read, they never *were* heard. Let but one of these sentences be rightly read, from any pulpit in the land, and there would not be left one stone of that meeting-house upon another.

In that social world of which Thoreau was willy-nilly (mostly nilly!) a part, the hold of dogmatic and institutional Christianity was, of course, weakening. Perhaps comparatively few went so far or expressed themselves so violently as he, but for the rejection of dogma and the rejection of the organized church he had example and encouragement. Relatively speaking, it could not have been too difficult for him to cast both aside and to uproot from his unconscious as well as from his conscious mind the influence which either would have exerted upon him. But formal, organized doctrines are more easily rejected than are pervasive habits of mind, and Thoreau never rejected certain socially inherited preferences and distastes so completely as he rejected the church. A long and still-living tradition of puritan tendencies and puritan habits was, inevitably, something which he had met at every side long before the critical thoughts either of himself or of others could have had any effect upon him. Timeless though he sought to be, timeless though some of his boldest and chilliest thoughts may have been, he was also a New Englander, and however effectively he might reject the New England church, many essentially puritan predilections survived, to wage ceaseless war in him against those pantheistic tendencies which defiantly asserted themselves from time to time. For whatever else puritanism may be, it is at least the opposite of pantheism. It is dualistic rather than, in the secular sense of the term, unitarian. It always insists upon the necessity of choice; is always grimly determined not to accept the All but to embrace the Good and reject the Bad, since into one or the other of these categories everything must fall, nothing being indifferent.

Moreover, certain of the thought patterns of puritanism fitted well enough into Thoreau's scheme. Like certain, at least, of the puritan sects, he too sought the inward light and would suffer no authoritative intermediary between himself and his God. His also was a salvation religion, and the empathy he sometimes felt was the assurance which his soul gave him that he was among the elect. Indeed it would be easy to interpret certain phases of his thought as merely a secularized puritanism, since, though he had discarded almost completely most of the vocabulary of puritanism, he had kept some of the conceptions as well as a few of the words. Thus, though there are, in all his writing, few references other than contemptuous ones to Sin or Redemption, there are many to Purity—which, by the way, is left mostly undefined. It is true that he fulminates against the Sense of Sin again and again. "Though you be a babe," he was writing in 1851, "the cry is 'Repent, repent.' The Christian world will not admit that a man has a just perception of any truth, unless at the same time he cries, 'Lord, be merciful to me, a sinner.'" And, as was pointed out a few pages back, he confidently asserted—with all the assurance in his knowledge of God's purpose which he would have jeered at in another—that repentance is "not a free and fair highway to God." But what, after all, is another, and one of his earliest paradoxes, propounded indeed in a college essay, if it is not a mere secularization of a puritan tenet? The purpose of life, he had said, is education; and what is that saying except the familiar puritan contention that this life is but a discipline to prepare us for higher things?

Elsewhere, in the earliest pages of the *Journal*, those which antedate the Walden period, this tendency to secularize puritan concepts is very strong; as it is, for instance, when we find him discovering at the beginning of the year 1841 that obedience to conscience and trust in God are really a retreat into oneself and a reliance upon one's own strength. But equally early, some six months earlier in fact, comes the protest that "life is not all moral," that the "actual phenomena" of life "deserve to be studied impartially" and that no "science of human Nature" has ever been attempted in the same spirit as men have attempted a science of the other aspects of nature. In *A Week on the Concord and Merrimack Rivers* a very curious passage develops the protest against a too exclusive concern with morality and turns the passage into a criticism of the New Testament itself, which Thoreau finds too continuously treating of so-called spiritual affairs. "It is not worth the while to let our imperfections trouble us always. The conscience really does not, and ought not to monopolize the whole of our lives." There is, he insists, an important life in this world as well as a concern for a future state and there is another kind of success than that which Christ preaches. A healthy wood chopper, for instance, is not a good subject for Christianity. The New Testament may be a good book for him on some days but not on most. He would rather go fishing in his leisure hours. The apostles, we are told, were fishers, too, but they "were of the solemn race of sea-fishers, and never trolled for pickerel on inland streams."

Even purity, one of his catchwords, is something which

nature does not always too rigidly insist upon. Her laws, so he says on an earlier page of *A Week on the Concord and Merrimack Rivers*, are immutable, but she seems content to let man relax a little and not to remind him too harshly of the things he must not do. Even men of vicious habit are allowed to persist strangely, and the tramp who has been abusing himself for years pops up from behind a hedge asking work and wages for a healthy man "as if consistency were the secret of health, while the poor inconsistent aspirant man, seeking to live a pure life, feeding on air, divided against himself, cannot stand, but pines and dies after a life of sickness, on beds of down." And from the *Journal* for June 1850 he picked up to incorporate in *Walden* the brief account of how he had found the lower jaw of a hog with sound teeth and tusks and of how it served to remind him that there is an animal vigor and health distinct from the spiritual. "This animal succeeded by other means than temperance and purity."

Yet the pull of puritan tendencies was equally strong; indeed, was stronger, or at least more frequently manifest. Something in his temperament as well as in his mind, something as much a part of his psychology as of his thinking, made a kind of austerity more congenial to him than the self-expression and *laissez faire* he sometimes seems to acknowledge as a significant aspect of the nature which he would have liked to accept. Neither the tramp nor the hog very warmly engaged his sympathy, and one would be tempted to identify him with the "poor inconsistent aspiring man" who was "divided against himself" and "seeking to lead a pure life" were it not for the fact that these inconsistencies seem actually to trouble him so little as to suggest that he had accepted the universe so completely that he was able, paradoxically, to accept puritanism as a somehow reconcilable part of it and to say both yea and nay to the nature which is indifferent to puritan prejudices.

In any case, Thoreau, a protestant against the habit of speaking as though man were exclusively a moral creature, was himself a very persistent moralizer, and though he occasionally celebrated nature's free and easy ways, he rather more frequently talked of discipline and the necessity for choosing the higher rather than the lower. He had, for all that was shiftless or sloppy in any man's way of life, the true New England hatred. Puritanlike, he insisted upon the necessity of choice ("For every inferior, earthly pleasure we forego, a superior, celestial one is substituted"); and puritanlike, he celebrated strenuous living—what he called life "on the stretch." "What is peculiar in the life of a man," he permits himself on one occasion to say roundly, "consists not in his obedience, but in his opposition, to his instincts. In one direction or another he strives to live a supernatural life." But where, then, is nature, or our right to follow her? If it is human nature to resist what the rest of nature obeys, then nothing more than a juggling with words is left of the proposition that we must unite ourselves with her.

Unlike many present-day naturalists Thoreau would never have felt the excitement rather than the horror of the teeming jungle. "The alert and energetic man," so he once wrote, "leads a more intellectual life in winter than in summer" and this preference for the season when nature is subdued rather than rampant suggests the strong strain of asceticism which runs through him. At thirty-four he was convinced that, as we grow older, we live more coarsely and cease to obey "our finest instincts." "We are more careless about our diet and our chastity. But we should be fastidious to the extreme of sanity." Emerson, it may be remembered, spoke with friendly derision of Henry's "edible religion," and we have already seen how keen a sensual delight he took in tasting the wild fruits—even those which were not commonly regarded as edible. But this same man who, as may also be remembered, sometimes felt that he could devour a woodchuck raw, could speak of food sometimes with something amounting almost to disgust. It was this ascetic tendency which, combined with his sympathy for the members of the animal family, produced the persistent, uneasy approval of the vegetarianism he never practiced for long with absolute consistency. His own statement in 1852 is: "Like many of my contemporaries I had rarely for many years used animal food, or tea or coffee, etc., etc., not so much because of any ill effects which I had traced to them in my own case, though I could theorize extensively in that direction, as because it was not agreeable to my imagination." As late as 1856 h() was exclaiming against "the pitiful kind of life ours is, eating our kindred animals." He was sure, so he said, that the repugnance to animal food was instinctive, not learned from experience.

As a boy Thoreau had smoked lily stems, but this seems to be the closest he ever came to any vice. Yet he was not, it should be added, too sourly censorious of individuals whose tastes were grosser than his, and one of the best of the humorous passages which deal with his neighbors is the one describing the consuming passion for cider which possessed a certain John L—— for whom, in 1853, he did some surveying. This man could not go into the woods without wishing he had brought a jugful, or even placed a barrel somewhere within reach. "This, or rum, runs in his head, if not in his throat, all the time." The very sight of gooseberries or currants set him to thinking whether or not they would make wine, and he evidently (as Thoreau charitably puts it) thought that cider "corrects some mistake in him." In somewhat similar vein he wrote in 1858 to Daniel Ricketson, who had evidently made some apologies for an Australian whose portrait he had drawn in a letter: "What do you mean by that ado about smoking, and my 'purer tastes'? I should like his pipe as well as his beer, at least. Neither of them is so bad as to be 'highly connected' which you say he is, unfortunately."

There is also redeeming humor in his remark that he liked to see tried such experiments as that of a young man who lived for a fortnight on hard raw Indian corn, using his teeth for the only mortar. "The squirrel tribe tried the same and succeeded." But Thoreau could also be deadly serious on both humanitarian and ascetic grounds against what Mr. Bernard Shaw calls the devouring of corpses. Hunting might be, as he had said it was, an inevitable stage through which men went in their approach to nature; but fellowship should succeed pursuit. "The hunter regards with awe his game, and it becomes at last his medicine." Or so, at least, it ought to be. What of the muskrats of Concord gnawing off their legs in the traps of George Melvin, who calmly remarked that muskrats are great fellows at that art? "Why I caught one once that had just gnawed his third leg off, this being the third time he had been trapped; and he lay dead by the trap, for he couldn't run on one leg." Animal food was not only evilly got, but evil in itself, for it dulled with gross sensuality the finer perceptions and made temperance impossible. "Any excess—to have drunk too much water, even, the day before—is fatal to the morning's clarity, but in health the sound of a cow-bell is celestial music."

No monk ever expounded in more extreme terms the monkish doctrine that the sin of gluttony is not incompatible with the most austere of diets, and Thoreau was, of course, also almost monkish in his attitude toward sensuality in any of its forms. Many, perhaps most, natural philosophers from Lucretius down to the present day have seen sex not only as an important feature of nature but as the very mainspring of the machine. Thoreau, on the other hand, seems to wish, first to rule it out of himself, and then almost to shut his eyes to its omnipresence in animate nature. Léon Bazalgette's *Henry Thoreau, Sauvage* was translated into English as *Henry Thoreau; Bachelor of Nature*, and in many ways the alternate title is the better. Thoreau never supposed that "wildness" was more than an element in his character and he was a "savage" in only a very special sense. But he was a bachelor at least as fundamentally and as all-pervasively as he was anything else—so much so, in fact, that when a woman suggested that he and she might be married, his mind boggled at the attempt to conceive the monstrous incongruity. That particular scheme of life whose practicality he triumphantly demonstrated to his own satisfaction took bachelorhood for granted.

On rare occasions he could be, as on the subject of vegetarianism, decorously humorous about sex—as he is, for instance, when he had read in a textbook of zoology that worker bees were barren females whose sexual attributes "seem to consist only in their solicitude for the welfare of the new generation, of which they are the natural guardians, but not the parents," and when he comments: "This phenomenon is paralleled in man by maiden aunts and bachelor uncles, who perform a similar function." But he was seldom prepared for even the mildly humorous touch in the treatment of anything which involved what he persistently calls "impurity." One of the very few occasions on which he confessed to having felt that sense of sin he thoroughly disapproved of is in a curious passage of the *Journal* where he speaks of having recently "swallowed a snake" and appears to be referring to some thoughts or desires which he regarded as impure. In 1851 he was writing: "I am sure that the design of my maker when he has brought me nearest to woman was not the propagation, but rather the maturation, of the species. Man is capable of a love of woman quite transcending marriage." In the next paragraph of the same entry, he passes on to a rather priggish—and whatever else he may have been, "priggish" is an adjective which Thoreau seldom suggests—observation on the fact that the Situations Wanted advertisements in the newspaper he has been reading generally refer to "respectable young women" but always "intelligent" or "smart" young men: "From which I infer that the public opinion of New York does not require young men to be respectable in the same sense in which it requires young women to be so." And then he concluded the day's entry with the curious question: "May it consist with the health of some bodies to be impure?"

That "impurity" was as respectable as antiquity could make it, he was well aware. In another passage as uncharacteristic as that in which he alludes to the mores of New York City, he comments on the rhymes scribbled by boys on the walls of privies. No doubt, he says, they are more ancient than Orpheus. "Filth and impurity are as old as cleanliness and purity. To correspond to man completely,

Nature is even perhaps unchaste herself"; and it is curious to note that the possibility he suggests is not that man, being part of nature, shares the "impurity" which is part of the All, but that her "impurity" is made necessary by him—thus, as it were, putting the blame on the human race instead, as is surely more usual, of excusing man by an appeal to his "natural" impulses. Here, as is so often the case, his equally characteristic protest against the insistent moralizing in which men commonly indulge gives way to something puritanical, and "higher" and "lower" become the most fundamental of all categories. If this does not negativate his pantheism, it at least tends to make it Hindu rather than Western.

His distaste for sexual phenomena obviously limits the scope of the observations he makes, and the fact is all the more striking since the animal kingdom attracted so strongly his interest. Those who are determined to find only purity and peace in nature are usually wisely inclined to direct their attention chiefly to the inanimate or the vegetable, to the ocean, the mountains and the trees—even though, as the grandfather of the great Darwin was delighted to learn, the flowers also have their love affairs, and even though, as John Muir once pointed out, a forest seems peaceful only because the slow ruthless battle for life which it represents is silent, and the dying trees cannot scream. A Wordsworth projects his idea of God into the light of setting suns, which is sexless, will-less, and inanimate. On the other hand, the student of animal behavior, even the laboratory student of protoplasmic behavior, usually finds himself, soon enough, less free to interpret nature in terms of his own predilections. Thoreau took it all in—the willful woodchuck and the persistent turtle no less than the soothing woods and the bland sunset. But the red tooth and the red claw were so far from obsessing him as they were to obsess many nineteenth-century students that they play only a minor role, and even the sexuality of nature passes with no more than an occasional acknowledgment.

Occasional acknowledgment it does get. Thus, though he usually exhibited little curiosity about such matters, he did allow himself to record at least once in the *Journal* a short account of how he had observed the copulation of frogs. Going from such a specific phenomenon to the opposite extreme of the widest possible generalization, he did also, occasionally, refer to the omnipresence of "love." As early as 1840, when he was just beginning to discover his own style and still often exhibited the effects of his effort to imitate the rather pretentious *aperçu* of some of his fellow Transcendentalists, he had written that "Love is the burden of all Nature's odes," that the flowers too have their marriages and that "this is the employment and condition of all things." But that is prettily sentimental rather than deeply felt, like a similar remark many years later: "The music of all creatures has to do with their loves" and like the question, apparently not wholly rhetorical, which follows: "Is it not the same with man?" Like most transcendentalists, perhaps, Thoreau did not want to climb the ladder of love but to begin at the top; and the sexual image which he once used when he wrote that "there must be the copulating and generating force of love behind every effort destined to be successful" since "cold resolve" can beget nothing, startles the reader because the image is uncharacteristic, though the sense in which "love" is used is not.

In 1852—possibly, it has been guessed, as a result of his

association with Lidian Emerson during his second residence in the Emerson household—he wrote, in the guise of
a letter to Harrison Blake, a formal disquisition on love,
sex, and marriage, which is much the frankest and fullest
expression of his feelings on these subjects that he ever
committed to paper. One surprising sentence—surprising
because it is so nearly unique—declares: "The intercourse
of the sexes, I have dreamed, is incredibly beautiful, too
fair to be remembered"; but the next sentence is either a
vast understatement or confirms one's impression that the
author was extraordinary in the extent to which he escaped
a preoccupation almost universally human. "I have had,"
he says, "thoughts about it, but they are among the most
fleeting and irrecoverable in my experience." Much of the
rest of the long letter is not only virginal, but almost ado-
lescently idealistic, in its vague but earnest distinction between "love" and "lust" and in the understatement involved
in such a pronouncement as "Men commonly couple with
their idea of marriage a slight degree at least of sensuality;
but every lover, the world over, believes in its inconceivable
purity." Another observation is: "What the essential difference between man and woman is, that they should be thus
attracted to one another, no one has satisfactorily answered," and even the moderately ribald are likely to find
that statement a real howler.

Also in the same letter, and in a somewhat similar vein
of adolescent radicalism, Thoreau is to wonder that men
so seldom speak openly of such important matters; and in
the *Journal* he once alludes scornfully to the fact that
human beings are largely unfamiliar with nakedness. But
in actual fact he was squeamish, and, in his horror at any
sort of coarseness where sex was concerned, just short of

being a prig. For other forms of grossness he sometimes showed a kind of amused tolerance because he recognized it as primitive or earthy, but he wanted no earthiness where sex was concerned. "Each man's mode of speaking of the sexual relation proves," he declared primly, "how sacred his own relations of that kind are. We do not respect the mind that can jest on this subject." At twenty-two he had expressed the opinion that to be shocked at vice was to reveal a lingering sympathy with it, and much later in life, when he met Whitman and read *Leaves of Grass*, he was to attempt to apologize for the book on somewhat similar grounds. But the truth seems to be that he was sometimes shocked in a way hardly becoming to a man who, sometimes at least, wished to accept all nature. When, at thirty-nine, he saw for the first time that rather startling fungus accurately denominated in the catalogues *Phallus impudicus*, he was not entertained as the scientist who named it obviously was, but genuinely shocked. "Pray, what was nature thinking of when she made this? She almost puts herself on the level with those who draw in privies."

Perhaps the reader needs to be reminded here that this rather long disquisition on the ascetic element in Thoreau's temperament and on that distaste for the sexual which is part of his asceticism took off from the discussion of certain conflicts or ambiguities in his conception of nature and of man's proper relation to it. We now return to the general discussion with the conclusion that he shied away from (though on a few occasions he seemed formally to acknowledge) that conception of nature as a sexual and teeming mother to which the biologist is so frequently drawn and which Lucretius, the progenitor of all scientific pantheism, enthusiastically celebrated. There was in him rather more of the Brahman than of the Lucretian. The Uranian Venus he honors. Of Venus Pandemos he recognizes the existence, though he tends to avert his eyes. Venus Creatrix he only sporadically seems willing to acknowledge. Those maiden aunts and bachelor uncles are more to his taste.

For all this, however, the fact, perhaps the most significant fact, still remains that Thoreau was not settled or consistent in any of these attitudes; that there is, as was previously maintained, a dialectic which animates his thought; and that this thought operates between poles. These poles have previously been identified as, respectively, an Emersonian assumption that nature is a hieroglyph, an allegorical representation of the same truths which the human mind may intuit, and, on the other hand, a scientific rather than transcendental assumption that objective familiarity with nature modifies or corrects the too-ready conclusions drawn by the humanly prejudiced intuitions of those who take it for granted that the hieroglyphs are part of their own language. But these poles may also be described in other terms. One is the center for those moral and ascetic predilections we have just been attempting to detail, while from the other radiate thoughts which sometimes startlingly contradict the others. It is possible, as the last ten or fifteen pages may have demonstrated, to select from Thoreau's *Journal* an anthology of opinions which would seem to define him as a puritan who was, at moments, almost a prig. It would, nevertheless, be possible to select others which, taken by themselves, would suggest a mind struggling toward a philosophical position "beyond good and evil" so far as "good" and "evil" have any purely human meaning. And though it is true that such passages are less numerous than those which point in the opposite direction, it is equally true that the most striking come from the later *Journal* and the later letters, where some of the most inhumanly detached opinions concerning both man and society find expression.

At thirty he had written to Harrison Blake in a passage quoted once before, "I know that another is who knows more than I, who takes interest in me, whose creature, and yet whose kindred, in one sense, I am." Here is a creed stated with theological precision almost as though intended, like the Thirty-nine Articles, to serve as a test. There is, it proclaims, a power which makes for righteousness, and though that power is not ourselves, it is kindred with ourselves—or, as one is tempted to say, homoiousian though not homoousian. Nor can it be said that Thoreau ever definitely repudiated that creed. But it is clear enough that he did question the closeness of the kinship, the extent to which he was a creature more important to, or more the concern of, the creator than were countless other very different creatures, and the extent to which righteousness was anything like what men commonly supposed it to be. From the very beginning he had tended, in moments of stress, to seek consolation by identifying himself with the nature which is indifferent to us rather than with a nature which is part of us—as he did for example when, at twenty-four, he wrote to Lucy Brown concerning the death of his beloved brother: "What right have I to grieve, who have not ceased to wonder? . . . Soon the ice will melt, and the blackbirds sing along the river which he frequented, as pleasantly as ever. The same everlasting serenity will appear on the face of God, and we will not be sorrowful if he is not." *A Week on the Concord and Merrimack Rivers*

is persistently transcendentalist and more persistently moralizing than either *Walden* or the subsequent portion of the
Journal, and yet even in *A Week on the Concord and
Merrimack Rivers* he was already dreaming of an escape
from morality: "To the innocent there are neither cheru-
bim nor angels. At rare intervals we rise above the necessity of virtue into an unchangeable morning light, in which
we have only to live right on and breathe the ambrosial
air." Somewhat later he recognized in himself, as so many
writers have recognized, a dual personality: the spectator
who observes alongside the participant who experiences;
and there were moments at least when it was the spectator,
not the participant, who seemed nearest to God. Nature's
gladness is beyond human institutions and human laws.
"There is no law so strong which a little gladness may not
transgress. . . . Pile up your books, the records of sad-
ness, your saws and your laws. Nature is glad outside, and
her merry worms within will ere long topple them down."

His conscious choice of nature rather than of society
was, of course, early made, but if we can believe the asser-
tions, repeated year after year in the *Journal*, his withdrawal was more and more complete. In 1852, many years
after the first renunciation had been made, he was still
noting that his intimacy with nature withdraws him from
man, and he makes then a curious effort to reconcile certain of the conflicts by the declaration: "My desire for
society is infinitely increased; my fitness for any actual
society is diminished." But the supposed desire did not lead
to any attempts to satisfy it, and joy seems to be more and
more assumed to be the privilege, not of man, but of the
rest of animate and even inanimate nature. When in 1857
he was asked if such and such persons were not as happy as

most, and when he perceived that the man who asked it did so because he had so little hope of happiness in himself, Thoreau, "speaking to his condition," replied: "Why! the stones are happy, Concord River is happy, and I am happy too. When I took up a fragment of a walnut-shell this morning, I saw by its very grain and composition, its form and color, etc., that it was made for happiness. . . . Do you think that Concord River would have continued to flow these millions of years by Clamshell Hill and round Hunt's Island, if it had not been happy—if it had been miserable in its channel, tired of existence, and cursing its maker and the hour that it sprang?"

Now a feeling of fellowship with the animals, with the vegetables even, can remain a warm thing. With the first we are linked by the common possession of consciousness and emotion, with the second at least by the fact that all protoplasm is the same and that hence we must possess in common certain characteristics. But fellowship with the rivers or the stars inevitably carries one on into a chilly region, and to ask that man be happy like the Concord River is to approach a sort of pantheism which seems on the point of breaking the last link with that humanity which Thoreau was still occasionally willing to declare the test of all things. Even as far back as the pre-Walden epoch, he sometimes recorded *pensées* which sound less puritan than like something in the manner as well as the mood of Blake or even Nietzsche. "We cannot well do without our sins; they are the highway of our virtue." "I never feel that I am inspired unless my body is also." "He who resists not at all will never surrender." "When a dog runs at you, whistle for him." "Say, Not so, and you will outcircle the philosophers." But it was in November 1860, only a year before illness put an end to the *Journal*, that he wrote the letter from which has been already quoted the passage about the winter goodness which is so far above "all mere sentimental, warm-blooded, short-lived, soft-hearted, *moral* goodness" and which goes on to declare that, "Whatever is, and is not ashamed to be, is good." Such phrases as those seem to put the final seal of approval upon a nonmoral and a nonhuman system of values which had elsewhere been suggested and which did more than merely survive alongside much that contradicted it in Thoreau's thought. In 1852 he had written: "If an Indian brave will not fear torture and aids his enemies who torment him, what becomes of pity and a hundred other Christian virtues? The charitable are suddenly without employment." And four years later he was expressing a similar idea more boldly, though its effect is perhaps softened by the fact that he is here rather rejecting sympathy for himself than denying it to others. "I cannot but think it nobler, as it is rarer, to appreciate some beauty than to feel much sympathy with misfortune. The Powers are kinder to me when they permit me to enjoy this beauty than if they were to express any amount of compassion for me. I could never excuse them that."

Contemplating such sentiments as these, the conclusion reached by some might be that one cannot withdraw oneself from society so completely as Thoreau did without running the risk of becoming completely unhuman. However that may be, it is obvious enough that it was only on those relatively rare occasions when Thoreau climbed up the chilliest peaks of his consciousness that he thought such thoughts, and obvious enough that most of his mental as well as emotional life was lived at a warmer level; that his interviews with animals met in the woods or his moments of silent communion with the little boy in the woodchuck hat were equally characteristic. It is not as a metaphysician but as a writer about man and nature whose writings are tinged with metaphysical notions that he won his audience.

To the tidy mind of a technical philosopher, Thoreau's thought must seem hopelessly confused. Puritanism, New England Transcendentalism, and Hindu mysticism made some sort of peace with one another because all were to some degree dualistic, but they were also all at war with both an objective, quasi-scientific curiosity and a tendency to deduce from the results of that curiosity a religion of nature in which the worshiper is tempted on beyond good and evil as either can be defined in humanistic terms. But Thoreau was well served by this constant balancing of possibilities, by his very inability to hold firm to a doctrine. Because of the doubts, his relentless persistence in what appeared to outsiders a mere routine actually took on the character of a ceaseless quest, and the moments of empathy were all the more eagerly sought because Thoreau himself could never be sure what they meant. His "nature writings" have a quality which immediately distinguishes them not only from the almost trivial tranquillity of Gilbert White but also from a John Burroughs or a W. H. Hudson. To some readers, at least, they are more varied, and they have, besides, a certain tenseness, a certain excitement which is unique. Thoreau is an observer without the mere observer's coldness, and he is a lover of wisdom without the mere teacher's monotonous dogmatism. The quest remains exciting because he himself does not know what he is going to find. No doubt he was, as he himself insisted, a happy man; but he was not settled or certain. A hunger and a thirst are elements in his happiness and make it something other than mere content. And it is the hunger and thirst which are responsible for the excitement of his writing.

The Reluctant Crusader

THOREAU'S SISTER HELEN had died of tuberculosis in 1849. Seven years later Henry himself was down with a serious illness, no doubt a crisis of the same malady. He forced himself, for a time, to continue his walks, but he was finally compelled to confess that he was seriously unwell and he spent an unwontedly inactive summer vacation on Cape Cod. By autumn he could again take on a job of surveying; but though he soon ceased to think of himself as a sick man, it is probable that he was never again quite so vigorous as before. He was not one, however, to dwell on the fact. Did he not once advise those who worried about their health to remember that they might, for all they knew, be dead already?

Certainly he made no obvious or outward change in his habits and professed the same delight with his lot, while remaining as aloof as he had always been in his relations with his fellow citizens. There seems to have been little contact between such intellectual companions as he did have and the members of his family with whom he lived; and it is possible that the very intimacy of his domestic life made it easier for him to keep his other acquaintances at a spiritual distance. As late as 1858 he was noting in the *Journal* the characteristic opinion that: "The gregariousness of men is their most contemptible and discouraging aspect." They follow one another like sheep, he says, and they prefer the religion of their fathers for the same reason—or lack of it— that makes them prefer their fathers' brand of shoe polish. "Generally speaking, they think more of their hen-houses than of any desirable heaven. If you aspire to anything better than politics, expect no co-operation from men. . . . You must prevail of your own force, as a plant springs and grows by its own vitality."

A willingness to walk was still the surest method of winning his tolerance, and it was no doubt that willingness which secured Thoreau's company (if not, apparently, a great deal more) for the schoolmaster F. B. Sanborn who came to Concord in 1855 and (since he boarded for a time with Mrs. Thoreau) could later boast not only of his walks but of the fact that he had seen Henry at table almost daily for three years. Thoreau did not, he said, know what to do with visitors who could not use their legs. One could, of course, get a horse to draw them, but that meant dealings with "stablers and dirty harness." Besides, though a ride might get them through the morning pretty well, the visitors were as heavy as a dumpling by midafternoon, and instead of taking an honest nap and letting Thoreau go about his business they would alarm him "by an evident disposition to sit."

Channing apparently lasted well because of his legs and despite a tendency to conversation either frivolous or, what was quite as bad, pretentious. Alcott continued on a footing of relative intimacy because Thoreau had a genuine admiration for his character, and from Alcott's journal one gets an occasional glimpse of his friend rather different from any that Thoreau gives of himself. On January 9, 1859, for instance: "Sanborn, Henry Thoreau, and Allen take tea and pass the evening with us. We discuss questions of philosophy and the Ideal Theory as applied to education." One will, it is hardly necessary to say, not find any mention of this very high-minded little party in Thoreau's own *Journal*, where, as a matter of fact, there is, for that day, only a one-sentence entry concerned with some eggs, believed to be those of the hen hawk, which a boy had collected three days before "from a pine near Breed's house site." These Thoreau evidently regarded (or was determined to regard) as more important than "the Ideal Theory and Personal Identity" which, according to Alcott, Henry "defended," to Alcott's great delight. It is true that in the same passage Alcott speaks of Thoreau as "large always and masterly in his own wild way." But there he was, nevertheless, discussing philosophy over the teacups.

It was Alcott, a very gregarious man, who had also been responsible a few years earlier for taking Thoreau on what, with a little stretching, might be called a literary pilgrimage —certainly the only one he ever made. In the autumn of 1856 he had been persuaded to go with Alcott on a trip to New York and, once there, to call on Walt Whitman, who was not at home on this first occasion, but whom they found on a second visit. Thoreau may have read *Leaves of Grass* in Emerson's copy the year before, though there is no direct evidence that he did, and Alcott, anxious to see what would happen when two of his many heroes met, tried, without apparent success, to play the Boswell. "Each seemed planted in fast reserves, surveying each other curiously—like two beasts, each wondering what the other would do, whether to snap or run; and it came to no more than cold compliments between them."

One's first impulse is to regard the whole incident as an example of pure comedy—something like Sir Max Beerbohm's account of the imaginary meeting of Henrik Ibsen and Robert Browning. What could the lover of crowds and the lover of solitude, the admirer of men en masse and the ferocious individualist, possibly have to say to one another? But the meeting was not actually so meaningless as it seemed at first sight to be, and it is surprising—or perhaps it is not surprising—that the theoretically all-embracing lover of his fellows was the one who seemed the less impressed. Whitman complained that Thoreau's writing smacked of the library and the fireside rather than of the out-of-doors; that he caught "a literary scent off his phrases." He complained also that the man himself had a "disdain for men" and "was impatient with other people." Thoreau, on the other hand, once he had got away by himself again, could not for some time get the strange phenomenon out of his mind. In *Walden* he had written that anyone who had lived sincerely must have lived in a land distant from him, and here was a very striking case in point.

Almost immediately he wrote an account of the meeting to Harrison Blake and a few months later sent a copy of *Leaves of Grass* to Cholmondeley in London. "He told us that he loved to ride up and down Broadway all day on an omnibus, sitting beside the driver, listening to the roar of the carts, and sometimes gesticulating and declaiming Homer at the top of his voice." Thoreau must have wondered how a man who liked Homer could like omnibuses also, but he found him "a remarkably strong though coarse nature, of a sweet disposition" and "essentially a gentle-

man." Next day he was more enthusiastic: "That Walt
Whitman, of whom I wrote to you, is the most interesting
fact to me at present. I have just read his second edition
(which he gave me) and it has done me more good than any
reading for a long time. . . . We ought to rejoice greatly
in him. He occasionally suggests something a little more than
human. . . . Though rude, and sometimes ineffectual, it is
a great primitive poem—an alarum or trumpet note ring-
ing through the American camp. . . . Since I have seen
him, I find that I am not disturbed by any brag or egotism
in his book. He may turn out the least of a braggart of all,
having a better right to be confident. He is a great fellow."
And when one considers what others who might have been
expected to be temperamentally less alien were saying
about Whitman, this tribute is impressive. Cholmondeley
acknowledged Thoreau's gift of the book with hoots of
derision and, according to Sanborn, Sophia Thoreau, Mrs.
Emerson, and Mrs. Alcott all refused to allow their re-
spective husbands to invite Whitman to their houses when
he visited Boston in 1860.

Inevitably Thoreau was puzzled (and it was puzzlement
more than shock) by Whitman's feverish sexuality, which
he did not recognize as the feebleness rather than strength
which apparently it was. "There are two or three pieces
in the book which are disagreeable, to say the least; simply
sensual. He does not celebrate love at all. It is as if the
beasts spoke." Then comes the very characteristic sentence:
"I think that men have not been ashamed of themselves
without reason"—a sentence which somehow suggests the
ring of Swift's, "I never wonder to see men wicked, but I
often wonder to see them not ashamed." And soon Thoreau
is going on very bravely to try to understand in his own

way even Whitman's sensuality. "As for its sensuality—and it may turn out to be less sensual than it appears—I do not so much wish that those parts were not written, as that men and women were so pure that they could read them without harm, that is, without understanding them. One woman told me that no woman could read it—as if a man could read what a woman could not. Of course Walt Whitman can communicate to us no experience, and if we are shocked, whose experience is it that we are reminded of?"

Thoreau realized well enough that he did not understand Whitman. "I . . . feel," he said, "that he is essentially strange, to me at any rate." But if he did not understand him, he did the next best thing, which was to realize that he did not. Not every man who professes, as Thoreau did, to believe that those who seem out of step with the rest of mankind may be only marching to the sound of a different drum are capable of actually making that assumption when brought face to face with a genuine practitioner of the art of being different. Thoreau recognized, though he did not entirely comprehend, some greatness which was alien to him. Like one of the beasts in Alcott's simile, he regarded with curious respect a creature of a different species with whom he could have no real intercourse but whose impressiveness was, in its own way, unmistakable. Or, to vary the figure, he realized that he was one of two ships, bound perhaps for the same distant port, but proceeding, certainly, on different routes. They passed with a hail and a farewell.

Meanwhile a genuine friendship, perhaps the most important of all, had never recovered from the effects of a deterioration which had begun a long time before. With no one outside his own family had Thoreau ever lived so closely as he had with members of the Emerson household.

Nor was there, it seems, any other man whom he was willing to admire as much as he had once been willing to admire Emerson—the only human being he had ever at any time come close to "looking up to." During the 'fifties, however, he obviously came not only to get along with Emerson less well but also, what was perhaps more important, to respect him less.

There was never any actual rupture or any crucial moment at which a definite rejection took place. Probably the long passage in the *Journal* for February 8, 1857, which contains the sentence, "And now another friendship is ended," does not refer to Emerson himself, though it may refer to Lidian, and to some misunderstanding on her part of what Henry wanted and expected from her. Certainly during most of the 'fifties, he had been an accepted, informal visitor to the household, and eight months after Thoreau had mourned the end of a friendship, in the passage referred to above, Emerson was referring in a letter to his "two gossips," Alcott and Thoreau. Nevertheless, disappointment, irritation, and a degree of estrangement are plain on both sides, though characteristically they are expressed with more downrightness by Thoreau. In the early days of their acquaintance, Henry had seemed to Emerson the most promising man in Concord, and Emerson had seemed to Thoreau the man among all others in whom the divine was most realized. But presently Emerson had begun to condescend just a little because Thoreau was not a success, and Thoreau had begun to condescend even more because Emerson was. The man who had remained content to be merely "the captain of a huckleberry party" spoke slightingly in the *Journal* of the man who was too much of a gentleman to trundle a wheelbarrow and too little aware of fundamental things not to know that it was his own calf which he drove out of the yard one day. Emerson, becoming far too genteel, indulged, he said, in "palaver"; he was suffering "the misfortune of being a gentleman and famous." By 1853 Thoreau had come to the point where he could record in his diary: "Talked or tried to talk, with R. W. E. Lost my time—nay, almost my identity. He, assuming a false opposition where there was no difference of opinion, talked to the wind . . . and I lost my time trying to imagine myself somebody else, to oppose him." And comically enough, Emerson, three years later, is complaining in *his* diary about what was evidently exactly the same kind of situation. "If I knew only Thoreau, I should think co-operation of good men impossible. Must we always talk for victory, and never once for truth, for comfort, and joy? . . . Always some weary captious paradox to fight you with, and the time and temper wasted." Nothing could better illustrate the essential blandness of Emerson's personality and the essential acidity of Thoreau's.

Emerson was, of course, to write what remains perhaps the most penetrating and laudatory account of his friend's personality, and nine years after Thoreau's death was to list him as one of "my men." But he had also, shortly after Thoreau died, set down in his journal the opinion which had long been and continued to be his estimate. Like Charles Newcomb, Bronson Alcott, and the elder Henry James, Thoreau had seemed, he said, in some one act, to prove himself a genuine master mind. But "he was only master-mind in that particular act. He could repeat the like stroke a million times, but, in new conditions, he was inexpert, and in new company, he was dumb." And so Thoreau, in the case of Emerson also, had to confess that he had failed to achieve the paradoxical and impossible friendship concerning which he had written some of his most cloudy passages and for which, despite all his porcupine prickliness, he liked to think he had always longed.

It was also about the time of his illness that the pages of the *Journal* begin to be more and more given over to the minute record of observations which are methodical and exact so far as they go, yet seem to lack method in the larger meaning of the term, because it is difficult to see what ultimate purpose they were intended to fulfill. As early as 1852 one might have found him making a chronological list of the flowers as they put in their spring appearance and toying with the idea that the most primitive and simplest were the first to bloom. But lists of one sort or another become more and more frequent. He planned a lecture on the succession of forest trees and a history, never even begun, of the American Indian. A collection of quotations intended for use in connection with this last project is preserved in the Morgan Library as well as various loose work sheets and large tables, setting forth the succession of plants, the phenomena of the seasons, etc. Apparently the book which he seems to have vaguely planned for the future was to be along the lines these materials suggest, but it is difficult to imagine that it could have had much interest either literary or scientific, or indeed that it could ever have become a book at all.

On the other hand, the two or three further attempts he was to make to write for a popular audience succeeded during his lifetime only very little better than the previous ones had. In 1853 George William Curtis published in *Putnam's Monthly* three travel pieces based on Thoreau's Canadian trip, but he irritated the author (who was very stiff-necked about such things) by omitting certain passages of "defiant pantheism," including the statement: "I am not sure but this Catholic religion would be an admirable one if the priest were quite omitted." Thoreau wrote to Harrison Blake early in 1853 that the liberty which the editor had taken in omitting without consultation what he did not like was "a privilege California is not rich enough to bid for," and as a result of the disagreement the series was discontinued, nearly half the MS being returned to its author. In 1858 another attempt to find a magazine market collapsed for precisely the same reason. James Russell Lowell had asked Thoreau for something about his latest trip to the Maine woods, and got the article which is now the second section of the volume called *The Maine Woods*. He omitted a sentence about a pine tree which read, "It is as immortal as I am, and perchance will go to as high a heaven, there to tower above me still," and got from the author a flaming letter first published in Mr. Canby's biography. The omission, Thoreau says, is mean and cowardly. "The editor has, in this case, no more right to omit a sentiment than to insert one, or put words into my mouth. . . . I should not read many books if I thought that they had been thus expurgated. I feel this treatment to be an insult, though not intended as such, for it is to presume that I can be hired to suppress my opinions." Thoreau went on to request that the sentence be printed in a subsequent number with an indication of the place from which it had been cut. When some four months later the request had not been complied with, he wrote again, asking for a settlement. He got one hundred and ninety-eight dollars and that was the end of his relations with Lowell as an editor.

It has already been suggested that there seems no reason

to regret that Thoreau never actually wrote his apparently ill-conceived book on the natural history of the Concord region. Neither, except so far as it may have affected his pride and his pocketbook, does it seem worth while to lament very actively his failure to find a market for the travel essays, which, as they now survive, are pleasant enough without contributing much to the higher reputation which *Walden* had earned. To Harrison Blake, he remarked of what he called "my Canada story": "It concerns me but little, and probably is not worth the time it took to tell it." By comparison not only with *Walden* but even with the best pages of *A Week on the Concord and Merrimack Rivers*, much in both the Canada and the Maine woods essays is tepid and journalistic.

Why, then, did Thoreau never utilize, or apparently have any definite plans for utilizing, the real riches of the *Journal?* Why go from the one extreme represented by the arid record of natural phenomena to the other extreme of merely popular travel writing when he was at the same time possessed of an accumulation of material (to which he never entirely ceased to add) sometimes as striking as the best of *Walden?* Why did he not at least plan the book which seems foreshadowed in dozens of the *Journal* entries; the book which would have described fully and taken as its professed subject that communion with nature which, even in *Walden,* is at best co-ordinated with, if not actually subordinate to, his plea for a simplification of existence, the purpose of which simplification being primarily the provision of sufficient leisure to make possible a "life in Nature"? One chapter of *Walden* is, to be sure, called "Where I Lived and What I Lived For"; but if *Walden* had been followed, as it might have been, by one or more volumes on the "What I Lived For," then *Walden* itself might have fallen into place as merely a sort of preliminary description of "How I Managed to Live."

If, as seems probable, *Walden* was substantially complete at least a few years before it was actually published, then nine or ten years of at least relatively good health produced neither any completely finished literary work of major importance, nor even, it would seem, any mature project for such a work. A mere volume of selections like Mr. Allen's *Men of Concord* is more interesting than anything Thoreau himself prepared for publication after *Walden* and, as has previously been remarked, other volumes equally interesting could have been quarried out in the same manner. Had he somehow lost his way completely and, having deluded himself into the belief that his record of New England seasons would have some significance we cannot imagine, committed himself irrevocably to it? Is it possible that those philosophical conflicts described at length in the preceding chapter of this book actually disturbed his mental equilibrium more than they seem to have done and, perhaps without his being aware of the fact, turned him toward record, on the one hand, or relatively superficial accounts of journeys, on the other, for the simple reason that in neither was it necessary for him to face squarely the moral and philosophical questions which his thought had raised? Or was it that the other conflict between his growing indignation over the handling of the slavery question and his never-conquered distaste for social reformers destroyed the equanimity which would have been necessary for the shaping of material really close to his heart?

So far as his material situation was concerned, the years after the illness of 1855 should have been easier than any of the years before. The family had become at least modestly affluent, and after the death of his father Thoreau was almost a capitalist. Moreover, the position of town surveyor had given him a certain dignity, and it was in 1859 that he undertook the rather important—and to him delightful—job of surveying the township's rivers for flood control; one result being a map inscribed rather surprisingly: "Henry D. Thoreau, Civil Engineer."

To the very end he continued to maintain that his had been a happy life. At no point is there any sign that he was even remotely tempted, after the fashion of those who come late to "social consciousness," to echo King Lear's "O, I have ta'en too little care of this." Nor does it appear certain, when the evidence is carefully examined, that at least up to the arrest of John Brown in 1859, his indignation concerning slavery and the role which his own state of Massachusetts had played was ever allowed to dominate his life or his thoughts except during the relatively brief periods when he interrupted (but no more than interrupted) his continuous chronicling of natural phenomena in order to write into the *Journal* a first draft of the jeremiads he was to deliver on the occasions when he felt it necessary to speak his mind before his fellow citizens.

Had he lived another twenty years he might, as some commentators seem to like to assume, have turned from communion with nature to become primarily a social reformer. But it is at least equally possible that once the Civil War was over and it had become evident that white slavery remained in North and South alike—evident that men of Massachusetts, still leading lives of quiet desperation, still followed false gods—he might, on the other hand, have returned to the conviction that organized society could achieve nothing worth achieving even when it professed, as it had been professing, a noble aim. At the very least, it is worth noting that his last days, with the war already waging, were spent in arranging the papers which he left to his sister Sophia for publication.

The question already posed, the question why *Walden* was his last major work written directly for a public, remains unanswerable. Perhaps only more time was needed since what he had actually published had, in the case of both *Walden* itself and *A Week on the Concord and Merrimack Rivers*, been long delayed. And if that is not the answer, one cannot by any means assume that his concern over the slavery question is a more obviously satisfactory explanation than the alternate possibility already suggested or even, perhaps, the possibility that a waning energy, sapped more than he realized by the hidden progress of disease, was insufficient for any major task. His own opinion seems to have been simply the one he expressed in 1856 in a letter to Harrison Blake: "I am still a learner, not a teacher, feeding somewhat omnivorously, browsing both stalk and leaves; but I shall perhaps be enabled to speak with the more precision and authority by and by—if philosophy and sentiment are not buried under a multitude of details."

To say this is not, of course, to deny that Thoreau's indignation against slavery was real and powerful. Neither is it to belittle the significance of the fact that what he said on the subject does not always seem consistent with earlier attitudes. We can, moreover, easily trace the growth of that inconsistency, and it is worth while for two reasons to examine briefly but carefully his successive attitudes. These attitudes were important to him and they have been made even more important by those to whom the question of Thoreau's "social philosophy" seems the only question worth asking. How far, then, did "social consciousness" carry him? Beyond what point did he refuse to go?

He had, it must be remembered, grown up in an abolitionist atmosphere. His sister Helen, his Aunt Maria Thoreau, and Mrs. Joseph Ward (the mother of Aunt Prudence) had all been active members of an abolitionist society. He himself read, as they did, *The Liberator*, and one of the pieces that he published in *The Dial* in 1844 was a rather perfunctory, rather clumsy, but friendly "notice" of the abolitionist weekly the *Herald of Freedom*. As a believer in every man's right to be heard, he insisted, against strenuous opposition, that Wendell Phillips be allowed to speak at the Concord Lyceum, and in 1845 he wrote a long letter to *The Liberator*, reporting the speech which Phillips had at last made, and characteristically stressing the fact that "It was the speaker's aim to show what the State, and above all the Church, had to do, and now, alas! have done, with Texas and slavery, and how much, on the other hand, the individual should have to do with Church and State."

But Thoreau was not a member of abolitionist societies and he would not at this time have called himself an abolitionist. Throughout the Walden period his attitude was clear. Slavery was, of course, an evil thing, but those who made so much of it were doubly ridiculous. In the first place, they were swallowing a camel while straining at a gnat, since they were themselves part of a society which encouraged white slavery at home while protesting against Negro slavery abroad. In the second place, and like most "reformers," they refused to realize that no man can reform anyone except himself.

The Mexican War increased Thoreau's sense of the reality and the immediacy of the problem. Here was the national government of which he was, willy-nilly, a part, actively promoting an abomination for which heretofore only distant men in distant states had had responsibility. The realization of this fact provoked his first active participation in the controversy, and in 1848 he wrote the lecture which became "Civil Disobedience." But that essay, as we have seen, is perfectly consistent with Thoreau's contempt for group action; perfectly consistent with what was, after all, his fundamentally anarchistic position. It reaches nonco-operation but it goes not one step beyond the advocacy of passive resistance on the part of the individual. Thoreau "washes his hands" and seems less concerned by the social wrong itself than by the possibility that he may be contaminated by it. It is his own soul, not the souls or bodies of black slaves, which seems to concern him, and he might easily be accused of a merely Pharisaical determination to maintain his own technical virtue by renouncing responsibility. Psychologically his sometimes desperate casuistry may well be a sign that he was desperately endeavoring to fight off a growing sense that social responsibility could not be repudiated, that he could not get rid of it merely by announcing that he had "signed off" all human institutions. But logically "Civil Disobedience" is perfectly consistent with what had always been his attitude. He is not joining the government or any group. Nonco-operation makes him more completely an individual than ever before. His hands are now clean and he serves notice that in the future he will continue to attend strictly to his own business. Two years later, when the newspaper disgusted him, he went out to find turtle eggs. They, he still thought, were his real business.

Presently, however, the passage of the Fugitive Slave Law once more disturbed the precarious equanimity which he hoped he had achieved after the crisis precipitated by the Mexican War. The latter had involved the national government; the new law involved his own state of Massachusetts and him as an individual; made him legally criminal if he failed to turn over to the authorities any escaping slave of whom he had knowledge. Man's "dirty institutions" (as he had called them in *Walden*) were catching up with him and they were undertaking to compel him not merely to a symbolical act, like the payment of a poll tax, but to a cowardly deed directly affecting another human being. Was the formula which he had evolved in "Civil Disobedience" still adequate? Was it enough merely to refuse as an individual to obey the law as he had once refused as an individual to pay his poll tax? His fellow citizens in Massachusetts, in Concord even, were capable of a brutality which probably he would not have believed possible five years before.

In part his reaction was sheer exasperation. Heretofore he had lived his own life; must he now sign on the rolls he had jubilantly signed himself off of? But there was more than mere exasperation, and perhaps nothing proves better how deeply disturbed he was than the fact that his indignation forces its way into the sacred pages of the *Journal*. Whatever he did not acknowledge as deeply important to himself had always been rigidly excluded. As late as November 1850 he was protesting that "My Journal should be the record of my love. I would write in it only of the things

I love, my affection for any aspect of the world, what I love to think of. . . . Notwithstanding that I regard myself as a good deal of a scamp, yet for the most part the spirit of the universe is unaccountably kind to me, and I enjoy perhaps an unusual share of happiness. Yet I question sometimes if there is not some settlement to come."

Now, both his irritations and his righteous indignations interrupt more and more lengthily the record of his love to interpolate a record of his hate. On occasion he himself had helped runaways on their journey to Canada, and when, in the spring of 1851, he read how one Daniel Foster had said a prayer of thanks on the wharf at Boston when the authorities rendered up a fugitive, he was shocked anew. Then in 1854 Anthony Burns was returned to slavery on a government cutter and Thoreau blazed again. He journeyed to Framingham, Massachusetts, and there on July 4, 1854, delivered himself of the outburst printed a few weeks later in *The Liberator* under the title of "Slavery in Massachusetts." "I have," he said, "lived for the last month —and I think every man in Massachusetts capable of the sentiment of patriotism must have had a similar experience —with the sense of having suffered a vast and indefinite loss. I did not know at first what ailed me. At last it occurred to me that what I had lost was a country." And the astonishing thing is this reference to "patriotism." Thoreau had never admitted, perhaps did not know, that he had "a country" until he knew that he had lost it.

"Civil Disobedience" had been a brilliant piece of casuistry; "Slavery in Massachusetts" is pure indignation. "Show me a free state, and a court truly of justice, and I will fight for them, if need be; but show me Massachusetts, and I refuse her my allegiance, and express contempt for her courts." That is a statement of principle. The second half of the sentence is only a reiteration of what he had always said, but the first half is Thoreau's first recognition of the possibility that any state could be worth fighting for. As a whole, however, the address throws logic of his usual sort to the winds. An outrageous fact has provoked an indignation in the face of which he no longer cares how (or if) that indignation can be reconciled with abstract theories. There never yet, says Leonato, was a philosopher who could endure the toothache patiently. No philosopher, Thoreau seems to say, can explain away a shameful indifference to such an outrage as he has seen accomplished.

"I walk," he said, "toward one of our ponds; but what signifies the beauty of nature when men are base? We walk to lakes to see our serenity reflected in them; when we are not serene, we go not to them." The audience at Framingham may not have felt the full force of that argument. To many it may have seemed that the spoiling of Thoreau's walks was not one of the worst things that could be said against the institution of slavery. But Thoreau himself could hardly have said more. His whole scheme of life had presupposed a stable society which would not only permit him to go his own way but would also refrain from misconduct too outrageous to be ignored. It presupposed, that is to say, just such a stable, decorous, and unviolent society as he had grown up in and been able to take for granted. It was threatened now; had, perhaps, already ceased to exist. The logic of his former position was no longer adequate and though he never formulated another, he realized the inadequacy.

Three years after the address at Framingham he met John Brown—once when Sanborn brought him to call and again the next evening at Emerson's house. Thoreau was impressed without being wholly satisfied, but when Brown was arrested in 1859, he delivered his "Plea for Captain John Brown" at Concord on October 30th, and, after the execution, his "Last Day of John Brown" at North Elba on July 4, 1860. Significantly, the speeches are primarily eulogies of a man, not discussion of a principle; they are arguments *ad hominem* so far as they are arguments at all. John Brown was a man of principle, a hero after the ancient, honorable model. As an individual he did what his individual conscience told him to do, and he shamed the citizens of Massachusetts, who talked only about the law and the will of the majority. But for all that, there is no mistaking the break with a previously inviolable conviction. In none of his previous outbursts had Thoreau gone beyond the advocacy of passive resistance, and whatever John Brown was or was not, he was certainly not passive. "I do not wish," Thoreau had written in his *Journal* during the trial, "to kill or to be killed but I can foresee circumstances in which both these things would be unavoidable. In extremes I could even be killed."

Cautious though this last statement may seem, it was as reckless as any he had ever made, and like his championship of John Brown it involves (as "Civil Disobedience" does not) some assumption of some "social responsibility." And it is upon the acceptance of some such "social responsibility" that Thoreau's salvation must, in the view of certain critics, depend. The "even be killed" is not comic, for Thoreau the individualist must have found it in theory almost as difficult to imagine himself dying for others as Thoreau the abhorrer of violence found it difficult to imagine himself killing another individual. In fact as opposed to theory, Thoreau might possibly have died on a scaffold. He could never have raided Kansas or shot down even a slaveholder.

Sanborn had been directly involved in Brown's danger. He had not only sponsored Brown's speeches but helped him to get arms from a Massachusetts committee, and he thought it necessary to flee Concord. Finally even Thoreau committed himself to what was probably a criminal act under the existing law, even though the state of Massachusetts refused to enforce it. In December 1859, Jackson Merriam, one of John Brown's raiders, with a price on his head, called on Sanborn for aid. Sanborn borrowed a horse from Emerson, and Thoreau drove the criminal to South Acton station where he could get a train for Canada. This was an act very different in its possible consequences from the much better known refusal to pay a tax some thirteen years before.

Late in 1860, only a few months after he had delivered his address at North Elba, Thoreau contracted the cold which marked the beginning of his last illness. His eulogy of John Brown was almost his last act before he became, to all intents and purposes, a dying man, and his career as a reformer—if reformer he would ever have been—was cut off almost as soon as it began.

In the paragraphs just preceding this, Thoreau's strongest expressions have been quoted and the stress laid on the extent to which he seemed at moments willing to join forces with the advocates of direct, if not of political, action. But he never committed himself beyond the speech that he made, and he never lost his distrust of organized movements. It may be worth remembering that when, in

1856, he spent nearly a month doing a job of surveying for the community of Eagleswood in New Jersey, where the very influential abolitionist, Theodore Weld, had established a school, he wrote his sister Sophia a characteristically contemptuous letter and complained about the difficulty of finding solitude. It is certainly significant that in April 1861, nine months after his last eulogy of John Brown, he was writing to Parker Pillsbury, an abolitionist and an old friend of the family, that he hopes a certain unnamed friend who wants to read *Walden*, "ignores Fort Sumter, and 'Old Abe,' and all that." "That [*i.e.*, ignoring] is," he goes on, "just the most fatal, and, indeed, the only fatal weapon you can direct against evil, ever." And if this seems to indicate a return to the advocacy of absolute non-resistance, just as his championship of John Brown had seemed a repudiation of it, the sentences that follow are even more astonishing. "I do not," he writes, "so much regret the present condition of things in this country (provided I regret it at all) as I do that I ever heard of it. . . . Blessed were the days before you read a President's message. Blessed are the young, for they do not read the President's message. Blessed are they who never read a newspaper, for they shall see Nature, and, through her, God." Those sentences were written a few days before the surrender of Fort Sumter, and part of the passage may be interpreted as an expression of Thoreau's disgust with what still seemed to him the temporizing, uncertain policies of the government, rather than a radical disbelief in the effectiveness or importance of any government. Yet it does seem difficult to reconcile with the crucial sentence beginning "I do not so much regret" the usual assumption that by this time Thoreau had completely reversed his previous attitude.

His friend Sanborn, an active abolitionist, feels it necessary to remark that these "petulant words" would hardly have been uttered only a few days later when, at Lincoln's call, "the people rose to protect their government," and every President's message became of thrilling interest, even to Thoreau. And it must be added that Alcott, after two visits to the dying man in early January of 1862, remarks each time in his journal that Thoreau "is interested . . . in our civil troubles especially, and speaks impatiently of what he calls the temporizing policy of our rulers."

John Brown's raid, being the act of an individual, would, one imagines, be less difficult for Thoreau to accept than government-sponsored mass action, and by what logic or by what readjustment of his principles he approved the war, if approve it he did, probably we shall never know. He himself lived only to see the war's beginning and never had an opportunity to judge its results.

At most, Thoreau was, then, a very reluctant crusader. He never supposed that social organization itself was an interesting subject, that politics should or could be one of the important sources of satisfaction, and one of the things a man might "live for." No one had ever more ardently insisted that "getting a living" ought to be a joyous part of living itself and that it inevitably was, when "getting a living" meant the business of supplying oneself with food and shelter and clothing as directly as possible; when it meant actually hoeing one's beans or cutting one's wood or building one's house. But government was a necessary evil—dubiously necessary and indisputably evil—which a wise man would avoid as completely as possible. He had, indeed, been perfectly explicit on the subject when, in November 1851, he wrote into the *Journal* a two-paragraph essay, describing what a really healthy society would be, and assuming, as a matter of course, not that it would be one in which all citizens actively participate, but rather one in which no part need be taken. Government, he seems to feel, is no doubt one of the vital functions of society, but such vital functions should be as unconsciously performed as the vital functions of the body are performed. A healthy citizen should be no more aware of his government than a healthy man is aware of the functions of his body. Such processes are infra-human and the society which is perpetually concerned with them is like a confirmed dyspeptic whose preoccupation with health is a sure sign that he has lost it.

The passage then trails off into a series of uncompleted sentences which struggle again to express Thoreau's recurrent attempt to identify himself with a grand scheme of nature in which man is only a trivial incident. "No true and absolute account of things—of the evening and the morning and all the phenomena between them—but ever a petty reference to man, to society, aye, often to Christianity. What these things are when men are asleep. I come from the funeral of mankind to attend to natural phenomena. The so much grander significance of any fact— of sun and moon and stars—when not referred to man and his needs but viewed absolutely!"

Thoreau's last surviving letter—preserved at the Huntington Library—is to a publisher and concerned with arrangements to reprint *Walden*. The last one printed in the standard edition of his correspondence expresses regret that he had not written his book on natural history. It contains not one word about politics or society, and even in the years when he was appearing in public as a crusader, the pages in the *Journal* making any reference to slavery or his protests against it are relatively very few. In 1861, it will be remembered, he could explain that he regretted the condition of the country less than he regretted the fact that he had ever heard of its condition, and the *Journal* seems to prove that whatever undercurrents of distress he may unwillingly have been aware of, he did not permit them to prevent him from devoting the major part of his time to what he believed to be his really important private business. Two of his latest entries, it has already been pointed out, concern the expressiveness of a cat's tail and the expertness of the squirrel who picks a pine cone. The times were out of joint. Society was not only hypochondriac but also desperately ill. Thoreau had heard of certain enormities, however much he might wish he had never done so, and his conscience would not permit him to maintain the detachment he would have preferred. But he was no happy warrior. If, on occasion, he went forth to fight, he went with an "O cursed spite" upon his lips in lieu of a battle cry.

For a longer time than most men know it, Thoreau knew that the end was at hand. The western trip which he began in May 1861, in the company of the young naturalist, Horace Mann, was frankly a trip in search of health, and it was no less frankly a failure. By late fall of the same year he was obviously sinking. Though unable to sleep, he was calm, cheerful, and perhaps unwontedly sociable. A rattan day-bed which he himself had made was brought down into the parlor where he received company, and as long as he could sit up, he came to the family table, saying that "It would not be social to take my meals alone." He looked out of the window; but he knew that he would never visit the woods again and apparently he preferred to avoid all reference to the world he had lived for, but which, so far as he was concerned, had now ceased to exist. He had been used, so Channing tells us, to say that if his out-of-door life was interrupted "all his living ceased," and now, standing at the window, he remarked: "I cannot see on the outside at all. We thought ourselves great philosophers in those wet days, when we used to go out and sit down by the wall-sides." And this, Channing goes on, "was absolutely all he was ever heard to say of that outward world during his illness; neither could a stranger in the least infer that he had ever a friend in field or wood." Finally, at nine in the morning of May 6, 1862, Henry Thoreau died, apparently without pain.

The last days of most men, even of most great men, are interesting only because convention and a certain inveterate morbidity in the reading public make them so. But the last days of a rebel have a real significance. They furnish a test, unfairly severe, but a test nevertheless. In the old days a priest offered the dying heretic a crucifix. The waiting spectators took the news to the world, and the world usually hoped that the message would be: "He is saved and he is cancelled out. You need let his paradoxes trouble you no more and you may cease to look for the answers you could not find. It was all merely pride and bravado. We were right and he admits it. He did not mean what he said." Some scene of which this is the simpified symbol must be acted out when any rebel comes to the end of his days and the question is always, "Did he or did he not persist to the end?"

The rebellion of very few men had ever been more radical on the one hand, or more ramifying on the other, than Thoreau's was. It was not merely that he was anti-Christian and that he rejected even the profession of social responsibility. These were specific and tangible heresies, but they were merely inevitable deductions from an antecedent rejection *in toto* of the way in which his fellow citizens lived and of the things they lived for. Withdrawing himself from them and professing to find nothing in life important except pursuits which to them were meaningless, he not only declared himself independent of their opinion and their assistance, but taunted them with their lives of quiet (and evil) desperation. What was, moreover, perhaps most galling of all, more galling even than his contempt for what they called the enterprise and progress of their nation, was the fact that he dared to say that he was always satisfied and happy, often deliriously so—thus by implication challenging any one of the orthodox to pretend that he could say the same. Nor could others claim that his opinions were merely opinions, for he dared not only to speak heretical thoughts but also, what is often more difficult, to live an eccentric life in a community where the most distinguished radical thinker was a substantial gentleman. He boldly risked the very thing that a "dangerous man" is usually least willing to risk—namely, the chance, nay, the probability even, that in the end he would seem merely ridiculous. What other great breaker of tablets ever calmly, good-humoredly, and for humble pay did chores for his neighbors?

There were many ways during a long, enervating illness in which he might have weakened or relented. He might at least have ceased to regret his "good behavior." Without so much as hinting anything that could be called a recantation, he might have exhibited some mere failure of nerve. Men who are sick and dying cannot always find the courage to hold out against the insistent human temptation to regret and sentimentalize. But Thoreau did more than merely hold out. He found, as we shall see presently, the courage and the strength to choose mocking, aphoristic words in which to reiterate, with all their pristine pungency, both his fundamental convictions and his acceptance of the universe.

Up until six months before his death, he had continued to make occasional entries in his *Journal*—mostly simple notations concerning natural facts that had interested him and including only one reference to the war, entered in October 1861. And even this seems to indicate more the survival of his old interest in the village worthies than any new interest in the conflict itself: "Prescott is not inclined to go to the wars again. . . . Cyrus Warren thinks that Derby, the first lieutenant (and butcher that was), would do for captain as well as Prescott, and adds, as his principal qualification, 'There isn't one in the company can cut up a crittur like him.' "

After he had become confined to the house and occupied himself with arranging his papers, the *Journal* is abandoned, perhaps because there was nothing to be added by a man to whom nature had at last closed her book. But it was his cheerful stoicism which came to the front. There was no complaining and there were no regrets. Though he could not sleep, he refused opiates, so Channing says, on the ground that he preferred to endure the worst sufferings with a clear mind rather than to sink into a turbid, narcotic dream. He retired, Channing goes on to say, "into his inner mind, into that unknown, unconscious, profound world of existence where he excelled." But there is no evidence that in whatever self-examinations he may have been holding, he found anything to regret or any cause for self-accusation. Less than two months before he died, he wrote in a dictated letter: "You ask particularly after my health. I *suppose* that I have not many months to live; but, of course, I know nothing about it. I may add that I am enjoying existence as much as ever, and regret nothing."

The testimony of those who saw him is, moreover, strangely consistent. A friend of Harrison Blake reported that Thoreau talked with the same curious combination of earnestness and fun which had always been his. Sam Staples, who had been his jailer long ago when the poll tax went unpaid, called upon him in March and reported to Emerson: "Never spent an hour with more satisfaction. Never saw a man dying with so much pleasure and peace." He thinks, Emerson adds, "that few men in Concord know Mr. Thoreau; finds him serene and happy." And only a month before the end, when he had not been able for many weeks to speak above a whisper, Sophia wrote: "It is not possible to be sad in his presence. No shadow attaches to anything connected with my precious brother. His whole life impresses me as a grand miracle. I have always thought him the most upright man I ever knew."

He was not, however, spared the challenge direct, and gnomic literature is the richer by two memorable sayings. Twice, near the end, a true believer offered the dying heretic the New England equivalent of a crucifix and got, for his pains, tremendous but heretical affirmations. Once was when Pillsbury, the abolitionist, made some reference to the future life and Thoreau responded with the now perhaps almost too familiar adjuration: "One world at a time." The other occasion was when some orthodox member of the family asked him if he had made his peace with God.

Now many men have answered this question in many different ways—some fearful and some hypocritical, some defiant and some flippant. But only Thoreau could have answered, as he did, that he was not aware that he and God had ever quarreled. Even at the end of his physical strength he thus demonstrated that he retained his grip upon the premises which had sustained him through life no less than upon a technique of expression which enabled him to make one of his last sayings one of his most characteristic. And it is not easy to decide which should provoke the greater admiration.

Here is, from one point of view, the most appalling and the most inclusive possible of blasphemies. Goethe, it is true, is said to have remarked that even in God he discovered defects, and Heine's reply to the question whether he thought God would forgive him has not been forgotten. But Heine's "That's what he is for," like Goethe's little shocker, is not much more than merely flip—is obviously the effort of an *enfant terrible* to live up to his reputation. On the other hand, Thoreau's tremendous statement seems, in some sense, innocent; and like all his most unforgettable observations, it springs not from a sense of his own cleverness but from an honest wonder that the obvious should need to be pointed out. By implication it embodies the most fundamental of his convictions, the conviction that is to say, that he—and he, almost, if not quite, alone—had discovered both what men should live for and how they could be happy. Years before, he had said to Channing: "God could not be unkind to me if he should try," and it was obvious either that this was true, or, if not, then that God had not tried. All his life, so it seemed to Thoreau at the end of it, confirmed his early conviction. He did not doubt his right to the deep satisfaction which was his, any more than he doubted the reality of the satisfaction itself. He was a man of many eccentricities, but none was more unusual than his happiness and his inability to regret it.

Legend, if legend still had the freedom it once had to select and modify, would probably make Thoreau's denial that he and God had ever quarreled his official "last words." They were not. But it is also not certain that they would have been any more appropriate than what these last words actually were. As consciousness faded, he sank down below the level of articulate thought into the depths of his being where he met again that instinctive sympathy with "wildness" which, in some way perhaps not altogether clear, had been the thing to which he must return in order to find again the point at which the path of so-called civilization had branched fatally away from the path of nature. "Moose," he whispered, and "Indians."

The Style and the Man

ELLERY CHANNING, whose pioneer attempt to interpret his friend's genius mingles some shrewd observations with a good deal that is foolish and feeble, observes of Thoreau that "No man had a better unfinished life." In a sense that is true since, when Thoreau died, possible books were unwritten and fame was still untasted. But his life was certainly not unfinished in the sense that it made no whole or that it seemed to the man who had lived it any more incomplete than all mortal things must be. Moreover, before the funeral services were finished in the village church, Emerson had read his eulogy and thus begun the process which was to transform Thoreau from "a Concord worthy (or unworthy)" into a world figure.

Other champions, determined that he should be given his due, were not wanting. Indeed, they were more numerous and fanatical than wise. Sister Sophia, to whom Thoreau had entrusted his papers, was fussily assiduous; Channing promptly wrote, though he did not publish until 1875, his diffuse recollections; Sanborn, though he also was not to publish his book until later, was soon busily engaged in the effort to claim Thoreau for the abolition movement to which he himself had been committed. But the champions did not love one another. Sophia, with a good deal of justification, protested that Sanborn had never been close to her brother; she and Channing presently ceased to be on speaking terms.

Sophia did, however, succeed in getting more of Thoreau's writing into print. "Life Without Principle" was published posthumously in *The Atlantic Monthly*. From time to time during the next dozen years, other magazine articles appeared. The volume called *The Maine Woods* (about half of which had never been printed in any other form) came out in 1863; the volume called *Excursions*, reprinted from the *Atlantic*, the same year; and *Cape Cod* in 1865. Concurrently, the two books that Thoreau had himself published were again made available when some rebound copies of *A Week on the Concord and Merrimack Rivers* were offered for sale in 1862 and when *Walden* was reprinted for the first time shortly thereafter.

A good deal of the writing which appeared for the first time after Thoreau's death was easier and more accessible to a large audience than either of his major works had been. Both *The Maine Woods* and *Cape Cod* belong, as neither *Walden* nor *A Week on the Concord and Merrimack Rivers* does, to a familiar genre; they are, that is to say, "travel books." Moreover, though both contain some fine passages and a scattering of knotty sayings, much of both is relatively relaxed, even relatively superficial. Thoreau seems to be subduing his personality to a point where he can seem merely an entertainingly original traveler, whose occasional crankiness is diverting rather than exasperating or challenging. In *Cape Cod* especially, though to some extent in *The Maine Woods* also, there seems to be a conscious attempt at journalistic jocosity and a willingness to make small jokes, which is pleasant enough but which seems at times almost unworthy of a man who was capable of strength so much greater than, except at intervals, he here permits himself to exhibit. Probably these books did get him an audience he had never had before, and they may have helped keep his memory alive during a period when he might otherwise have been forgot; but they also exposed him to the danger of becoming best known for his least important work.

The influential makers of literary opinion were not, moreover, yet ready to recognize the real Thoreau. The first two essays written about him by men whose opinions still carry some weight—James Russell Lowell and Robert Louis Stevenson—were in the main depreciatory. Indeed, it seems reasonable to suppose that Lowell's estimate, first printed in *The North American Review* for October 1865 and republished in *My Study Windows*, actually served for a time its purpose—which seems to have been to "place" Thoreau definitely as a mere eccentric, and to forestall any attempt to consider him a major figure.

Lowell had long been aware of Thoreau, for not only had he reviewed *A Week on the Concord and Merrimack Rivers*, but had also, before that, made brief reference to him in *A Fable for Critics*, where Thoreau appears as merely one of Emerson's hangers-on. For the new essay, he seated himself comfortably by his study window and, secure in a sense of superior learning, superior manners, and superior worldliness, put the quaint provincial in his place. Every reader past a certain age will, he begins, remember the Transcendental movement of some thirty years ago. Properly understood, it was not wholly contemptible because it was a phase of the war against Philistinism, and because Emerson, narrow though he may be, gave the receptive (which by implication includes Lowell himself) "a mental and moral nudge." But the Transcendental movement had its lunatic fringe, and "Every possible form of intellectual and physical dyspepsia brought forth its gospel." Among the minor figures, "the pistillate plants kindled to fruitage by the Emersonian pollen," Thoreau is probably the most interesting. He had a gift for expression within the limits of a sentence or a short poem, though he was incapable of shaping any large unit of expression; and he was a man "with so high a conceit of himself that he accepted without questioning, and insisted upon our accepting, his defects and weaknesses of character as virtues and powers peculiar to himself." "Was he indolent, he finds none of the activities which attract or employ the rest of mankind, worthy of him. . . . Was he poor, money was an unmixed evil. Did his life seem a selfish one, he condemns doing good as one of the weakest of superstitions."

After a few pages, Lowell's criticism then takes another turn. "We look upon a great deal of the modern sentimentalism about Nature as a mark of disease. It is one more symptom of the general liver-complaint. To a man of wholesome constitution the wilderness is well enough for a mood or a vacation, but not for a habit of life." And presently one perceives that the not-quite-expressed core of Lowell's objection is simply that Thoreau has refused to commit himself, as Lowell had, to "this bustling nineteenth century." "A greater familiarity with ordinary men would have done Thoreau good, by showing him how many fine qualities are common to the race. . . . To a healthy mind, the world is a constant challenge of opportunity." Thoreau is, in other words, an "escapist," though to Lowell that term would have meant, not someone who is escaping from the duty of remaking the world, but someone who is refusing to co-operate with the manifest destiny opening ever more delightful prospects to those who will consent to go along with the spirit of the age.

It is true that Lowell ends the essay with a paragraph in which he pays tribute to the excellence of Thoreau's style at its best, and that his last sentence reads: "He belongs with Donne and Browne and Novalis; if not with the originally creative men, with the scarcely smaller class who are peculiar, and whose leaves shed their invisible thought-seeds like ferns." But what, one inevitably asks, is more creative than a seed? And the very illogicality of Lowell's sentence reminds us that the seeds could not be expected to germinate into any flourishing growth until they should fall, later, upon a soil better prepared to receive them. Optimism—the conviction that, fundamentally, all was well with America and with the world—was, for them, stony ground. A sympathetic understanding of Thoreau's retreat from civilization into nature was not to be expected until some suspicion should arise that what Lowell called "the general liver-complaint" was more than hypochondria and that an acceptance of modern urban life was not necessarily proof of a "wholesome constitution." Thoreau's other reputation—his reputation as a social reformer rather than as a man who washed his hands of responsibility for modern man and his ways—was also inevitably delayed for a similar reason. Tolstoi and Gandhi, two of the world leaders who first acknowledged the importance of his seed, shared his conviction that not only was there something wrong with the world, but also that this something wrong was to be traced back to what was wrong in the souls of the men who make it.

Slowly, however, he made his way. The first English edition of *Walden* appeared in 1884, and there were six American reissues of the same book between 1889 and 1902—which amounts almost to one every two years. The first collected edition, in eleven volumes and including selections from the *Journal*, was dated 1894, and the twenty-volume edition, which is the most nearly complete, came out in 1906. Few American books have been translated into so many languages, and by now Thoreau's reputation is international in the widest possible sense.

Critical recognition was accorded him increasingly as his writings became better and better known. The first series of Paul Elmer More's *Shelburne Essays* (1904) contained a highly laudatory essay; Mark Van Doren published in 1916 the first study based upon a careful consideration of the *Journal;* and by the time the *Cambridge History of American Literature* appeared in 1918, Thoreau was recognized as indisputably one of our major writers. Paul Elmer More was perhaps the first clearly to recognize in Thoreau "the creator of a new manner of writing about nature," and, in a second essay published a few years later, to attribute the newness of the manner to the fact that Thoreau's "awe and wonder" distinguished it both from the manner of Gilbert White on the one hand, and from the sentimental-romantic manner on the other.

More recently the tendency has been to stress the political or social aspects of Thoreau's philosophy and to interpret it in terms of the special convictions of the commentator. To Vernon Parrington he was, first of all, an inheritor of the late eighteenth-century tradition of atomic individualism and hence a philosopher whose conception of the proper relation of man to the state is indistinguishable from that of William Godwin. Still more recently, the Marxian left-wing has made at least halfhearted attempts to claim Thoreau as a Marxian *manqué* or, if not quite that, as a man whose thinking was frustrated by his failure to find the magic key. Thus Bernard Smith's *Forces in American Criticism* (1939), which may be regarded as an attempt to sum up the attitude of the then-fashionable left-wing toward the American intellectual past, undertakes to point out just where Thoreau failed. Thoreau, says Smith, attacked American materialism, not from the point of view of a Marxian materialist but from the point of view of a mystic. "Once he had accepted an untenable metaphysical premise, he *had* to go on (such was his character) to an acceptance of propositions which later proved irrelevant to the problems and struggles that have disturbed his country."

Now to say that Thoreau was not a materialist, dialectical or otherwise, is hardly news, and to add that he is therefore irrelevant is to beg the question. But the real objection to such summations as that just quoted is not so much that they are merely opinions (which any man is entitled to hold) but that the simplicity to which they reduce the issue tends to obscure the complex implications of Thoreau's position. If that position, whether right or wrong, is arresting and interesting, it is not because it can be summed up by saying that he was a mystic, but because, by being one, he was able to challenge at so many points fundamental assumptions which, in this our present day, are seldom challenged.

To read him with any understanding at all is, for instance, to be compelled to reopen the whole question whether men are what they are because of the kind of society in which they live, or whether the kind of society in which they live was created because men are what they are. To some it may seem that the problem is in the same class as that concerning the aboriginal priority of the chicken or the egg, but actually it is far from being the same for the simple reason that a great deal depends upon which assumption we make. Because Thoreau assumed—merely as moralist rather than necessarily as mystic—that ultimately it is men who make institutions rather than institutions which make men, his whole approach to the question what men can do to better their condition was fundamentally different from that of those who assume, as nine-tenths of even the unthinking assume today, that institutions make men.

In Thoreau's understanding of the world, men do, of course, fall victim in their turn to the evil institutions which the evil in them has created. But because the head of the snake which thus holds its tail in its mouth and so creates the evil circle is, indeed, a head that thinks and feels and chooses and wills, it can be appealed to, and men will be saved when they can be persuaded to desire salvation. Moreover the effect of this is not merely to make Thoreau primarily a moralist rather than an economist, but also, by so doing, to imply a challenge to various other elements in a complex of now usual assumptions.

The theory that every man is necessarily "the product of his times" strikes at the root of every man's confidence in himself, but it also fits curiously well into what seems to be a general readiness to give up any immediate hope in exchange for a glad release from any sense of responsibility.

It is as difficult to imagine Thoreau a Freudian as it is to imagine him a Marxian, and the two great prophets of the nineteenth century, so often regarded as opposed one to the other, have in common at least the very important fact that both, whether or not they intended anything of the sort, have often been assumed to be assuring us that no man can be charged with responsibility for what he is. From one point of view it makes little difference whether he is the product of his psychic or of his sociological environment since in neither case is there a responsible "I" which did or could choose to be one kind of person rather than another. Freudianism and Marxism have, moreover, so extensively infiltrated even the less dogmatic philosophies which do not explicitly recognize either Freud or Marx as supreme prophet, that very few such philosophies as are now current do not in one way or another assume that man is, in his most significant aspect, inevitably a victim rather than a maker of his own fate.

To be sure, Thoreau, also, saw most men as victims. But the essential difference is his conviction that they, or at least some among them, did not need to be. The whole theory that men are, more significantly than anything else, the "products" of "forces" leads directly to the theory that all revolutions, either of an individual or of a group, are "inevitable." And that theory, leaving quite aside the question whether, or in what sense, it is true, cannot but have a very profound effect upon the whole tone which the experience of living takes on.

Thoreau's lifework was the writing of a spiritual biography and it is impossible to understand what he is talking about unless one can accept the fact that the whole of his mental and emotional life could exist only in so far as he assumed that it was possible for a man to resist "forces," to refuse to be "a product" or, what is the same thing, "a victim." Thoreau can, as has previously been admitted, be accused of having on occasion—it is his own phrase—"washed his hands" of society. But unlike many who profess to be concerned with society, he accepted responsibility for himself. One result of this is that he would not wait for a new world, and refused to put off anything. Instead of complaining with the poets who protest that poetry, which was possible once and will be possible again, is impossible today; or, for that matter, with the sociologists who complain that a good life, which was possible once and will be possible again, is not possible now—he went off to Walden to demonstrate that if you do not like the world you find yourself in and do not think you can change it very soon, you can at least move away from it. Thus he brings tidings of great joy and demonstrates their truth by being himself filled with that joy. He did not need to delay; he simply refused to wait until the dialectic (or any other) process made happiness possible, and he insisted upon taking the directest route toward what he wanted. Had he ever heard the theory that the state will ultimately wither away but that we must make it all powerful first, he would undoubtedly have replied as he did when he heard of the would-be poet who proposed to get rich in order that he might have leisure for poetry, "He should have gone up to the garret at once." To the complaint that it is impossible for a man to be happy "under present conditions," he would have answered very simply: "But I am." And to that there is no answer.

None of this is to be taken to mean that Thoreau was unaware of the importance to men of the economic system or of the society in which they live. It means only that to him the existing economic system is the expression, rather than the cause, of what is wrong with them, and that he was convinced that the only way to change the system was to persuade men to live for things other than those for which, despite all their quiet desperation, they did live. In the first chapter of *Walden*, he expounds a theory of value based upon labor as the only creator of value which should satisfy any left-wing economist. When he reviewed Carlyle, he remarked that no man has yet really spoken for the man of labor, and while even a man like Whittier defended the American industrial system, Thoreau denounced it in a very Carlylesque passage in *Walden* on the ground that "the principal object is not that mankind may be well and honestly clad, but, unquestionably, that corporations may be enriched." He remembered that even as a child he had asked, "Who owns all the land?" and he was so far from believing in the primacy or even in the existence of property rights that he can say roundly apropos those who complain of the trespass of the Irish laborers gathering wood: "The highest law gives a thing to him who can use it." Yet he differed radically from most modern major prophets of economic reform, not only in his insistence that any real improvement must proceed from within outward, but also in the fact that the ideal society would be technologically simple, not complex; and characterized, not by the multiplicity of goods that everyone could have, but by the number of things we had discovered we no longer needed. He offered men contemplation and the joy of performing simple, essential tasks—not what is commonly called "a high standard of living." Nothing would have seemed to him more absurd than the theory that the worth of a civilization can be measured by the amount of its production per man-hour. What he wanted, if one insists upon putting it that way, was not an economy of abundance but an economy of deliberately chosen scarcity. "Getting and spending we lay waste our powers"— and for him the truth remains true, no matter how much we get or how much we spend.

Perhaps this is sufficient to constitute an adequate warning to both the right and the left of the danger of interpreting, without consideration of the whole context of the man and his writings, any of the isolated sentences which might seem to give comfort or support to one side or the other. Often they cannot be assumed to mean or to imply quite what they would legitimately be taken to mean, if made today. In "Civil Disobedience," for instance, he wrote: "Government is an expedient by which men would fain succeed in letting one another alone. . . . Trade and commerce, if they were not made of India-rubber, would never manage to bounce over the obstacles which legislators are continually putting in their way." And unless one is willing to assume that such a statement might properly be quoted by the most reactionary of Chambers of Commerce to prove that Thoreau believed that "business" should run the country, it is well to avoid the opposite assumption that he would be, today, sympathetic to left-wing totalitarianism. Writing to Harrison Blake about the panic of 1857, he said: "If thousands are thrown out of employment, it suggests that they were not well employed," but it is no more rash to conclude from this that he would have opposed the WPA in the nineteen-thirties than it is to conclude from other remarks that he needed only the hint he never got in order to accept the gospel of dialectic materialism.

Specifically political criticism of contemporary society has become so dominant a feature of our intellectual life that it is hard to get an undistorted view of a man like Thoreau who is only peripherally related to it. In the present volume no further attempt will be made to define his position as a social thinker. Instead, the few remaining pages will be devoted to some consideration of his habits and style as a writer, with special reference, first to the characteristics of his best-known style and then to both the manner and the substance of what, for want of a better word, we are still compelled to call his "nature writing."

Any such discussion had perhaps best begin with a reminder that Thoreau was, after all, a writer almost as much as he was a reformer or a "savage"; that a great many of the hours allotted to him were spent in putting words upon paper; that his now printed works cover about ten thousand large pages; and that he was very consciously concerned to develop the highly individual style which was his.

Emerson told Sanborn that Thoreau "always looked forward to authorship as his work in life, and fitted himself for that." It was with literature rather than nature that he was consciously concerned in college, and in earliest young manhood he seems to have thought himself first of all a poet, in the usual sense of the term. At least it was as such that Emerson was enthusiastically hailing him soon after the two met, and though Emerson's enthusiasm was soon to cool considerably, both no doubt thought that the poems contributed to *The Dial* were the beginning of a literary career. According to one of Thoreau's statements, he destroyed a considerable body of verse after Emerson had criticized it harshly, and it has sometimes been assumed both that Emerson was thus responsible for Thoreau's turning to prose and that Thoreau regretted, if he did not actually resent, the fact.

A few years ago, all of his verse that is known to survive was collected from manuscript as well as from published sources and edited by Carl Bode. Stripped of the critical apparatus, it would fill only a small volume, and there is little if anything to make one regret that Thoreau devoted himself to writing of other kinds. Neither is there very strong reason to suppose that he himself regretted it. It is true that Mr. Bode quotes a passage from the *Journal* for 1852 in which Thoreau says sadly: "The strains from my muse are as rare nowadays, or of late years, as the notes of birds in the winter"; but he so habitually uses "poet" and "poetry" in the broadest sense that one cannot even be quite sure he was here referring to verse. Some years before, he had written into *A Week on the Concord and Merrimack Rivers* a passage that seems conclusive: "Great prose, of equal elevation, commands our respect more than great verse, since it implies a more permanent and level height, a life more pervaded with the grandeur of thought. The poet often only makes an eruption, like a Parthian, and is off again, shooting while he retreats; but the prose writer has conquered like a Roman, and settled colonies."

The man who wrote that was obviously not a man to whom the formal restrictions of verse were congenial or stimulating, and by itself it would be sufficient to make us anticipate what we actually find—namely, that most of even the better of Thoreau's poems seem only to say with less originality, and ease, and finish, what he says more satisfactorily elsewhere. But it is equally obvious that the author of that same passage was one who had a high ideal of what prose might be and understood that the writing of it was a difficult art.

When, then, it came to writing prose, he was conscious of addressing himself to a task which called for a dedication at least as continuous and as exalted as that of any versifier, and the most obvious indication of the seriousness with which he took the problems of expression is the fact that he was, from the beginning, an indefatigable reviser of what he wrote. He valued individuality in expression and in thought almost as much as he valued sincerity, but he was one of those who realize early that there is nothing more difficult to find than oneself, and that he who simply lets go on paper will write, not originally, but like other writers. Even the *Journal* was by no means left merely as first written. According to Sanborn, it commonly went through three forms—the notes hastily written down, the expansion of these notes and, finally, the version copied into the volume. Then the *Journal* itself was sometimes re-written again and again before a section of it was put into print, as Mr. Odell Shepard has demonstrated by comparing passages in *Walden* with both the *Journal* and the work sheets for the published version.

"Homely" is a word everyone is frequently tempted to use in connection with both Thoreau's phraseology and his vocabulary, but even when the adjective is in some sense appropriate, it must be remembered that the homeliness is something deliberately striven for, not something which expressed instinctively Thoreau's nature, and that literary influences—especially of the seventeenth-century writers—were strong and pervasive. His critical awareness exercised itself upon both the turns of his phrase and the words he used, leading him deliberately to compare first the elements and then the structure of alternate sentences so that he might choose the one which best represented not only what he wanted to say but the manner of saying he most approved of. When in that part of the *Journal* which belongs to the years just before the publication of *Walden*, he speaks contemptuously of "such words as 'humanitary' which have a paralysis in their tails," one may suspect that it is not merely the word that offends him; but some four years later he was reiterating a similar complaint: "Some men have a peculiar taste for bad words . . . words like 'tribal' and 'ornamentation,' which drag a dead tail after them. They will pick you out of a thousand the still-born words, the falsettos, the wing-clipped and lame words, as if only the false notes caught their ears. They cry encore to all the discords." Margaret Fuller said, "I accept the Universe." Thoreau's way of advising others to do just that was: "However mean your life is, meet it and live it; do not shun it and call it hard names. It is not so bad as you are." He noted that the dandiacal Channing was cursed with a predilection for feeble elegance which led him to refer to walks along the river bank as "riparial excursions," and that Alcott, as he remarks with amused contempt, wanted him to call the *Walden* book *Sylvania*.

In 1857 he wrote Daniel Ricketson a letter in which he discussed the style of one Wilson Flagg, a writer on scenery and natural history, and then went on to generalize: "As for style of writing, if one has anything to say, it drops from him simply and directly, as a stone falls to the ground. There are no two ways about it, but down it comes, and he may stick in the points and stops whenever he can get a chance. New ideas come into the world somewhat like falling meteors, with a flash and an explosion, and perhaps somebody's castle-roof perforated. To try to polish the stone in its descent, to give it a peculiar turn, and make it whistle a tune, perchance, would be of no use, if it were possible."

Now that is itself not a bad example of one of Thoreau's styles—of the one in which homely simplicity alternates with bold metaphor. And if it seems at first sight to contradict what has just been said about his own devotion to polishing, it should be noted that what he is recommending is merely to get the sudden thought down as it comes, leaving the problem of phraseology until afterwards. A few months later he was advising Harrison Blake to set himself the task of writing an answer to some such question as what a certain walk over a mountain had meant to him. "Don't suppose that you can tell it precisely the first dozen times you try, but at 'em again. . . . Not that the story need be long, but it will take a long while to make it short." And on still another occasion: "Nothing goes by luck in composition. . . . The best you can write will be the best you are. Every sentence is the result of a long probation. The author's character is read from title-page to end. Of this he never corrects the proofs."

Even in vocabulary, then, "homeliness" was not good in itself, nor always appropriate, nor usually to be achieved without effort. It was merely one of the means for achieving a certain effect, and Thoreau's own name for the effect which he desired above all others to produce was "poetry," though his attempts to explain just what he meant by that word were, as might be expected, not always satisfactory. Sometimes—especially in his earliest years—the term seemed to imply chiefly no more than the discovery of the analogical significance of some observed fact, the pointing out of its human or moral meaning, the decoding of one of Emerson's hieroglyphs; and this conception of "poetry" was responsible for some of the more vapid of his juvenile pseudo-profundities. More often—and more maturely—he understood poetical writing to be something both more inclusive and less likely to be influenced by his youthful notion that nature is primarily an allegory whose tropes it is the poet's business to explain in terms of human prejudices.

When he used the word "poetry" in the most inclusive of his senses, he seems to have intended it to indicate any kind of writing which communicates the full effect—including of course the full emotional effect—of the thing which the writer is attempting to communicate; any kind of writing, that is to say, which conveys a sense of familiarity with, as well as knowledge about, its subject. "Poetry," so he wrote in the *Journal* for 1852, "*implies* the whole truth; Philosophy *expresses* a particle of it." And again a few weeks later: "Color, which is the poet's wealth, is so expensive that most take to mere outline or pencil sketches and become men of science." The first of these quotations does, to be sure, indicate that "poetry" is necessarily suggestive as well as explicit, yet the definition is nevertheless so broad as to include nearly all good writing which has as its purpose more than the communication of information addressed to the practical intellect alone, and hence it is no wonder that he once concluded: "Every man will be a poet if he can" or that he confessed his inability to maintain a distinction which he had attempted to make between poetry and science—or at least between poetry and science of the only kind which had any interest for him. "I have a commonplace-book for facts and another for poetry, but I find it difficult always to preserve the vague distinction. . . . I see that if my facts were sufficiently vital and significant . . . I should need but one book of poetry to contain them all."

But if almost any kind of vivid, effective writing might seem to be included within these descriptions of what he recognized as "poetic," it is possible to define somewhat more narrowly his own special effects and methods. As we shall see later, what he wanted above all in description or in narration was to communicate not merely the object or the event but the empathy which had been established in his own consciousness between himself and it. In exposition or argument, to which for the moment we will confine ourselves, he sought to achieve that sudden astonished agreement which is one of the characteristic effects of wit or, as he himself put it in the passage just quoted, of the sudden expression of one of those new ideas which "come into the world somewhat like falling meteors, with a flash and an explosion, and perhaps someone's castle-roof perforated." He had, moreover, his own methods of achieving this effect.

Sometimes he speaks as though nothing were necessary except passionate sincerity and as though a good style were no more than simple, direct statement with conviction behind it. Thus he once referred in the *Journal* to "sentences uttered with your back to the wall," and it is perhaps worth remarking that the most widely known of all his own sentences—"The mass of men lead lives of quiet desperation" —not only sounds as though it had been uttered by a man with his back to a wall but makes no use of either metaphor or any other rhetorical device, seeming to be a statement as bald as any it is possible to make. Much the same

might be said of "Money is not required to buy one necessary of the soul."

But Thoreau did not always have his back against the
wall, and he was aware that good writing, which aimed to
induce a state of the soul, could not confine itself to bald
statement. He realized that suggestiveness and implication
were often the best, and sometimes the only, way of saying what it was most worth while to say. "It is the fault of
some excellent writers—De Quincey's first impression on
seeing London suggests it to me—that they express themselves with too great fullness and detail. . . . They lack
moderation and sententiousness. . . . Their sentences are
not concentrated and nutty. . . . [They do not write]
sentences—which contain the seed of other sentences, not
mere repetition, but creation. . . . His style is nowhere
kinked and knotted up into something hard and significant,
which you could swallow like a diamond, without digest-
ing."

To Thoreau, then, "suggestiveness" does not mean anything dreamy or musical. He makes what may seem a paradoxical demand for the hard and definite which shall at the
same time suggest much that it does not say, and he meets
the demand by the use of metaphors whose literal aspect is
often simple and concrete but whose full meaning defies
direct translation into prose by the mere literal expansion
of the suggested comparison. Homer, not Shakespeare, was
for him the perfect embodiment of the idea of The Poet,
and it may be guessed that the homely materials of Homer's
full-dress similes and metaphors are in part responsible for
his admiration. But Thoreau himself, though he liked as
well as Homer did the reference to homely things, does not
usually formally elaborate a comparison, and frequently

his metaphors are not, in the strictest sense of the term, metaphors at all, but merely figurative terms of speech in which the metaphor is at most implied.

Even when he begins with a simile as simple as "The life in us is like the water in the river," he is likely to go on in such a way as to introduce suggestions more and more mystical, less and less statable in terms of a direct comparison—as he does in this instance where he continues: "It may rise this year higher than man has ever known it, and flood the parched uplands; even this may be the eventful year, which will drown out all our muskrats." And it is noteworthy that the climax of his exaltation introduces the homeliest, most specific of the words—namely, "muskrats."

Often his language is figurative only to the extent that some particular instance stands for a whole class of phenomena, as in the statement: "There are nowadays professors of philosophy, but not philosophers," or to the extent that what begins with the statement of a concrete fact goes on to use that concrete fact as a symbol, as in the passage: "I see young men, my townsmen, whose misfortune it is to have inherited farms, houses, barns, cattle, and farming tools; for these are more easily acquired than got rid of. . . . How many a poor immortal soul have I met well nigh crushed and smothered under its load, creeping down the road of life, pushing before it a barn, seventy-five feet by forty, its Augean stables never cleansed, and one hundred acres of land, tillage, mowing, pasture, and woodlot!"

When he was less hortatory (less on the defensive) and more concerned to communicate his own delight than to scold others for missing it, his best phrases are often made by a single word in which the implied metaphor is reduced to the compass of one suggestive adjective. Thus, a November day is "finger cold" and one must "put his hands in winter quarters." On one occasion he speaks of "the Royal month of August"; on another of "That grand old poem called winter." And when in *Walden* he is attempting to describe what satisfaction he took in raising a crop he did not intend to eat, he remarks: "Making the earth say beans instead of grass—this was my daily work." Here, of course, the figurative use of the one simple word "say" is wholly responsible for an effect which would be completely destroyed if "produce" or "grow" were substituted. The choice of that one word is sufficient to constitute him what he called A Poet.

Emerson concluded his eulogy by quoting twenty-odd brief excerpts from Thoreau's then unpublished manuscripts. Among them was: "Nothing is so much to be feared as fear," and this seems the most likely source (if source there was) for Franklin Roosevelt's famous pronouncement. But Emerson also quoted: "The bluebird carries the sky on his back." That statement achieves a sort of coy prettiness—reminiscent of the present-day greeting card —and it illustrates the fact that when Thoreau, considered merely as a phrasemaker, does fail, it is most likely to be on those occasions when he is either abandoning his usual astringency for an Emersonian sweetness or straining too hard for something transcendental after the usual fashion of the Concord school rather than in his own very special way. There are few if any such failures in *Walden*, but there are some in *A Week on the Concord and Merrimack Rivers*, and there are others which he wisely left buried in the *Journal*. When he writes, "Methinks the hawk that soars so loftily and circles so steadily and apparently without effort has earned this power by faithfully creeping on the ground as a reptile in a former state of existence," that is merely feeble. "Love never perjures itself, nor is it mistaken" sounds suspiciously like mere guff. So, too, does the self-conscious demand: "Have not the fireflies in the meadow relation to the stars above, *étincelant?*" Even leaving aside the question what Thoreau, of all men, is doing with a French word of no unique appropriateness, one is surprised to discover that he too should on occasion find it worth while to strain after a significance when so many significances thrust themselves upon him. He might well have remembered then the warning words in *Walden* addressed to other over-earnest seekers: "Any truth is better than make-believe. Tom Hyde, the tinker, standing on the gallows, was asked if he had anything to say. 'Tell the tailors,' said he, 'to remember to make a knot in their thread before they take the first stitch.' His companion's prayer is forgotten." But lapses of the sort just illustrated would not be so striking if they were not astonishingly few, and they usually occur, not when Thoreau is too exalted, but when he is not sufficiently so. His homeliest statements are among his very best; but so, too, at the opposite extreme, are those which all but lose themselves in mystical exclamation. "There is more day to dawn. The sun is but a morning star."

In Emerson's case it is notorious that the unit of composition is the sentence, and that some of his essays are no more than a series of apothegms. The same might be said of certain pages of Thoreau; notably, for example, of those which make up the last chapter of *Walden*—which was, it will be remembered, a mosaic of collected fragments put together as Emerson is said to have put together certain of his essays. But Thoreau did not always write in this way and neither his composition nor his thinking about composition stopped with the consideration of the individual sentence. He had, it is interesting to notice, ideas rather in advance of his time about architecture and these ideas were closely related to his conception of the proper architecture of prose. Describing, in the first chapter of *Walden,* how he built his cabin, he turns aside to remark that he has heard of at least one architect in this country "possessed with the idea of making architectural ornaments have a core of truth, a necessity, and hence a beauty"; but even this, he goes on, is little better than the common dilettantism because it begins "at the cornice, not at the foundation." "What reasonable man ever supposed that ornaments were something outward and in the skin merely—that the tortoise got his spotted shell, or the shell-fish its mother-o'-pearl tints, by such a contract as the inhabitants of Broadway their Trinity Church? . . . What of architectural beauty I now see, I know has grown from within outward, out of the necessities and character of the indweller, who is the only builder."

In his *American Renaissance* Mr. F. O. Matthiessen has cited the passage just quoted and used it interestingly to illustrate his discussion of what he calls Thoreau's "organic" conception of style. That is perhaps the best word, not only because "functional" happens to be at the moment a much overworked term, but also because "organic" actually suggests, not a machine made for a purpose, but rather, as Thoreau himself suggested, a growth originating from "the indweller." And in any case, the meaning is clear. Though good architecture or good writing is good for something and cannot exist for its own sake, the mere absence of frivolous, extraneous ornament is a negative virtue. Ornament that reveals character and meaning is a positive one.

Sometimes—more frequently perhaps than one would suspect if one did not take pains to note the occasions—Thoreau can employ an almost Gothically intricate ornamentation when he summons to his aid a splendor of bookish rhetoric obviously caught from Sir Thomas Browne; as, for example, in the passage that concludes the sixteenth chapter of *Walden*, or, to take a less hackneyed one, the paragraph from *A Week on the Concord and Merrimack Rivers* which begins, "It is remarkable that the dead lie everywhere under stones" and ends: "Fame itself is but an epitaph; as late, as false, as true. But they only are the true epitaphs which Old Mortality retouches." Perhaps the most remarkable thing about these bookish passages is the completeness with which they have been assimilated into the texture of a prose which is elsewhere so seemingly direct and simple. And that is, of course, an indication of the fact that Thoreau had, in his own consciousness, assimilated Concord into the universe so that he not only said but felt that the local and the temporal were indistinguishably a part of the universal and the eternal. The grand style and the homely were not appropriate respectively to ancient and to contemporary, but indiscriminately to both; so that Therien, the woodchopper, could on occasion be seen as Homeric, and on other occasions Agamemnon could be treated like a Yankee.

These elaborately ornamented passages are, however, most likely to be reserved for Thoreau's more serenely elevated moments. For his hortatory and vituperative outbursts he is more likely to employ that strong, direct, hard-hitting, more austerely functional prose which, unjustly perhaps, we are more likely to think of as characteristic of him. Sometimes, for example, a paean in praise of wild nature will turn into a denunciation of the despoilers of wildness like that diatribe quoted on page 60, and on such occasions thunderbolts of eloquence fall. When he excoriated the defenders of slavery he spoke with the curt, businesslike vehemence of a man whose rage was only increased by the fact that he did not want to waste much precious time in the irritatingly necessary business of blasting them. But slavery itself scarcely enraged him more than the thought of men whose highest ambition was to live uselessly and without work on California gold, and the passage quoted on page 151 is one of his most successful expressions of indignation. He was enough of an economist to see that to "live by luck," to get the means of commanding the labor of others, was itself to practice a form of slaveholding, and in the most characteristic sentence of the paragraph he exclaims: "The hog that *roots* his own living, and so makes manure, would be ashamed of such company."

Most writers who impress by their extraordinary vigor do so, in part at least, because they are able to go one step farther than one is expecting even them to go; because they astonish us by reaching some sort of climax following a penultimate which we have already accepted as an ultimate. The sentence about the pig serves, in the passage just under examination, as such a gratuitous or supererogatory demonstration of energy, and one of Thoreau's frequent tricks, if trick it can be called, is to startle the reader with just some such piling on of one more analogy, or image, or paradox. "The greater part of what my neighbours call good I believe in my soul to be evil" is a sentence which any but the most incompetently feeble dealer in paradoxes might have written. The clause that comes next, "and if I repent of anything, it is very likely to be my good behaviour," is still not, in phraseology or any other way, strong enough or individual enough to identify the author. But the exclamation that follows, "What demon possessed me that I behaved so well?" adds precisely the touch of powerful extravagance which makes it unmistakably Thoreau's.

"Powerful extravagance" would, indeed, serve as well as any mere pair of words could serve to describe the general effect of his most often remembered paragraphs, and the effect of power usually is produced by bold tropes which employ a reference to some familiar object or situation to drive home a point or make clear an attitude. Moreover, the individual sentences are frequently both deliberately extravagant in themselves and arranged, one after another, to create a mounting climax of what calmer writers would call overstatement. "I fear chiefly," he wrote in *Walden*, "lest my expression may not be *extra-vagant* enough," and it is clear that though extravagance was sometimes a rhetorical device, it was also, and perhaps more frequently, the inevitable result of his conviction that the truth about neither man's potentialities nor his failure to realize them could possibly be overstated. When he wrote to a friend the advice not to worry about his health because "you may be dead already," that was both a deliberately shocking statement and an expression of Thoreau's sincere conviction that most men were actually, in the realest possible sense, not alive.

These most often remembered passages of powerful extravagance are, it should be observed, usually argumentative or scornful. In intention they are almost always, directly or indirectly, didactic or hortatory. They are concerned with what Thoreau did not approve of rather than with what he did; with what he blamed others for "living for," not with what he lived for himself. And there is another whole body of writing markedly different in style and purpose which is considerably less well known—partly because readers have, on the whole, tended to understand and sympathize with his criticism of life as it is commonly lived rather more than they have with the positive aspects of his philosophy, partly because his protestant writing is more adequately represented outside the little-read *Journal* than the other kind is.

Probably he himself would have been distressed to think that he might be remembered chiefly as a satirist or a critic; as a man who had managed to convey only his dissatisfaction with the world and not the happiness which he believed to have been his. In the essay on Persius, which is lugged by the ears into *A Week on the Concord and Merrimack Rivers*, he is explicit on this subject, and indeed he seems to be interested in Persius only in so far as that poet will serve him to make a point. "Satire," he says, "will not be sung." Indeed, since no man can write except out of himself, the rebuker of follies confesses that he shares in them. Fault-finding is at best a waste of time. "If you light on the least vestige of truth . . . an eternity will not suffice to extol it, while no evil is so huge but you grudge to bestow on it a moment of hate." Even the greatest of poets —even Homer and Shakespeare and Milton and Marvell and Wordsworth—are only apprentices in the art of praise which is the poet's true business. They are "but the rustling of leaves and the crackling of twigs in the forest, and there is not yet sound of any bird." There was, he thought, "a sort of necessary order in the development of Genius," from Complaint, to Plaint, to Love; and he would have been distressed indeed if he had not felt that he had got often beyond the first and sometimes beyond the second. "This life," he was writing a friend as late as 1860, "is not for complaint, but for satisfaction."

Certain of the intermediate chapters of *Walden* are devoted to the life he loved rather than the life he hated, and so too are a good many pages of *A Week on the Concord and Merrimack Rivers*. But much of the second is juvenile, and the *Walden* chapters do not seem to contain the best of his writing of the sort they attempt—perhaps because they actually do not, or perhaps only because their gentler tone cannot successfully compete for our attention against the powerful urgency of the sermonizing in the first chapter and the last. The posthumous *The Maine Woods* and *Cape Cod* are too nearly mere travel books, too deliberately directed at a relatively vulgar audience, to represent him at his best, though they contain some very fine passages; and so it is to the unquarried *Journal* itself that one must go for any adequate idea of the bulk or importance of a kind of writing which will contribute more to Thoreau's fame than it yet has, if it should ever be collected, as it easily might, into volumes selected to illustrate its own special intention and quality.

Much the largest part of the *Journal* is, it must be remembered, devoted not to Thoreau's criticism of his neighbors and their society but to a vast record of his intercourse with trees and flowers, with animals, wild and domestic, and with inanimate nature as well. The record of this intercourse varies in manner from the barest quasi-scientific, or sometimes merely perfunctory, jotting down of facts and observations to the most elaborately worked-up set pieces—many of which exhibit unmistakable evidence of having been carefully composed and suggest that they were probably several times rewritten. Reporting a certain incident he might, on some occasions, have said only something like "Stood within seven feet of a nesting hawk which kept her nest." On one particular occasion he wrote, instead, the long passage entered under the date June 7, 1853, which describes the motionless creature who "looked so saturnian" and who impressed him "with the venerableness of the globe." The working up involves the attempt to capture what Thoreau himself on occasion calls "poetry," since that was (as has already been pointed out) his word for almost any kind of writing that actually communicates something; but it is a "poetry" of a very different kind from the "poetry" of the last chapter of *Walden*, for instance, and it is far less dependent upon epigram or gnomic utterance, far more upon the building up of an effect through a paragraph whose impressiveness depends less upon the individually striking sentence, more upon the generation of an atmosphere.

A number of admirable passages of this sort have already been quoted in the present book to illustrate various parts of the discussion, and they have served less than half of their purpose if they did not also·illustrate the second, less well known, of Thoreau's styles. But the reader who wishes to turn back to refresh his memory will presently be given page references to some of the passages already cited.

Most interesting, because most nearly unique, are those of the set pieces where the working up consists in a process for which dramatization rather than poetizing might be an appropriate word. Here the attempt is to keep the attention fixed on the object itself; to return again and again to its own various aspects rather than merely to use the object as something from which the mind can take off. It is not the meaning of the hieroglyph but the thing itself which the writer is trying to grasp and which he wishes the reader to grasp also, so that experience itself rather than any explanation or interpretation of it is what he is trying to communicate.

The two things are of course not always, or perhaps ever, kept entirely distinct. A good example of their successful combination is the extraordinary passage about snow (quoted on page 187 of this book), where the physical fact is vividly presented and then made the occasion for one of the most striking of Thoreau's meditations upon the universe, which is there considered, not as something arranged for man's instruction, but as a vast self-sufficient system of wonders—some glimpses of which man is occasionally privileged to catch. His account of the little game that he played with a fox (quoted on page 35) is a minor example of his manner when he wishes merely to dramatize rather than to moralize an incident; and a more elaborate specimen of the same sort of thing is the report of his interview with a woodchuck, which is too long to be quoted but which may be found in the *Journal* of April 16, 1852. Here it is the sense of fellowship with all living things which is communicated, and it is this that constitutes the charm of so much of his less spectacular but very characteristic writing. The description of the little boy in the homemade fur cap (quoted on page 159) has almost precisely the same quality, and so too does the half-tender,

half-humorous account in 1850 of the calf with whom he
all but rubbed noses. "As I walked, she followed me, and
took an apple from my hand, and seemed to care more for
the hand than apple. So innocent a face as I have rarely
seen on any creature, and I have looked in face of many
heifers. And as she took the apple from my hand, I caught
the apple of her eye. . . . By the kindred spots I knew her
mother, more sedate and matronly, with full-grown bag;
and on her sides was Asia, great and small, the plains of
Tartary, even to the pole, while on her daughter it was
Asia Minor."

Thoreau despised fiction and most fashionable literature,
but he read the old travelers and historians who were "not
cursed with a style." Captain John Smith, he felt, introduced him directly into "a wilder country and a little
nearer to primitive times." William Bradford's account of
the Plymouth plantation was direct enough to reveal the
fact that "Nature has not changed one iota." And Wood's
New England's Prospect both delighted and saddened him
by its account of so many once common animals now gone
or going. But though he read also Gilbert White and even
Ruskin's *Modern Painters*, the moderns pleased him less,
and there is probably nothing which will better illuminate
the intention of his own writing about the fields and woods
or its relation to the whole tradition of modern "nature
writing" from White to William Beebe and Donald Cul-
ross Peattie than his remarks upon certain of the then recent
books he read.

In 1852, while *Walden* was still unpublished, he began
to read *Forest Scenery*, a late-eighteenth-century work by
William Gilpin. No other writer on "nature" seems to have
provoked him to so much comment, for Gilpin reappears

again and again in the *Journal* over a period of years, while Ruskin, for example, was briefly dispatched. But Thoreau's opinion of Gilpin went steadily down as he understood more and more clearly what the spiritual difference between himself and such a writer was. In the beginning *Forest Scenery* was "a pleasing book, so moderate, temperate, graceful, roomy, like a gladed wood," though it was also "somewhat spare indeed in the thoughts as in the sentences." A few months later, "Have just finished Gilpin's 'Lakes of Cumberland.' . . . I wish he would look at scenery sometimes not with the eye of an artist. It is all side screens and fore screens and near distances and broken grounds for him." Two years later, when what he regarded as the full enormity of Gilpin's soulless perversity had gradually dawned upon his imagination, he was writing with all the indignation of Blake annotating Sir Joshua.

What disgusted him—or perhaps shocked is the better word—was not mere vapidity. That amused as much as it irritated him in the elaborate literary musings about nature indulged in by Channing and in the writings about scenery and natural history by his contemporary, Wilson Flagg, of whom Thoreau wrote: "He is not alert enough. He wants stirring up with a pole. He should practice turning a series of somersets rapidly, or jump up and see how many times he can strike his feet together before coming down." Gilpin's sin was positive. What his exclusive concern with the picturesque really meant was, as Thoreau finally realized, an insensitiveness to everything else; a kind of dull heartlessness; a sort of blind atheism. "Gilpin talked," he said, "as if there was some food for the soul in mere light and shadow."

Gilpin had, for example, undertaken to explain how a

sleek, well-fed horse might, no less than a shaggy one, be picturesque; and these were his words: "It is not his smooth, and shining coat, that makes him so. It is the apparent interruption of that smoothness by a variety of shades, and colors, which produces the effect." "Mark," Thoreau exclaims, "that there is not the slightest reference to the fact that this surface, with its lights and shades, belongs to a horse and not to a bag of wind. The same reasoning would apply equally well to one of his hind quarters hung bottom upwards in a butcher's stall. . . . I should say that no arrangement of light and shade without reference to the object, actual or suggested, so lit and shaded can interest us powerfully, any more than paint itself can charm us." Gilpin had no fellow feeling, no sense of oneness. He, no less than the driest of laboratory scientists, had cut himself off, had become a mere observer, not a sharer in the wonder and joy of living things.

The term Thoreau finally chooses to describe what Gilpin lacks is "moral suggestion," not "poetry"; but it is clear that he means a pantheist's, not a transcendental puritan's, moral. In one sense of the word Ruskin is, on the contrary, certainly moral enough, but to Thoreau he is, significantly, "prose" instead of "poetry"; and Ruskin's concern, not with nature herself but with nature as she has been painted, had the same effect as Gilpin's inability to realize that a horse was alive: it drove Thoreau back to the older writers —specifically, to Topsell's translation of Konrad Gesner. Of the antelopes "bred in India and Syria, near the river Euphrates" Topsell says that "they delight much to drink of the cold water thereof," and Thoreau adds a comment: "The beasts which most modern naturalists describe do not *delight* in anything, and their water is neither hot nor cold.

. . . These men had an adequate idea of a beast, or what a beast should be . . . and they will describe and will draw you a cat with four strokes, more beastly or more beast-like to look at than Mr. Ruskin's favorite artist draws a tiger. They had an adequate idea of the wildness of beasts and of men."

"Delight" is certainly one of the things Thoreau gets into his own accounts of his adventures in nature, and the distinguishing character of that delight arises out of the fact that it is something that he is *sharing*, both with the beasts themselves and with the universe as a whole; not, as in the case of Gilpin, something which natural arrangements of light and shade enable him, as a detached observer, to enjoy. If, instead of Darwin, Thoreau had been able to read Alfred Russel Wallace's autobiography, for instance, he might have perceived that an instinctive sympathy with wildness was not dead even in nineteenth-century Englishmen; the whole question of Thoreau's "influence" on subsequent writers about nature is confused by the fact that others were discovering for themselves attitudes quite different from those of either the official scientists on the one hand or the admirers of the merely picturesque on the other.

Many of the more recent writers, though no doubt influenced by him, were also at least as strongly influenced by something of which he knew little. While he was first introduced to mysticism as formulated in non- if not actually antiscientific terms, they were led on from scientific fact to an emotional attitude, and it was the omnipresence of the same protoplasm rather than any transcendental intimations concerning the over-soul which drew them towards their sense of union with the One and the All. But the two paths converge. Thoreau himself tended more and more to draw his conclusions from phenomena rather than from intuitions, even though he lacked the key to any systematic arrangement of these phenomena; and what the later writers found expressed in his writing they had no difficulty in understanding, even if it was in a slightly different way.

"Thoreau," wrote Lowell without qualification or explanation, "had no humor." What he must have meant is that Thoreau deliberately avoided and consciously scorned mere jocosity; that he despised both the pseudo-rustic and the unconsciously cockney banter in which Lowell himself sometimes indulged and is guilty of in the very essay which undertakes to put Thoreau in his place. Such jocosity is a special manner reserved for special occasions and deliberately advertises the fact that it is of the surface only. Thoreau's humor is, of course, inseparable from his seriousness; it is merely a grotesque or a witty way of saying what he profoundly believes.

As a matter of simple fact it is not even true that he always avoided, in everyday life, the vulgar kind of humor. According to Channing—who certainly had seen much of Thoreau, however little real intimacy there may have been between the two—Thoreau delighted in making bad puns (of which Channing gives a rather gruesome example); and, as has already been noted, he danced and sang with gusto. But it *is* true that except for some passages of merely journalistic "funny writing" in *The Maine Woods* and *Cape Cod*, he kept mere jocosity both out of his published works and out of the *Journal*. Moreover he repeatedly declared his determination to do so, for he despised a man who did not mean his jokes.

Humor of another kind plays ambiguously over many of his most serious passages. Sometimes, as in the description of his living arrangements at Walden or in his suggestion that the hard-pressed might use a toolbox for shelter, it takes the curse of mere fanaticism off his most extreme pronouncements. Sometimes, as in the description of his conversation with the half-wit, it serves to reveal the tenderness just below the surface of his realism. Sometimes it is itself the vehicle of that realism and so loaded with scorn that it is, in effect, a particularly intense form of seriousness. "By and by some Dr. Morton may be filling your cranium with white mustard seed to learn its internal capacity. Of all the ways invented to come at a knowledge of a living man, this seems to me the worst, as it is the most belated. You would learn more by once paring the toenails of the living subject." But even here the unexpected parenthesis, "as it is the most belated," is sheer joy—one of those sudden supererogatory amplifications which must have been as delightful to write as it is to read.

Though Emerson's essay made famous Thoreau's observation: "Some circumstantial evidence is very strong, as when you find a trout in the milk," this is not really typical since it is too close to the spirit of the best professional cracker-barrel philosophers, of whom Thoreau was certainly not one. Far more typical are, on the one hand, the isolable, hard-hitting phrases that crystallize an exposition or an argument, and on the other hand those descriptive passages suffused by a warm sense of fun which promotes rather than impedes a kind of empathy. "When I came downstairs this morning, it raining hard and steadily, I found an Irishman sitting with his coat on his arm in the kitchen, waiting to see me. He wanted to enquire what I thought the weather would be today! I sometimes ask my aunt, and she consults the almanac. So do we shirk the responsibility." And who that has ever read the passages in which they occur can forget the Irishman's kitchen in which a hen wandered about "looking too humanized to roast well," or the description in *Walden* of the country auction from which the buyers carry away the accumulated rubbish of the deceased's attic and then store it away in their own until such time as their goods are dispersed after another funeral? "Among the rest was a dried tapeworm. . . . When a man dies he kicks the dust."

The intermingling without incongruity of Thoreau's humor with his seriousness is a phenomenon essentially similar to the intermingling of his homely style with his bookishly elaborate one, and of his delight in simple physical things with his mystical exaltation. Indeed it might be maintained that to unite without incongruity things ordinarily thought of as incongruous *is* the phenomenon called Thoreau, whether one is thinking of a personality or of a body of literary work. This is what constitutes his oneness, and the oneness of a man is the most important thing about him; is perhaps the man himself.

Mr. T. S. Eliot has popularized the phrase "unity of sensibility," to indicate, if I understand him aright, that power which enables a writer to present the totality of a varied experience in such a way that it makes a whole and that there is no sense of any distinction between the serious and the comic, the temporal and the eternal, the poetic and the prosaic, or the religious and the secular. Mr. Eliot believes, of course, that the English writers of the seventeenth century were peculiarly blessed with the ability to achieve this kind of unity, and it is perhaps significant both that they, like Thoreau, were often men who could be serious and humorous, not alternately but at the same time, and that Thoreau had read the seventeenth-century writers more assiduously and with greater appreciation than he had any other writers in his own tongue.

In the course of the present discussion, a good deal has been made of the separateness in the public mind of Thoreau's two reputations: of his reputation as critic of society and as a nature mystic. A good deal has also been made of the extent to which he himself may have been aware of certain conflicts not only between his hatred of slavery and his desire to lead his own isolated life but also between his pantheistic tendencies and moral ideas hardly compatible with these. But though the conflicts undoubtedly to some extent exist, and though they must at moments have disturbed him, it is certainly not of them that the reader of his writing is most frequently aware; and when one considers his literary work in and by itself, the unity of sensibility rather than any undercurrent of conflict is what gives to the literary work its dominant tone. Richness, not disharmony, is the usual consequence of the diversities of which he is simultaneously aware. He is one of the few writers who can smile, not mockingly but with joy, while exclaiming, "*O altitudo!*"

Index

· 289 ·